Hugh Charles Clifford

Studies in Brown Humanity

Being Scrawls and Smudges in Sepia, White, and Yellow

Hugh Charles Clifford

Studies in Brown Humanity
Being Scrawls and Smudges in Sepia, White, and Yellow

ISBN/EAN: 9783337339180

Printed in Europe, USA, Canada, Australia, Japan

Cover: Foto ©Suzi / pixelio.de

More available books at **www.hansebooks.com**

STUDIES

IN

BROWN HUMANITY

BEING

SCRAWLS AND SMUDGES IN SEPIA
WHITE, AND YELLOW

BY

HUGH CLIFFORD

AUTHOR OF
'IN COURT AND KAMPONG'

𝕷𝖔𝖓𝖉𝖔𝖓
GRANT RICHARDS
9 HENRIETTA STREET, COVENT GARDEN, W.C.
1898

To J. E. C.

As helpless Debtors come to lay
   Poor presents at the feet
Of those they ne'er can hope to pay,
   So come I, as 'tis meet,
To lay this book on thy dear knee,
   In token that I know,
Of love and sacrifice for me,
   How great the debt I owe.

H. C.

PREFACE

THE tales and sketches of which this book is composed have a very definite object underlying their apparent lightness. To some extent, it must be confessed, they wear the garb of fiction ; but, none the less, they are studies of things as they are,—drawn from the life. The facts related in the stories which I have named 'In the Valley of the Tĕlom,' 'The Fate of Leh the Strolling Player,' 'His Little Bill,' 'At the Heels of the White Man,' 'A Malay Othello,' 'The Weeding of the Tares,' and 'From the Grip of the Law,' are all things which have actually occurred in the Malay Peninsula during the last ten or twenty years. The tale told by Tûkang Bûrok, which is peculiarly painful and characteristic, is known to many people in the interior of Pahang, and is, I believe, true in every detail. I can only claim these stories as my own in that I have filled in the pictures from my knowledge of the localities in which the various events happened, and have generally told my tales in the fashion which appealed to me as the most appropriate. Ûmat, who is the subject of one of the sketches, is a very real person indeed, and as I write these lines he is sleeping peacefully over the *punkah* cord, with which he has become inextricably entangled. The purely descriptive chapters are the result of personal observation in a land which has become very dear to me, which I know intimately, and where the best years of my life have hitherto been spent. The remaining stories are somewhat more imaginative than their fellows ; but 'The Spirit of the Tree' and 'The Strange Elopement of Châling the Dyak' were both related to me as facts, in the manner which I have described. As regards the former, the man whom I have called Trimlett certainly had an exceedingly ugly wound on his foot, for which he accounted in rather a curious manner. As for Châling, I have no hesitation in expressing my own profound disbelief in its main features ; but this is merely a private opinion, by which I would ask no man to be unduly influenced. I am indebted to the Editor of *Macmillan's Magazine* for permission to republish the story of the Schooner. The tale is one which has long been current among the native and European pearlers of the Archipelago, from whom I heard it, and by whom it is unquestioningly believed.

In writing these tales and sketches it has mainly been my design to illustrate, in as readable a manner as I am able, the lives lived by those among the natives of the Peninsula who have not yet been changed out of all recognition by the steadily increasing influence of Europeans; to picture their habits and customs, their beliefs and superstitions, their tortuous twists of thought, and incidentally to give some idea of the lovely land in which they move and have their being. These things have seemed to me to be all the better worth recording because innovation is doing its work in the Peninsula with surprising rapidity, and the people, and to some extent even their surroundings, are undergoing a complete and radical change, which will leave them quite other than they were before we came amongst them, and as a few of them still are in some of the remoter places of which my stories tell.

For more than fourteen years I have dwelt in the Peninsula in almost hourly contact with natives of all classes, from Sultâns and Râjas to Chiefs and Dâtos, from villagers and fisher-folk to the aboriginal tribes of Sakai and Semang, who people the forests of the remote interior, and I have ever found the study of my surroundings of absorbing interest. I shall probably hurt no man's self-complacency, if I say that the things and places of which I tell are matters concerning which the ideas of the vast majority of my countrymen are both hazy and fragmentary. But, none the less, the Peninsula and its sepia-coloured peoples are curious and worthy of attention, and therefore they deserve to be better known by the men of the race which has taken the destiny of the Malays of the Peninsula under its especial charge,

In the selection of the subjects of my illustrations I have frequently experienced considerable difficulty, because I have often been driven to choose the exception rather than the rule, the abnormal rather than the normal, if my tales are to be rendered acceptable to any save the very few who are personally and directly interested in my brown friends. Had I received my training in the Kailyard School, instead of among the wilds of the Malay jungles ; had I the genius of a Barrie, instead of the facility of a mere writer of official reports,—it is possible that I might so paint the commonplace, everyday life of the Malays that I should move my readers to tears and laughter over every incident of the village on the river banks, and of the rice-fields which lie behind it. But, alas, these things are far beyond my reach, and I must whip my Pegasus over break-neck leaps, must charge him through barbarous combats, and must tumble him head-over-heels into some ugly depths, if his antics are to excite any particular emotion   On the flat, and across the grass, he has no special grace of action to distinguish him above his fellows.

HUGH CLIFFORD.

British Residency,
Pahang, Malay Peninsula,
November 24, 1897.

CONTENTS

For always roaming with a hungry heart *Irruppn*
Much have I seen and known.
Ulysses.

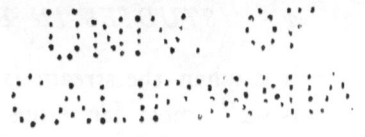

IN THE VALLEY OF THE TĔLOM

Where the forest yields to the open space,
    And the trees stand back to see
The waters that babble and glisten and race
    Thro' woodlands trackless and free ;
Where the soil is ploughed by a thousand feet,
    And the salt lies sweet below,
Here nightly the beasts of the jungle meet
    To wallow, and bellow, and blow.
                            The Salt-Lick.

VERY far away, in the remote interior of Pahang, there is a river called the Tĕlom—an angry little stream, which fights and tears its way through the vast primæval forest, biting savagely at its banks, wrestling impatiently with the rocks and boulders that obstruct its path, rippling fiercely over long beds of water-worn shingle, and shaking a glistening mane of splashing, troubled water, as it rushes downwards in its fury. Sometimes, during the winter months, when the rain has fallen heavily in the mountains, the Tĕlom will rise fourteen or fifteen feet in a couple of hours, and then, for a space, its waters change their temper from wild, excited wrath, to a sullen anger, which it is by no means pleasant to encounter. But

B

it is when the stream is shrunken by drought that it
is really most dangerous ; for, at such times, sharp and
ragged rocks, over which a raft is usually able to pass
in safety, rise up, from the river-bed, to within an inch
or two of the surface, and rip all things cast against
them with keen firm cuts, that need no further hacking
to complete their work of dismemberment. At the
very foot of the largest rapid in the river, one of these
boulders forms, in dry weather, a very efficient trap
for the unwary. The channel of the stream, at this
point, narrows somewhat, and is confined between high
walls of rock, and the boiling waters of the fall are
further troubled by the jagged blocks of granite, with
which the river-bed is studded. One of these leans
slightly up stream, for the friction of ages has worn
away a cavity where the force of the current strikes
most fiercely ; and, when the waters are low, it is
impossible for a raft to avoid this obstacle.

The rafts, which are used upon the upper reaches
of the Malayan rivers, are formed of about eighteen
bamboos, lashed side by side, and firmly kept in place
by stout wooden stays above and across. They are
usually some twenty feet in length, and, though they
have great flotage, their very lightness causes them to
wallow knee-deep when the furious waters of a rapid
roar over them and about them, while they whirl
down stream at a headlong, desperate pace. The more
shrunken the stream, the greater the speed at which a
raft spins down a fall, for the rapid itself is unchanging,
while, at such times, the volume of water is in-
sufficient to break the drop, and soften the descent.

Thus it is that, at the rapid in the Tĕlom, of

which I speak, a raft charges down the channel between the high walls of granite, and comes to eternal grief upon the leaning rock, which obstructs the passage, waiting so calmly and so patiently for its prey.

A harsh, sharp crack—the agonised pain-cry of the bamboos—sounds above the roar of the waters, as the raft strikes the boulder fairly and squarely. Another second, and the bow is fast wedged beneath the projecting ledge of the slanting rock. The bamboos give another despairing shriek ; and the tail of the raft rises swiftly to a perpendicular position, waggling irresolutely, while the bow is buried more deeply beneath the boulder, which grips it fast. Then, like the sail of a windmill, the raft whirls round in the air, the fixed bow serving as its axis, and, with a flap, it smites the racing waters beyond the obstructing rock. Every one of the bamboos is smashed in an instant into starting, shrieking slivers, which have power to cut more sharply than the keenest knife. The men, who lately manned the raft, are cast high into the air. Then they are broken pitilessly upon the rocks, are cut and wounded cruelly by the matchwood that was once their raft, or are to be seen struggling powerlessly in an angry torrent.

Jĕram Mûsoh Kâram—the Rapid of the Drowned Enemy—the place is named in the vernacular, and native tradition tells of an invading expedition utterly destroyed in this terrible rock-bound death-trap. But men who know the records of the river are aware that the Tĕlom spares friend no more than it once spared foe ; and the tale of its kills waxes longer and longer as the years slip away.

None the less, it is during the driest season, when the stream, shrunken to the lowest limits, is most angry and vicious, that the valley of the Tĕlom fills with life. It is then that the black tin ore, found in the sands and shingles of the river-bed, is most accessible, and the Malays come hither, in little family parties, to wash for it. Men, women, and little children stand in the shallows, deftly shaking their great flat wooden trays, with a circular motion, and storing small pinches of tin in the hollows of bamboos. At night-time, they camp in rude shelters on the banks of the stream, roast such fish as they have caught in the cleft of split sticks, and discuss the results of the day's toil. The amount of their earnings is very small, but Malays are capable of a great deal of patient labour when it chances to take a form that, for the moment, they happen to find congenial.

At this season, too, the jungles are one degree less damp and sodden than they are at other times, and the searchers for *gĕtah* and rattans seize the opportunity, and betake themselves to the forests, for well they know how unpleasant life can be when the rain falls heavily, and what sun there is cannot force its way through the tangled canopy of leaves and creepers, to dry what the rain has soaked.

Meanwhile, the magnificent *dûri-an* groves of the upper reaches of the Tĕlom are rich in a profusion of splendid fruit, and the semi-wild tribes of Sâkai [1] come from far and near to camp beneath the shade of the giant trees, and there to feast luxuriously. No man

---

[1] Aboriginal tribes of the Malay Peninsula, belonging to the Mon-Annam family.

knows who planted these gardens, for the Sàkai asks
no questions as long as food is plentiful, and the
Malays are equally lacking in curiosity upon the
subject. But the trees are very ancient, and the fruit
has formed one of the main food-supplies of the Sàkai
since first they roamed through these forests.

So the wild tribes gather together in the groves,
camping there for weeks at a time, and gorging rap-
turously. In the silent night-time, the dulled thud of
the fruit, falling upon the rank grass, sounds in the
ears of the watchers, and a wild stampede ensues from
under the shelters of the forest-dwellers, in order that
the fruit may be instantly secured. This is a somewhat necessary. precaution, for tigers love the *dúri-an*,
and a man must be quick in the gathering, if he would
avoid a fight for possession with one of these monsters.

But it is not only by human beings that the valley
of the Télom is overrun during the dry season of
the year ; for it is then that the great Salt-Lick of
Mìsong is crowded by game. The Mìsong is a
small stream, which falls into the Télom on its left
bank, some miles above the rapids. About a couple
of thousand yards up the Mìsong, from its point of
junction with the Télom, there is a spot where the
right bank, though covered with virgin forest, is much
trodden by the passage of game. The underwood is
worn down, and has become thin and sparse. The
trees are smooth in places, and here and there are
splashed by great belts of mud, eight feet from the
ground, which mark the spots where wild elephants
have stood rocking backwards and forwards, gently
rubbing their backs against the rough bark. In many

places, the earth is trodden down to the water's edge
in great deep clefts, such as the kine make near Malay
villages, at the points where, in the cool of the afternoon, they go to wallow in the shallows of the river.

A bold sweep of the Mîsong, at this spot, forms of
the left bank a rounded headland, flat and level, and
covering some two acres of ground. In places, short,
closely-cropped grass colours the soil a brilliant green,
but, for the most part, this patch of open bears the
appearance of a deeply-ploughed field. This is the
Salt-Lick of Mîsong.

The earth is here impregnated with saline deposits, and
the beasts of the forest come hither in their hundreds to
lick the salt, which, to them, and to the lowest of our
human stock also, is 'sweeter' than anything in the
world. When the waters of the Mîsong are swollen,
the salt cannot be got at, and the lick is deserted, but
in the dry weather, the place is alive with game.
Here may be seen the tracks of deer ; the hoof-marks
of the *sĕlâdang*, the strongest of all the beasts ; here is
found the long, sharp scratch made by the toes of the
rhinoceros ; the pitted trail, and deep rootings left by
the wild swine ; the pad-track of the tiger ; the tiny
footprints of the *kanchil*, the perfectly formed deer
which, in size, is no larger than a rabbit ; and the
great round sockets, punched by the ponderous feet of
the elephants in the soft and yielding soil. Here
come, too, the tapir, and the black panther, and packs
of wild dogs, and the jungle cats of all kinds, from the
brute which resembles the tiger in all but bulk, to the
slender spotted animal, built as lightly and as neatly as
a greyhound. Sitting in the fork of a tree, high

above the heads of the game, so that your wind cannot disturb them, you may watch all the animal life of the jungle come and go, and come again, within a few yards of you, and, if you have the patience to keep your rifle quiet, you may see a thousand wonderful things.

It was to the Salt-Lick of Mîsong that my friend, Pandak Âris, came, one day, with two Sâkai companions, from his house below the rapids. When I knew him, he was an old man of seventy or thereabouts, wizened and dry, with deep furrows of wrinkle on face and body. His left arm was stiff and powerless, and he bore many ugly scars besides. His closely cropped hair was white as hoar-frost, and, on his chin, grew a long goat's beard of the same hue, which waggled to and fro with the motion of his lips. Two yellow fangs were set in his gums, and his mouth was a cavern stained dark-red with betel-nut juice. His words came indistinctly through his quid, and from his toothless gums, but he had many things to tell concerning the jungles, in which he dwelt, and, when I camped near his house, we were wont to sit talking together far into the night.

In his youth, he had come to Pahang from Rĕmbau, drifting aimlessly, as young men will, to the fate which awaited him, he knew not where. She—these fates are always feminine—proved to be a Jĕlai girl, who lived near the limits of the Sâkai country, and, after he had married her, they took up their abode a couple of days' journey up the Tĕlom river, where they might be completely alone ; for no other Malays live permanently in this valley. Here, she had borne him

three sons, and two daughters, and he had planted
cocoanut and fruit trees, which now cast heavy shade
about the roof of his dwelling.   That all happened
nearly fifty years before I first met Pandak Âris, and,
during all that long, long time, he had lived contentedly
without once leaving the district in which he had his
home.   He remained wrapped up in his own joys and
sorrows, and in his own concerns, rarely seeing a
strange face, from year's end to year's end, and entirely
undisturbed by the humming and throbbing of the
great world without.   Think of it, ye White Men !
He had only one life on earth to live, and this is how
he spent it—like the frog under the cocoanut-shell, as
the Malays say, who dreams not that there are other
worlds than his.   Wars had raged within sixty miles
of his home, but his peace had not been broken ; great
changes had taken place in the Peninsula, but they had
affected him not at all ; and the one great event of his
life, which had left its mark scored deeply upon both
his mind and his body, was that which had befallen
him at the Salt-Lick of Mïsong, a score of years and
more, before I chanced upon him.   He told me the tale,
brokenly as a child might do, while we sat talking in
the dim light of the *dâmar* torch, which guttered in
its clumsy wooden stand, set in the centre of his mat-
covered floor, and, as he spoke, he pointed, ever and
anon, to his stiff left arm, and to the ugly scars upon
his body, calling upon them, like Sancho Panza, to
prove that he did not lie !

It was in the afternoon that Pandak Âris, and his
two Sâkai followers, reached the Salt-Lick of Mïsong.
They had been roaming through the forest, blazing

gĕtah trees since morning, for it was Pandak Âris's intention to prepare a large consignment of the precious gum, against the coming of the washers for tin, in the next dry season. They all three knew the Salt-Lick well, and as it was an open space near running water, and they were hungry after their tramp, they decided to halt there, and cook rice. They built a little fire near the base of a giant tree, which grows a hundred yards or so inland from the left bank, at a point where the furrowed earth of the Salt-Lick begins to give place to heavy jungle. The dry sticks blazed up bravely, the flame showing pale in the brighter sunlight of the afternoon, while the thin vapours danced furiously above it. The black rice-pot was propped upon three stones in the centre of the crackling fuel, and while one of the Sâkai sat stirring the rice, and the other plucked leeches from his bleeding legs, and cut them into pieces with his wood-knife, Pandak Âris began preparing a luscious quid of betel-nut, from the ingredients contained in the little brass boxes which he carried in a small cotton handkerchief. The gentle murmur of bird and insect life, which precedes the wild clamour of the sunset hour, was beginning to purr through the forest, and the Mîsong sang drowsily as it pattered between its banks. Pandak Âris's eyes began to close sleepily, and the Sâkai, who had dismembered his last leech, stretched himself elaborately, and then, rolling over on his face, was asleep before his nose touched the grass ! This is the manner of the Sâkai, and of some of the other lower animals.

Suddenly, a wild tumult of sound broke the stillness.

The Sâkai who was cooking had screamed a shrill cry of warning to his companions, but, above his frightened cry, came the noise of a furious trumpeting, like a steam siren in a fog, the crashing of boughs and branches, and a heavy tramping which seemed to shake the earth. The cooking Sâkai had swung himself into a tree, and was now swarming up it like a monkey, never pausing to look below, until the topmost fork was reached. His sleeping fellow, at the first alarm, had awaked with a leap, which carried him some yards from the spot where he had been lying, for the Sâkai, who can fall asleep like an animal, can also wake into complete alertness like any other forest creature. A second later, he, too, was sitting in the highest fork of a friendly tree, and all this had happened before Pandak Âris, who had been merely dozing, was completely awake to the fact that danger was at hand. Then he, also, leaped up, and, as he did so, two long white tusks with a trunk coiled closely about one of them, two little fierce red eyes, and a black bulk of dingy, crinkled hide, came into view within a yard of him.

Pandak Âris sought shelter behind the big tree from the onslaught of the squealing elephant, and, a moment later, he also swung himself into safety among the branches overhead, for a jungle-bred Malay is quick enough, if he be not compared with the Sâkai, whose activity is that of a frightened stag.

The elephant charged the fire fiercely, scattering the burning brands far and wide, trampling upon the rice-pot, till it was flattened to the likeness of sheet tin, kneading the little brass betel-boxes deep into the earth, and keeping up all the while a torrent of angry squealings. The whole scene only lasted a moment or two, and then the furious brute whirled clumsily round, and, still sounding his war-cry, disappeared into the echoing forest, as suddenly as he had emerged from it.

Pandak Âris and the two Sâkai sat in the trees, and listened to the trumpeting of the elephant, as it grew fainter and fainter in the distance.

'How can one name such ferocity as this?' murmured Pandak Âris, with the aggrieved half-wondering patience of the much-enduring Oriental. He looked down very sadly upon the flattened metal, which had once been a rice-pot, and at the shapeless lumps of brass, deeply imbedded in the soil, which had so lately contained his betel quids.

The two Sâkai, chattering in the upper branches of the trees, shook the boughs on which they were seated, in the agony of the fear that still held them.

'The Great Father was filled with wrath!' said one of them. He was anxious to speak of the elephant that had assailed them, with the greatest respect. Both he and his fellow felt convinced that the rogue was an incarnation of their former friend and tribesman Pa' Pâtin—the 'Spike-Fish'—who had come by his death on the Salt-Lick two years before, but they were much too prudent to express this opinion yet awhile. Pa' Pâtin had been a mild enough individual during his lifetime, but he seemed to have developed a temper since he joined the other shades, and the two Sâkai would not willingly outrage his feelings by speaking of him by name.

Presently, Pandak Âris climbed down from his tree,

and began somewhat ruefully to gather together his
damaged property. He cried to the two Sâkai to
come to his aid, but they sat shuddering in their lofty
perches, and declined to move.

'Come down! Descend out of the branches!
Are your ears deaf that ye obey me not?' shouted
Pandak Âris; but the frightened Sâkai showed no
signs of complying. He cursed and miscalled them
with that amplitude of vocabulary which the Malays
know how to use upon occasion. He threatened all
manner of grievous punishments; he tried to bribe
the shuddering creatures with promises of food and
tobacco; at last, he even condescended to entreat
them to come down. But all was in vain, for the
Sâkai remained firm, and cared for none of these things.
Pandak Âris knew how hopeless would be an attempt
to chase these creatures through the branches, and,
at last, very much out of temper, he gave up all hope
of making the Sâkai rejoin him that night.

Meanwhile, much time had been wasted, and the
waters of the Mîsong were dyed scarlet by the reflections cast from the ruddy clouds overhead. The
tocsin of the insect world was ringing through the
forest, and the birds' chorus was slowly dying down.
High above the topmost branches of the trees, the
moon, not yet at the full, was showing pale and faint,
but each moment the power of its gentle light grew
in strength. Pandak Âris glanced at all these things,
and, almost unconsciously, he drew a number of in-
ferences from them. It was too late for him to push
on alone to the mouth of the Mîsong, near which their
camp had been pitched that morning, for no Malay

willingly threads the jungle alone when the darkness
has fallen upon the land. It was too late also to erect
a camp on the Salt-Lick, for, after the shock which
his nerves had received from the attack of the rogue
elephant, he had no fancy for penetrating into the
forest to cut leaves and sticks for a hut, unless he
was accompanied by at least one of the Sâkai. Thereupon, Pandak Âris decided to camp on the bare earth,
at the foot of the giant tree near which he stood.
It would be fairly light, he told himself, until within
three hours before the dawn, and though his rice-pot
was smashed, and he must go to bed supperless, he
would light a fire and sleep beside its protecting blaze.
But here an unexpected difficulty presented itself.
The flint and steel, with which the fire was to be
kindled, was nowhere to be found. With the rest of
Pandak Âris's gear, it had been cast to the winds by
the rogue elephant, and the fast-waning light refused
to show where it had fallen. Pandak Âris searched
diligently for an hour, but without result, and at
length he was forced to abandon all hope of finding
it. If he could have put his hand upon a seasoned
piece of rattan, he could easily have ignited a dry
stick, by pulling the former backwards and forwards
across it, but rattan grows green in the jungle, and
is useless for this purpose until it has been dried.

Pandak Âris lay down upon the warm earth between the roots of the big tree, and swore softly under
his breath. He cursed the Sâkai to the fifth and sixth
generation, and said bitter things of Fate and Destiny.
Then he rolled over on his side, and fell asleep. The
tree near which he lay, like most jungle giants, threw

out long ridges of root, which, at their junction with
the trunk, rose above the surface of the ground to a
height of two or three feet. Thence they sloped
down at a sharp angle, and meandered away through
the grass, and the rank underwood, in all manner of
knotty curves and undulations. Pandak Âris lay in
the space between two of these roots, and was thus
protected by a low wall on either side of him, extend-
ing from his head to his hips. The placid moonlight
bathed the jungle with a flood of soft radiance, and
fell upon the sleeping face of the Malay, and upon the
Sâkai hunched up, with their heads between their
knees, snoring uneasily in the tree-tops. The ants
ran hither and thither over Pandak Âris's body, and
a lean leech or two came bowing and scraping towards
him as he slept. The jungle hummed with its myriad
sounds caused by birds and insects, but the rhythm of
this gentle murmur did not disturb the sleepers.

Suddenly, the two Sâkai awoke with a start. They
said never a word, but they listened intently. Very
far away, across the Mîsong, a branch had snapped
faintly but crisply. The ear of a European would hardly
have detected the sound, had he been listening for it,
but it had been more than sufficient to arouse the
sleeping Sâkai into an alert wakefulness. The noise
was repeated again and again. Now, several twigs and
branches seemed to snap simultaneously ; now, there
was a swishing noise, as of green leaves ripped from
their boughs by a giant's hand ; and then for a space
deep silence once more. The sounds grew gradually
louder and more distinct, and for an hour the Sâkai sat
listening intently, while Pandak Âris slept placidly.

Suddenly, there came a soft squelching noise, followed shortly by a pop, sounding in the distance like that of a child's gun. This was repeated many times, and was succeeded by the splashing of water sluiced over hot rough hides. Even a White Man could have interpreted the meaning of this, but the Sâkai could beat him even now, for their ears had told them not only that a herd of elephants had come down to water, but even the number of the beasts, and moreover that one of them was a calf of tender age.

The wind was blowing from the jungle across the Mĭsong to the trees where the men were camped, so the elephants took their bath with much leisure, splashing and wallowing mightily in the shallows, and in such pools as they could find. Then they came ashore, and began working slowly round under cover of the jungle, so as to get below the wind before venturing out upon the open space of the Salt-Lick. The Sâkai high up in the trees, could watch the surging of the underwood, as the great beasts rolled through it, but the footfall of the elephants made no noise, and, save when one or another of the animals cracked a bough, in order to feed upon the leaves, the progress of the herd was wonderfully unmarked by sound. The wind of the Sâkai passed over their heads, but presently they scented Pandak Âris. And in a moment a perfect torrent of trumpetings and squealings broke the stillness. This was followed by a wild crashing, tearing noise, and Pandak Âris, awake at last, fancied that the whole herd was charging down upon him. It is often difficult to tell in which direction big game are moving, when they rush through the jungle, but, on this occasion, the herd had been seized with panic, and was in full flight.

Over and over again, while the light of the moon held out, game of all kinds made its way to a point below the wind, whence to approach the Salt-Lick, and each time their noses told them that men were in possession. The savage blowing and snorting of the wild kine ; the grunting of a pack of pig ; the loud frightened barking of a stag : all sounded in turn, and each was succeeded by the snapping of dry twigs, and the crashing of rent underwood, which told of a hasty retreat.

At first, Pandak Âris sought shelter in the branches of the tree, but, in a little space, the agony of discomfort he suffered from his uneasy seat, and from the red ants swarming over him, drove him once more to brave the perils of the earth.

At about 2.30 A.M. the moon sank to rest, and a black darkness, which must be experienced to be understood, fell upon the forest. Though Pandak Âris squatted or lay at the edge of the open, he was unable to see his own hand when he waved it before his eyes ; and the impenetrable gloom, that surrounded him, wrought his already overstrained nerves to a pitch of agonised intensity.

And now a fresh horror was lent to the situation, for the game no longer troubled themselves to approach the Salt-Lick from below the wind. At intervals, Pandak Âris could hear some unknown beast splashing in the waters of the Misong, or treading softly upon the kneaded earth, within a few feet of him. He was covered with a thousand biting sand-flies—the tiny

insect which the Malays say has a bet that he will
swallow a man, and seems anxious on all occasions to
try to win his wager. They came from the beasts,
which now crowded the Salt-Lick, and they clung
to the Malay's bare skin, and nestled into his hair,
driving him almost frantic with the fierce itching
they occasioned.

Now and again, some brute would pass so near to
him that Pandak Âris could hear the crisp sound of its
grazing, or the rhythm of its heavy breath. Occasionally, one or other of them would wind him, as the
sudden striking of hoofs against the ground, and an
angry snorting or blowing would make plain. But
all this time Pandak Âris could see nothing.

Many times he clambered into the tree, but his
tired bones could not rest there, and the fierce red ants
bit him angrily, and drove him once more to the earth.

Shortly before the dawn, Pandak Âris was startled
out of an uneasy, fitful sleep, by the sound of some
huge animal passing very near him. He could hear it
even more distinctly than he had yet done any of the
other beasts which had peopled his waking nightmare.
Then, suddenly came a mighty blowing, a fierce
snort, and some monster—he knew not what—charged
him viciously. Pandak Âris lay flat upon the ground,
and the beast passed over him, doing him no harm,
save that a portion of the fleshy part of his thigh was
pinched violently by a hoof which cut cleanly, for
Pandak Âris could feel the warm blood trickling freely.
He still lay flat upon the earth, in the dead darkness,
too frightened to move, with his heart leaping chokingly
into his gullet. But his assailant had not yet done

c

with him. A warm blowing upon his face, which almost deprived him of reason, told him that some animal was standing over him. Almost instinctively, he felt for his *párang*, or long, keen wood - knife, and drew it gently to his side, grasping the handle firmly in his right hand. Presently, amid a tumult of angry snortings, something hard seemed to be insinuated beneath his body. Pandak Âris moved quickly to avoid this new horror, and clung convulsively to the ground. Again and again, first on one side, and then on the other, this hard prodding substance sought to force itself below him. It bruised him terribly, beating the wind from his lungs, sending dull pangs through his whole body at each fresh prod, and leaving him faint and gasping.

Pandak Âris never knew how long this lasted. To him it seemed a month or two, but the situation was still unchanged when the light began to return to the earth.

Dawn comes rapidly in the Peninsula, up to a certain point, though the sun takes time to arise from under its bed-clothes of white cloud. One moment all is dark as the Bottomless Pit ; another, and a new sense is given to the watcher—or so it seems—the sense of form. A minute or two more, and the power to distinguish colour comes almost as a surprise —the faint, dim green of the grass, the yellow of a pebble, the brown of a faded leaf, each one a new quality in a familiar object, hitherto unnoticed and unsuspected. So it was with Pandak Âris. All in a moment he began to see ; and what his eyes showed him did not tend to reassure him. He looked up at a vast and overwhelming bulk of blackness, that seemed to completely overshadow him, and he knew his assailant for a *sělâdang*, the largest of all beasts, save only the elephant, though many say that in strength the wild bull can outmatch even him. Presently, as the light grew in power, Pandak Âris could see the black hairy hide, the gray belly, the long fringe of shaggy hair at the beast's throat, the smoking nostrils, wide open, and of a dim red, and the cruel eyes looking angrily into his.

Almost before he knew what he had done, Pandak Âris had seized his wood-knife in both hands, and with the instinct of self-preservation, had drawn its long, keen edge across the monster's throat. A deluge of blood fell into the man's face, and the *sělâdang*, snorting fiercely, stamped with its off fore-foot. The heavy hoof fell on Pandak Aris's left arm, reducing it to a shapeless mass, but the wounded limb telegraphed no signal of pain to the brain, which was working too eagerly on its own account to take heed of aught else.

Still standing upon the arm of its victim, the *sělâdang* tried again and again to force its horn beneath Pandak Âris's body, and all the while the wood-knife, worked by the still uninjured hand, sawed relentlessly at the brute's throat. Presently, the bull began to feel the deadly sickness which comes before death, and it fell heavily upon its knees. It floundered up again, bruising Pandak Âris once more as it did so. Then it reeled away, sinking to its knees again and again, while the blood poured, in great, far-carrying jets, from the widening gap in its throat. Presently it sank to the ground, and, after tearing up the earth angrily in its death agony, lay still for ever.

'Yonder lies much meat!' grunted one of the Sâkai to his neighbour. That was their only comment on what had occurred.

Now that the fight was over, and that daylight had come, they climbed down out of the tree. They stooped over the insensible body of Pandak Âris, and when they found that he still lived, they bandaged his wounds, not unskilfully, with strips of his *sárong*. Then, they built a make-shift raft, and placed the wounded man upon it, together with as much *sélâdang* beef as it would carry. Wading down stream, one at the bow, and one at the stern of the raft, they reached the camp that they had left the preceding morning, and there they feasted in plenty on the good red meat.

Pandak Âris was tough and blessed with a mighty constitution, so, when he regained consciousness, he also ate of the body of his enemy.

'I cut his throat, and, while doing so, I mind me that I murmured the word *Bishmillah*—in the name of God—wherefore it was lawful for me to eat of a beast which had been killed according to the rites of Muhammad,' he said to me, in after days, and I was less surprised at the ease with which he had salved his conscience, than I was at his ability to eat meat at all, after such an adventure.

The Sâkai got him back to his house, rafting him gently down stream, and his wife, Mînah of the soft-eyes, tended him devotedly, till naught but scars, and a useless left arm, remained to tell of his encounter with the *sélâdang*.

This was the one incident that served to break the dead monotony of Pandak Âris's many days of life ; and perhaps he was right in thinking that this single night held sufficient excitement and adventure to last any man for all his years.

THE FATE OF LEH THE STROLLING PLAYER

I made them to laugh till their ribs were sore,
I made them to weep till their eyes were red,
I bore their hearts through the carnage of War,
I bore them back to the day they were wed.
I gave them to think of the babe in the hut,
Of the soft-eyed wife, with a tender love ;
I carried them out of their life's dull rut,
And wafted them up to the World Above !
Ah, my skill was great in the playing !

I fill'd them with Hate, till their hands ran blood,
I scourged them with Lust, like a raging fire,
I whipped their souls to a hurrying flood,
I fill'd them with torture of Vain Desire ;
Their skins grew parch'd, and their eyes wax'd hot,
While I drove them whither no man should go ;
Their souls were my toys, to play with, I wot,
And I toss'd them down to the World Below !
Ah, my skill was great in the playing !

The Chant of the Minnesinger.

AT Kôta Bharu, the Capital of Kĕlantan, the Powers that be are at great pains to preserve a kind of cock-eyed, limping, knock-kneed Morality, which goes on all fours with their notion of the eternal fitness of things. Yam Tûan Mûlut Mêrah—the Red-Mouthed

King—did his best to discourage theft ; and with
this laudable intention killed, during his long reign,
sufficient men and women to have repeopled a new
country half the size of his own kingdom. Old Nek
'Soh, the Dâto' Sri Paduka, who stood by and saw
most of the killing done, still openly laments that all
the thieves and robbers were not made over to him,
instead of being wasted in the shambles. With so
large a following, he says, he might have started a new
dynasty in the Peninsula, and still have had enough
men and women at his disposal to enable him to sell
one or two, when occasion required, if ready money
was hard to come by. Nek 'Soh is a wise old man,
and he probably is sure of his facts, but though his
influence with his master, the Red-Mouthed King,
was great in most things, he never succeeded in
persuading him to try the experiment. So the King
continued to slay robbers, suspected thieves, and the
relations and relatives of convicted or accused persons,
while Nek 'Soh mourned over the sinful waste of
good material, and the bulk of the population thieved
and robbed as persistently and as gaily as ever.

It must be owned that these efforts at reform were
not encouraging in their results, and perhaps this is
why, so long as the Red-Mouthed King, with Nek
'Soh at his side, was responsible for the government of
the country, no other attempts to improve the morality
of the people of Kĕlantan were made by the dis-
heartened rulers.

At length, in the fulness of time, old Mûlut Mêrah
died, and his son, and later his grandson, ruled in his
stead. Nek 'Soh continued to have a hand in the

government of the country, but a younger man than he, was now the principal adviser and soon the real ruler of Kĕlantan.   This person bore the title of Maha Mĕntri, which means the Great Minister, and since he was young and energetic he plunged hotly into reforms which were destined, as he forecast them, to revolutionise the ways and manners of the good people of Kĕlantan.   Quite oblivious of the fact that mutilation and sudden death, to which an added horror was lent by some ingenious contrivances cunningly devised with the amiable object of increasing the intensity of the pain inflicted upon the unfortunate victims, had completely failed to cure the Kĕlantan folk's innate propensity to rob and thieve, Maha Mĕntri conceived the bold idea of forthwith converting an irreligious people into fervent and bigoted Muhammadans.   To this end, he insisted upon attendance at the Friday congregational prayers, even to the breaking of the heads of recalcitrant church-goers ; he observed, and personally superintended the observance of Fasts ; he did his best to prevent the use of silk garments by any save the women-folk, and this, be it remembered, in a country which is famed for its silk fabrics ; he put down cock-fighting, bull matches, prize-fights, hunting, and the keeping of dogs,—all the sports of the wealthy, in fact ; and while he pried into the home of every family in the capital, with the laudable object of ascertaining whether the inmates prayed regularly at each of the Five Hours of Appointed Prayer, he dealt an even more severe blow to the bulk of the population by forbidding the performance of the *ma'iong*, or heroic plays, such as are acted throughout the length and breadth of the Peninsula by troupes of strolling players, but which are an amusement that is specially dear to the hearts of the good people of Kĕlantan.

These plays are performed inside a small, square paddock, enclosed by a low bamboo railing, but otherwise open on all four sides, so as to give the spectators an unobstructed view of all that goes forward within. A palm-leaf roof protects the players from the sun by day, and from the heavy dews of the tropics by night ; and whenever a *ma'iong* shed is erected upon a new site, the Pâwang, or Medicine Man, who is also the Actor-Manager of the company, performs certain magic rites with cheap incense, and other unsavoury offerings to the Spirits, reciting many ancient incantations the while to the Demons of Earth and Air, beseeching them to watch over his people, and to guard them from harm. First he calls upon Black Âwang, King of the Earth, who is wont to wander in the veins of the ground, and to take his rest at the Portals of the World ; next to the Holy Ones, the local demons of the place ; and finally to his Grandsire, Pĕtĕra Gûru, the Teacher who is from the Beginning, who is incarnate from his birth, the Teacher who dwelleth as a hermit in the recesses of the Moon, and practiseth his magic arts in the Womb of the Sun, the Teacher whose coat is wrought of green beads, whose blood is white, who hath but a single bone, the hairs of whose body stand erect, the pores of whose skin are adamant, whose neck is black, whose tongue is fluent, whose spittle is brine ! All these he prays to guard his people, and then he cries to them to aid him by opening the gates of Lust and

Passion, together with the gates of Desire and Credulity, and the gates of Desire and Longing, the Longing which lasteth from dawn unto dawn, which causeth food to cease to satisfy, which maketh sleep uneasy, which remembering maketh memory unceasing, causeth hearing to hear, seeing to see !

These exhortations to Spirits, which should find no place in the Demonology of any good Muhammadan, were naturally regarded as an Uncleanness and an Abomination by the strait-laced Maha Měntri ; and not content with prohibiting the performances of the *ma'iong*, he made life so excessively unattractive to the actors and actresses themselves, that many bands of them trooped over the jungle-clad mountains, which divide Kělantan from Pahang, to roam the country playing for hire at the weddings and feasts of a people who, no matter what other faults they may have, cannot justly be accused of bigotry or fanaticism.

So great joy was brought to the natives of Pahang, and from end to end of the land the throbbing beat of the *ma'iong* drums, the clanging of the gongs, the scrapings of the ungainly Malay fiddles, the demented shrieks and wailings of the *sěrúnai*, and the roars of hearty laughter, which greet each one of the clown's jests, made merry discord in the villages. The gates of Lust and Passion, the gates of Desire and Longing,— that Longing which lasteth from dawn unto dawn, which causeth food to cease to satisfy, which maketh sleep uneasy,—were opened wide that tide, and there were tales of woe brought in from many a village in the long Pahang valley. While the *ma'iong* was a-playing no one had any care for the crops, the women left their babies and their cooking-pots, and the elders of the people were as stage-struck as the boys and maidens. When the strolling actors moved forward upon their way, having squeezed a village dry of its last copper coins, many of the *kampong* folk followed in their train, cadging for their food from the people at each halting-place, enduring many hardships often enough, but seemingly unable to tear themselves away from the fascinations of the players and of the actresses. Many lawful wives found themselves deserted by their men, and the husbands and fathers in the villages had to keep a sharp eye upon the doings of their wives and daughters while the *ma'iong* folk were in the neighbourhood; for when once the dead monotony of their lives is broken into by some unusual occurrence, the morality of the Malay villagers, which is generally far better than that of the natives of the Capitals, quickly goes to pieces, like a wrecked ship in the trough of an angry sea.

Of all the Actor-Managers who were then roaming up and down Pahang, none were so successful both with the play-goers and with the women, as Saleh, or Leh, as he was usually called, for Malay energy is rarely equal to the effort necessary for the articulation of the whole of a proper name. In their mouths the dignified Muhammad becomes the plebeian Mat, Sulehman,—our old friend Solomon,—is reduced to plain Man, and a like evil fate is shared by other high-sounding, sonorous names. This is worth noticing, because it is very typical of the propensity, which the Malay can never resist, to scamp every bit of labour, no matter how light its nature, that falls to his share in this workaday world.

Leh was a man of many accomplishments. He played the fiddle, in most excruciating wise, to the huge delight of all the Malays who heard him ; he was genuinely funny, when he had put his hideous red mask, with its dirty sheepskin top, which stood for the hair of his head, over his handsome, clever face, and roars of laughter greeted him at every turn ; he had a keen eye for a topical joke, a form of satire much appreciated by his Malay audiences ; he had a happy knack of imitating the notes of birds, and the cry of any animal ; and above all he was a skilled Rhapsodist, and with that melodious voice of his would sing the wonderful story of Âwang Lôtong, the Monkey Prince, which is a bastard, local version of the Ramayana, until the cocks were crowing to a yellow dawn. He travelled with me, on one occasion, for a fortnight, and I had the whole of the Folk-Tale written down, and when completed it covered the best part of sixty folios, yet Leh knew every word of it by rote, and could be turned on at any point, continuing the story every time in precisely the same words. He had learned it from an old man in Kĕlantan, and he was reputed to be the only surviving bard to whom the whole of the tale was known. In due course I sent the manuscript, with a translation, and elaborate notes to a Learned Society, where it was lost with the usual promptitude and despatch.

It was always a marvel to me that Leh escaped having some angry man's knife thrust deftly between his fourth and fifth ribs, for the natives of Pahang are

wont to discourage too successful lovers by little
attentions of this sort, and Leh was much loved by the
women-folk, both high and low, throughout the length
and breadth of the land. Perhaps he was as cunning
as he was successful, for he certainly lived to return to
his own country.

This was rendered possible for all the *ma'iong* people
by the sudden death of Maha Měntri. This great
and good man,—the self-appointed Champion of
Muhammadanism, the enforcer of Prayer, the orderer
of Fasts for the mortification of the erring flesh,—like
some other zealous people, who in the cause of Religion
have contrived to make their neighbours' lives as little
worth living as possible, had one little weakness which
marred the purity and consistency of his character.
This was an irrepressible impulse to break the Seventh
Commandment, a strange failing in a man who was
so scrupulous that he would not even suffer himself to
be photographed when a view of Kôta Bharu, in which
several hundreds of people figured, was being taken.
This is but one of the startling inconsistencies which
are to be remarked in the religious Oriental. Until
one has become familiar with an Eastern People, it
is difficult to realise how far the Letter of the Law
may be pushed by a man who, all the while, is daily
defying its Spirit.

The good people of Kělantan bore with Maha
Měntri and his little peculiarities for a considerable
time, and they might, perhaps, even have suffered
him for a longer period, had it not been for the fact
that his religious fanaticism, on subjects which did
not happen to hit him in a tender place, had the effect

of making life a more evil thing than seemed to be altogether necessary. Be this how it may, upon a certain night Maha Měntri was shot through the flooring of another man's house by the owner thereof, ably and actively assisted by two other men, who were entirely convinced that there was not sufficient room for them and for Maha Měntri upon the surface of one and the same Planet.

Everybody knew who had done the deed, and the Rája would dearly have loved to take a life for a life, but the murderers were under the protection of a young prince, with whom, for political reasons, the Rája could not afford to precipitate a quarrel. Therefore he and his advisers professed to wonder very much indeed who could have been so unmannerly as to shoot Maha Měntri in three several places ; and there the matter ended, in spite of the clamorous protests of the dead man's relatives.

Very soon the news of Maha Měntri's death spread through Pahang, word being brought by the trading boats lurching down the Coast, or by the sweating villagers who trudged across the mountains to bring the glad tidings to the exiles from Kělantan, to whose return the presence of Maha Měntri had hitherto been a very sufficient obstacle.

So the *ma'iong* folk packed their gear, and started back for their own country, and many men and maidens were left lamenting, when the players who had loved them strode away.

Leh went back by sea, with half a dozen broken hearts in his *gendong* (bundle), and soon after his return, he was appointed to the post of Court Minstrel,

and Master of the royal Dancing Girls. For the
Kělantan to which he came back, was a very different
place from the land which he had quitted when he
started out for Pahang. As soon as the worthy Maha
Mĕntri had been laid in his grave, the reaction, which
always follows any paroxysm of religiosity, set in in
full force, and for a season Kělantan was a merry land
for a pleasure-lover to make his home in. The Five
Hours of Appointed Prayer were suffered to slip by
unregarded of the people ; no man troubled himself to
fast more than his stomach thought fitting ; and the
music of the *ma'iong* was once more heard in the land.

In this new and joyful Kělantan, Leh found himself
very much in his element. The old Pillar Dollars,
which are the standard currency of the country, came
rolling merrily in, and Leh was able to go abroad
among his fellows lavishly clad, from the waist downwards, in a profusion of gaily-coloured silk *sârongs* and
sashes, such as the souls of the Kělantan people love.
He wore no coat, of course, for in this State that
garment is never used, except by the Nobles on official
occasions when strangers chance to be present.

Leh was never a man to keep all his good fortune
to himself, and not only a select few of the King's
Dancing Girls, but a countless troop of other dames
and maidens, who should rightly have been entirely
occupied with their lawful lords and masters, came in
for a large share of the spoil. Given a well-set-up
figure, a handsome face, gay garments, a witty tongue,
and a superfluity of ready money, and a far less clever
and engaging fellow than Leh, the Strolling Player,
might be expected to win the facile heart of any average

Malay woman. It was not long before the best-favoured half of the ladies of Kôta Bharu,—and that means a surprisingly large proportion of the female population of the place,—were, to use the Malay phrase, 'mad' for Leh. The natives of the Peninsula recognise that Love, when it wins a fair grip upon a man, is as much a disease of the mind as any other form of insanity ; and since it is more common than many manias, they speak of the passion as 'madness' *par excellence*. And this was the ailment from which a large number of the ladies of Kôta Bharu were now suffering with greater or lesser severity, according to their several temperaments.

This state of things naturally caused a considerable amount of dissatisfaction to the whole of the male community, and the number of the malcontents grew and grew, as the 'madness' spread among the women-folk. The latter began soon to throw off all disguise, for they were too numerous for even the most extensive system of wife and daughter beating to effectually cope with the trouble. When they were not occupied in waylaying Leh ; in ogling him as he swaggered past their dwellings, cocking a conquering eye through the doorways ; the ladies of Kôta Bharu were now often engaged in shrill and hard-fought personal encounters one with another. Each woman among them was wildly jealous of all her fellows ; mother suspecting daughter and daughter accusing mother of receiving more than her fair share of Leh's generous and widely scattered attentions. Many were the scratches made on nose and countenance, long and thick the tussocks of hair reft from one another by the angry ladies, and the men beholding these impossible goings-on with horror and dismay said among themselves that Leh, the Strolling Player, must die.

He was a good man of his hands, and badly as they felt about him no one saw his way to engaging him in single combat, though enough men and to spare were ready to have a hand in the killing. At last, a committee of three angry men was appointed, by general consent, and these lay in wait for Leh, during several successive evenings, in the hopes of finding him returning alone from the *ma'iong* shed.

It was on the third night of their vigil that their chance came. The moon was near the full, and the heavy, hard shadows lay across the ground, under the gently waving palm-fronds, like solid objects. The footpath which leads from the main thoroughfare into the villages around Kôta Bharu branches off some twenty yards from the spot where the watchers lay concealed. The Committee of Three sat huddled up, in the blackness cast upon the bare earth by a native house just within the clustering compounds, and the vivid Eastern moonlight gave up the colour of the yellow sun-baked soil, the green of the smooth banana leaves, even the red of the clusters of *rambut-an* fruits on a neighbouring tree.

Presently the sound of voices, talking and laughing lightheartedly, came to the ears of the listening men, and as the speakers drew nearer, the Committee of Three were able to distinguish Leh's mellow tones. At the parting of the ways Leh turned off by himself along the footpath, the others, with whom he had been walking, keeping still to the main road. Leh took leave of them, with a farewell jest or two which

sent the others laughing upon their way, and then he
strolled slowly along the footpath, humming the air
of Âwang Lôtong under his breath. The Three, in
the shadow of the house, could see the colour of the
gaudy cloths wound about Leh's waist, the fantastic
peak into which his head-kerchief was twisted, the
glint of the polished yellow wood and the gold settings
of his dagger-hilt, and the long, broad-bladed spear
that he carried in his hand. They watched him draw
nearer and yet more near to them, still humming gently,
and wearing a half smile upon his face. They suffered
him to come abreast of them, to stroll past them, all
unsuspicious of evil; but no pity for him was in their
hearts, for they had all been injured in a deadly manner
by this callous, lighthearted libertine, who now went
to the death he knew not of with a smile on his face,
and a stave of a song upon his lips.

As soon as Leh had passed them, the Committee
of Three stepped noiselessly out of the shadow, and
sounding their *sôrak*, or war-cry, into which they
threw all the pent-up hatred of their victim which for
months had been devouring their hearts, plunged their
spears into his naked brown back. Leh fell upon his
face with a thick choking cough, and a few more
vigorous spear-thrusts completed the work which the
Committee had been appointed to perform.

They left the body of Leh, the Strolling Player,
lying where it had fallen, face downwards in the dust
of the footpath, and though the King did all that lay
in his power to discover the secret of the identity of
the murderers, and though half the women-folk in the
Capital seconded his efforts to the utmost, hoping

that thereby their lover's death might be avenged, the
men who had planned the deed kept their secret well,
so no punishment could be meted out to those who had
actually brought about the destruction of the Warden
of the King's Dancing Girls. But in the eyes of Malay
Justice,—which is a very weird thing indeed,—if you
cannot punish the right man, it is better to come
down heavily upon the wrong one, than to allow
everybody to get off scot free. The house near to
which the body of Leh had been found, chanced to
be tenanted only by an old crone and her widowed
daughter, with her three small children, but none the
less, this hut was taken as the centre of a circle of
one hundred fathoms radius, and all whose dwellings
chanced to lie within its circumference, whether men
or women, old or young, whole or bedridden, women
great with child, or babes at the breast, were indiffer-
ently fined the sum of three dollars each—a large sum
for a Malay villager to be called upon to pay, and a
delightfully big total, from the King's point of view,
when all heads had been counted.

This new system of punishment by fine has several
advantages attaching to it. In the first place it en-
hances the revenue of the King, which is a matter of
some moment ; and secondly, if you chance to have
a quarrel with some one whom you are unable to get
even with in any other way, you need only leave a
corpse at his front door, which, in a land where life is
as cheap as it is in Kĕlantan, is an easy matter to
arrange. If the corpse, by any chance, should be that
of a man who has done you an injury, you will kill
two birds with one stone. Which is economical.

ÛMAT

Fat rice to eat and viands sweet,
        A mat on which to lie,
No feckless toil to mar and spoil
        The hours that saunter by ;
Man-child and wife to cheer my life,
        What need a man ask more?
Save just my sight and God's own light
        To see as once I saw.

THE *punkah* swings freely for a space ; then gradually shortens its stride ; hovers for a moment, oscillating gently, in answer to the feeble jerking of the cord ; almost stops ; and then is suddenly galvanised into a violent series of spasm-like leaps and bounds, each one less vigorous than the last, until once more the flapping canvas fringe is almost still. It is by signs such as these that we know that Ûmat, the *punkah*-puller, is sleeping the sleep of the just.

If you look behind the screen which cloaks the doorway, you will see him, and, if the afternoon is very warm and still, you may even hear his soft, regular breathing, and the gentle murmur with which his nose is wont to mark the rhythm of his slumber. An old cotton handkerchief is bound about his head, in such a manner that his bristles of hair stand up stiffly, all over his scalp, in a circular enclosure, like the trainers in a garden of young *sirih* vines. On his back he wears an old, old coat of discoloured yellow *khaki*, once the property of a dead policeman. The Government buttons have been taken away from him, by a relentless Police Inspector, and their place is supplied by thorns, cunningly arranged pieces of stick, and one or two wooden studs. The shoulder-straps flap loosely, and their use is a problem on which Ûmat often ponders, but which he is never able to satisfactorily solve. A cotton *sârong*—not always of the cleanest, I fear—is round Ûmat's waist, and, falling to his knees, supplies the place of all other lower garments. For Ûmat is both comfort-loving and economical, and Pahang is now a free country where a man may go clad as he likes, without fear of some ill-thing befalling him. Less than ten years ago, a man who went abroad without his trousers ran a good chance of never returning home again, since Pahang Malays were apt to think that such an one was no lover of war. Among Malays, who are the most personally modest people in the world, it is well known that no man may fight with a whole heart when, at every moment, he runs. the risk of exposing his nakedness ; and, in days gone by, the natives of Pahang were well pleased to display their prowess in mangling one from whom little resistance could be expected. But, in Kĕlantan, where Ûmat was born, few men possess trousers, and no one who loves to be comfortable wears them, when he can avoid doing so.

Below his *sârong*, goodly lengths of bare and hairy

leg are visible, ending in broad splay feet, with soles
that seem shod with horn ; for Ûmat could dance barefoot in a thorn thicket with as much comfort as upon
a velvet carpet.

He half sits, half lies, huddled up in a wicker-work
arm-chair, his head canted stiffly over his right shoulder,
his eyes tight shut, and his mouth wide open, exposing
two rows of blackened tusks, and a fair expanse of gums
and tongue stained scarlet with areca-nut. His feet
are on the seat of the chair, one doubled snugly under
him, with the suppleness of the Oriental, and the other
supporting the knee upon which his chin may rest as
occasion requires. The pull-cord of the *punkah* is
made fast about his right wrist, and his left hand holds
it limply, his arms moving forward and backwards
mechanically in his sleep. At his feet, humming
contentedly to himself, sits a tiny brown boy, dressed
chastely in a large cap and a soiled pocket-hand-
kerchief ; and thus Ûmat dreams away many hours of
his life. If his sleeping memory takes him back to
the days when he followed me upon the war-path,
when we went a-fishing on a dirty night, or when
the snipe were plentiful, and the bag a big one, the
punkah dances merrily, and takes a violent part in the
action of which he dreams. But, if Ûmat's mind
plays about the tumble-down cottage in my compound,
which he calls 'home,' and dwells upon his soft-eyed,
gentle wife, Sĕlĕma, and upon the children he loves so
very dearly, or if his dreams conjure up memories
of good meals, and quiet sleepy nights, then in sympathy
the *punkah* moves softly, sentimentally, and stops.

' *Tárek!* Pull !' comes a voice from the inner room,

and Ûmat, awakened with a start, bursts into voluble
reproaches, addressed to himself in the guttural speech
of the Kĕlantan people. Then he falls asleep more
soundly than ever.

If you run up the East Coast of the Peninsula, past
the smiling shores of Pahang and Trĕnggânu, you at
last reach the spot where the bulk of the Kĕlantan
river-water formerly made its way into the China Sea.
The better entrance is now a mile or two farther up
the Coast, but the groves of palm-trees show that the
people have been less fickle than the river, and that the
villages at the old mouth are still tenanted as of yore.
It is here that Ûmat was born and bred, the son of a
family of Fisher Folk, countless generations of whom
have dwelt at Kuâla Kĕlantan ever since the beginning
of things.

If you look at Ûmat's round face, and observe it
carefully, you may read therein much that bears upon
the history of his people. The prevailing expression
is one of profoundly calm patience—not that look of
waiting we understand by the term, the patience which,
with restless Europeans, presupposes some measure of
anticipation, and of the pain of hope long deferred—
but the contented endurance of one who is satisfied to
be he is; of one whose lot is unchanging, and
whose desires are few. It is a negative expression,
without sadness, without pain, or the fever of longing,
and yet sufficiently far removed from dulness or
stupidity. It speaks of long years during which Ûmat's
forebears have laboured stolidly, have been as driven
cattle before prince and chief, and yet, since the curse

of knowledge that better things existed had not fallen upon them, have accepted their lot as they found it, unresisting and uncomplaining.

This is what one reads in Ûmat's face when it is in repose, but, when emotion changes it, other things may be seen as clearly. Suddenly, his features break up into a thousand creases, the brown skin puckering in numberless spreading lines, like the surface of a muddy puddle into which a stone has fallen. A laugh like the crowing of a cock, combined with the roaring of a bull, accompanied this phenomenon, and you may then know that Ûmat's keen sense of humour has been tickled. It does not take much to amuse him, for, like most Malays, he is very light-hearted, and anything which has a trace of fun in it delights him hugely. Almost every Kĕlantan fishing boat that puts to sea carries its *âlanâlan*, or jester, along with it, for toil is lightened if men be merry, and, in days gone by, Ûmat was the most popular man in his village. A quaint phrase; a happy repartee, not always in the most refined language; the rude mimicry of some personal eccentricity; a word or two of rough chaff; or a good story; such things are his stock in trade, and this is why Ûmat is so well beloved by his fellows.

But he can be grave, too. As my raft whirls down a rapid, a clumsy punt sends it reeling to what looks like certain destruction. Ûmat's face sets hard. His teeth are clenched, his lips compressed tightly. His bare feet grapple the slippery bamboos with clinging grip, and his twenty-foot punting-pole describes a circle above his head. The point alights, with marvellous rapidity, and unerring. aim, upon the only projecting ridge of rock within immediate reach, and all Ûmat's weight is put into the push, while his imprisoned breath breaks loose in an excited howl. The raft cants violently, and wallows knee-deep, but the danger of instant destruction is averted, and we tear through the fifty yards of foaming, boiling, rock-beset water, which divides us from the rapid's foot, without further mishap. Then, Ûmat's face relaxes, and his queer laugh resounds, as he chaffs the man, whose clumsiness had nearly been our ruin, with unmerciful disregard for his feelings.

His promptness to see the nature of the emergency, his ready presence of mind, his quick, decisive action, that saves us from a break-up, which, in a boiling, foaming rapid, is no pleasant experience, have little to do with Ûmat himself. He owes all to his kinsmen, the Fisher Folk, who have been accustomed to risk their lives on the fishing banks, amid the sandy river bars, the rocky headlands, and the treacherous waves of the China Sea, for many unrecorded centuries. Readiness to face a danger, prompt and fearless action, quick apprehension of the best means of escape, are qualities without which the race would long ere this have become extinct, and in Ûmat these things amount to absolute instincts.

But he can, on occasion, show pluck of quite another kind—the courage which is no mere flash-in-the-pan, born of excitement, and owing its origin to an instinct of self-preservation—that long-enduring fearlessness in the face of a danger, before which a man must sit down and wait. It is no light thing to stare death in the eyes for days or weeks together, to expect it in some cruel, merciless form, and yet to possess one's soul in patience, and to keep a heart in one's body that does not sink and quail.   Yet, Ûmat is capable of this higher form of courage, as you shall presently hear, and though the limitations of his imagination stand him in good stead, and doubtless make the situation easier to him than it can be to the white man, cursed with the restless brain of his kind, yet one must give Ûmat credit for valour of no mean order.   The merriment dies out of his face at such times, for, unlike my friend, Räja Haji Hamid, whose eyes were wont to dance, and whose mouth smiled cheerily when danger was afoot, Ûmat comes of a class to whom a gamble with death is a hated thing.   The look of calm patience is in his eyes, but now he is enduring consciously, and the hard puckers in his forehead show that his nerves are tightly strung, and that there is little gladness in his heart.

But Ûmat's face is capable of yet another change. When his brown eyes blaze, when his face is full of excitement, and a torrent of hardly articulate words bursts headlong from his lips, you may know that Ûmat is angry.   A tumult of wrathful sound, at the back of the bungalow, where the servants congregate, in the covered way which joins the cook-house to the main building, begins the uproar, and, if you fail to interfere, some Chinese heads will infallibly be broken in several places.   Knowing this, I run to the spot, and reduce my people to silence.   On inquiry, it will prove to be that the cook has accused Ûmat of adulterating the milk, or the water-coolie, whose business it also is to make lamps smell and smoke, has charged

him with purloining the oil. No words can describe
Ûmat's fury, and indignation, if he is indeed guiltless;
but he is a bad liar, and, if the charges are true, his
manner soon betrays him, and his wrath fails to convince. In a little time, he will produce the bottle of
lamp-oil from the folds of his *sárong*, and, laughing
sheepishly, will claim that praise should be his portion,
since the bottle is only half full. He takes my pungent
remarks with exaggerated humility, and, five minutes
later, the compound will be ringing with the songs he
loves to bellow. It is not possible to be angry with
Ûmat for long. He is so very childlike, and I, in common
with many others, love him better than he deserves.

I first met Ûmat in 1890, when, after a year spent
in Europe, I returned to Pahang, and took charge of
the interior. I was very lonely. My Malay followers
had been scattered to the winds during my absence in
England, and I had none but strangers about me.
The few European miners scattered about the district
were only met with from time to time. The Pahang
Malays stood aloof from us, and I found the isolation
dreary enough. Pahang had had an ill name on the
Coast, any time these last three hundred years, and,
until the white men protected the country, few
strangers cared to set foot in a land where life was held
on such a precarious tenure. But, presently, the
whisper spread through the villages of Trĕnggânu and
Kĕlantan that work found a high price in Pahang
under the white men, and a stream of large-limbed
Malays, very different in appearance from the slender
people of the land, began to pour over the borders.

On this stream Úmat was borne to me, and, since then, he has never left me, nor will he, probably, till the time comes for one or the other of us to have his toes turned up to the love-grass.

Úmat saw that I was lonely, and perhaps he dimly realised that I was an object of pity, for he would creep into my bungalow, and, seating himself upon the floor, would tell me tales of his own people until the night was far advanced. His dialect was strange to me, at that time, and the manner in which he elided some of his vowels and most of his consonants puzzled me sorely. I could not understand the system under which *ánam* (six) shrank into *ne'*, and *kérbau* (buffalo) became *kúba'*; but I let him talk on—for was he not my only companion?—and, in the end, I not only learnt to understand him, but actually to speak his barbarous lingo.

So Úmat and I became friends, and life was to me a trifle less dreary because he was at hand. He taught me many things which I did not know, and his simple stories, told with little skill, served to enliven many an hour of crushing, overwhelming solitude.

Then came a period when trouble darkened the land, and I turned to the war-path, which to me was then so strange and unfamiliar, with Úmat stamping along at my heels. He never left me all that time, and I had many opportunities of testing the quality of his courage. At last, it became necessary for me to visit a number of almost openly hostile Chiefs who, with their six hundred followers, were camped about half a mile from my stockade. I had only a score of men at my disposal, and they were needed to hold our frail fort, so it became evident to me that I must go alone. I was not altogether sorry to have the opportunity of doing so, for I knew how susceptible to ' bluff' Malays are apt to be, and I was aware that in a somewhat ostentatious display of fearlessness—no matter what my real sensations might be—lay my best hope of safety. Therefore, I armed myself carefully, and prepared to set out, though most of my Malay friends were clamorous in their efforts to dissuade me. As I started, Ûmat, armed with *kris* and spear, and with a set look of resolve upon his face, followed at my heels.

' It is not necessary for thee to come,' I said. ' If all goes well, there is no need of thee, and, if aught goes amiss, what profits it that two should suffer instead of one ? '

Ûmat grunted, but he did not turn back.

' Return,' I said. ' I have no need of thee.'

I halted as I spoke, but Ûmat stood firm, and showed no signs of obeying me.

' *Tûan*,' he said, ' for how long a time have I eaten thy rice, when thou wast in prosperity and at ease ; is it fitting that I should leave thee now that thou art in trouble ? *Tûan*, where thou goest I will go. Where thou leadest I will follow after.'

I said no more, but went upon my way with Ûmat at my heels. I was more touched than I liked to say, and indeed his courage was of the highest, for he believed himself to be going to certain death, whereas I was backing my own opinion of the character of those with whom I had to deal, and, though the stake was a big one, I was sufficiently conceited to feel confident about the result. During the long interview

with the Chiefs, the knowledge that Ûmat's great,
fleshy body was wedged in securely between my
enemies and the small of my back, gave me an added
confidence, which was worth many points in my
favour.   We won through, and the hostile Chiefs
dispersed their people, and, that night, Ûmat made
darkness hideous by the discordant yellings with which
he celebrated the occasion, and gave token of the
reaction that followed on the unstringing of his tense
nerves.

Later I was promoted, and Ûmat came with me to
the Capital, and since then he has lived in a house in
my compound with Sĕlĕma, the Pahang girl, who has
made him so gentle and faithful a wife.   It was soon
after his marriage that his trouble fell upon Ûmat, and
swept much of the sunshine from his life.   He con-
tracted a form of ophthalmia, and for a time was blind.
Native Medicine Men doctored him, and drew sheafs
of needles and bunches of thorns from his eyes, which
they declared were the cause of his affliction.   These
miscellaneous odds and ends used to be brought to me
for inspection at breakfast-time, floating, most un-
appetisingly, in a shallow cup half full of water ; and
Ûmat went abroad with eye-sockets stained crimson,
or black, according to the fancy of the native physician.
The aid of an English doctor was called in, but Ûmat
was too thoroughly a Malay to trust the more simple
remedies prescribed to him, and, though his blindness
was relieved, and he became able to walk without the
aid of a staff, his eyesight could never really be given
back to him.

But Ûmat is sanguine, and, though he has now

been blind for years, and each new remedy has proved
to be merely one more disappointment, he still believes
firmly that in time the light will return to him.
Meanwhile, his life holds many emotions. His laugh
rings out, and the compound at night-time resounds
with the songs he loves to improvise, which have for
their theme the marvellous doings of ' Ûmat the Blind
Man whose eyes cannot see.' His patience has come
to the rescue, and the sorrow of his blindness is a
chastened grief, which he bears with little complaining.
He has aged somewhat, for his sightless orbs make his
face look graver, heavier, duller than of old, but his
heart is as young as ever.

Though his affliction has been a heavy one, other
good things have not kept aloof. One day, as I sit
writing, Ûmat comes into the room, and presently the
whole house resounds with the news that he expects
shortly to become a father. Ûmat's face dances with
delight, and excitement, and pride ; but it wears also
an uneasy look, which tells of his anxiety for Sĕlĕma,
and another new expression which speaks of a fresh-
born love for the child whose arrival he prophesies so
noisily. When the latter feeling is uppermost, Ûmat's
ugly old face is softened until it looks almost sentimental.

Ûmat rushes off to the most famous midwife in the
place, and presents her with a little brass dish filled with
smooth green *sirih* leaves, and sixpence of our money
(25 cents) in copper, for such is the retaining fee
prescribed by Malay Custom. The recipient of these
treasures is thereafter held bound to attend the patient
whenever she may be called upon to do so, and when

the confinement is over, she can claim other moneys in payment of her services. These latter fees are not ruinously high, according to our standard, two dollars being charged for attending a woman in her first confinement, a dollar or a dollar and a half on the next occasion, and twenty-five, or at the most fifty cents being deemed sufficient for each subsequent event.

When Ûmat has placed the *sirih* leaves, he has done all he can for Sĕlĕma, and he resigns himself to endure the anxiety of the next few months, with the patience of which he has so much at command. The *pantang bĕr-ânak*, or birth taboos, hem a husband in almost as rigidly as they do his wife, and Ûmat, who is as super-stitious as are all Malays of the lower classes, is filled with fear lest he should unwittingly transgress any law, the breach of which might cost Sĕlĕma her life. He no longer shaves his head periodically, as he loves to do, for a naked scalp is very cool and comfortable ; he does not even cut his hair, and a thick black shock stands five inches high upon his head, and tumbles raggedly about his neck and ears. Sĕlĕma is his first wife, and never before has she borne children, where-fore no hair of her husband's must be trimmed until her days are accomplished. Ûmat will not kill the fowls for the cook now, nor even drive a stray dog from the compound with violence, lest he should chance to maim it, for he must shed no blood, and must do no hurt to any living thing during all this time. One day, he is sent on an errand up river, and is absent until the third day. On inquiry, it appears that he passed the night in a friend's house, and on the morrow

found that the wife of his host was shortly expecting
to become a mother. Therefore, he had to remain at
least two nights in the village. Why? Because, if he
failed to do so, Sělěma would die. Why would she
die? God alone knows, but such is the teaching of
the men of old, the wise ones of ancient days. But
Ûmat's chief privation is that he is forbidden to sit in
the doorway of his house. To understand what this
means to a Malay, you must realise that the seat in
the doorway, at the head of the stair-ladder that
reaches to the ground, is to him much what the fire-
side is to the English peasant. It is here that he sits,
and looks out patiently at life, as the European gazes
into the heart of the fire. It is here that his neighbours come to gossip with him, and it is in the doorway of his own or his friend's house, that the echo of
the world is borne to his ears. But, while Sělěma is
ill, Ûmat may not block the doorway, or dreadful
consequences will ensue, and though he appreciates
this, and makes the sacrifice readily for his wife's sake,
it takes much of the comfort out of his life.

Sělěma, meanwhile, has to be equally circumspect.
She bridles her woman's tongue resolutely, and no
word in disparagement of man or beast passes her
lips during all these months, for she has no desire to
see the qualities she dislikes reproduced in the child.
She is often tired to death, and faint and ill before her
hour draws nigh, but none the less she will not lie
upon her mat during the daytime lest her heavy eyes
should close in sleep, since her child would surely fall
a prey to evil spirits were she to do so. Therefore,
she fights on to the dusk, and Ûmat does all he can

E

to comfort her, and to lighten her sufferings, by constant tenderness and care.

One night, when the moon has waxed nearly to the full, Pëkan resounds with a babel of discordant noise. The large brass gongs, in which the devils of the Chinese are supposed to take delight, clang and clash and bray through the still night-air; the Malay drums throb, and beat, and thud; all manner of shrill yells fill the sky, and the roar of a thousand native voices rises heavenwards, or rolls across the white waters of the river, which are flecked with deep shadows and reflections. The jungles on the far bank take up the sound, and send it pealing back in recurring ringing echoes, till the whole world seems to shout in chorus. The Moon which bathes the Earth in splendour, the Moon which is so dear to each one of us, is in dire peril, this night, for that fierce monster, the *Gĕrhâna*, whom we hate and loathe, is striving to swallow her. You can mark his black bulk creeping over her, dimming her face, consuming her utterly, while she suffers in the agony of silence. How often in the past has she served us with the light; how often has she made night more beautiful than day for our tired, sun-dazed eyes to look upon; and shall she now perish without one effort on our part to save her by scaring the Monster from his prey? No! A thousand times no! So we shout, and clang the gongs, and beat the drums, till all the animal world joins in the tumult, and even inanimate nature lends its voice to swell the uproar with a thousand resonant echoes. At last, the hated Monster reluctantly retreats. Our war-cry has reached his ears, and he slinks sullenly away, and the pure, sad, kindly Moon looks down in love and gratitude upon us, her children, to whose aid she owes her deliverance.

But during the period that the Moon's fate hung in the balance, Sělěma has suffered many things. She has been seated motionless in the fireplace under the tray-like shelf, which hangs from the low rafters, trembling with terror of—she knows not what. The little basket-work stand, on which the hot rice-pot is wont to rest, is worn on her head as a cap, and in her girdle the long wooden rice-spoon is stuck dagger-wise. Neither she nor Ûmat know why these things are done, but they never dream of questioning their necessity. It is the custom. The men of olden days have decreed that women with child should do these things when the Moon is in trouble, and the con-sequences of neglect are too terrible to be risked ; so Sělěma and Ûmat act according to their simple faith.

Later, comes a day when Sělěma nearly loses her life by reason of the barbarities which Malay science considers necessary if a woman is to win through her confinement without mishap. Ûmat's brown face is gray with fear and anxiety, and drawn and aged with pain. He paces restlessly between the hut, where Sělěma is suffering grievous things, and my study, where he pours his terror and his sorrow into my ears, and wets the floor-mats with his great beady-tears. Hours pass, and a little feeble cry comes from Ûmat's house, the sound which brings with it a world of joy, and a wonder of relief that sends the apple

lumping in one's throat, and tears rising to one's eyes.
Ûmat, mad with delight, almost delirious with relief
that the danger is over, laughing through his tears,
and sobbing in his laughter, rushes to me with the
news that a man-child has been born to him, and that
Sĕlĕma is safe.   Nightly for many weeks after, the
cries of Âwang—as the boy is named—break the
peace of my compound during the midnight hour.
The poor little shapeless brown atomy is being
ruthlessly washed in *cold* water, at this untimely hour,
and thereafter is cruelly held face downwards over a
basin filled with live embers, whence a pungent,
reeking wood smoke ascends to choke his breath, and
to make his tiny eyes smart and ache fiercely.   No
wonder the poor little thing yells lustily ; the marvel
is that he should survive such treatment.   But he
does outlive it, and, so soon as he is old enough to
leave the house, he becomes Ûmat's constant friend
and companion.   Long before the child can speak, he
and Ûmat understand one another, and you may hear
them holding long conversations on the matting outside my study-door with perfect content for hours at
a time.

Love is infectious, and as Âwang grows big enough
to use his legs and his tongue, the little brown mite
patters nimbly around his blind father, with an air
which has in it something of protection.   He is
usually mother naked, save that now and again a hat
is set rakishly upon one side of his little bullet head,
and, when I speak to him, he wriggles in a most
ingratiating manner, and stuffs his little hand half-
way down his throat.   Ûmat's eyes follow him con-

stantly, and, though they are very dim, I fancy that he sees Âwang more clearly than anything else on earth.

So much love cannot go for nothing, and I hope that Âwang will grow up to repay his father for the devotion he lavishes upon him. But whatever gifts he may be able to bring to Ûmat, he can never win him back to sight, and the best that we can hope for is that, in the days to come, Ûmat may learn to see more clearly through Âwang's eyes. Meanwhile, I think he is not altogether unhappy.

HIS LITTLE BILL.

A STUDY IN CHINESE PSYCHOLOGY

'Tis the added straw breaks the elephant's back ;
'Tis the half turn more kills the man on the rack ;
'Tis the little wrong, too hard to be borne,
By one who for long has been harassed and worn,
That can utterly break and undo him.

He put me to shame, while he saved his ' face,'
They held me to blame, while he thrived apace,
He passed me by with a mock and a jeer ;
His time to die grew near and more near.
Ah, my heart was well pleased when I slew him !

HUMAN Beings are most unaccountable creatures, and
the feelings and secret motions of their hearts, that
serve on occasion as the mainsprings of their actions,
are perhaps the least probable things about them. As
we get lower down the scale of humanity, the more
difficult it becomes to appreciate the attitude of mind
of a man who is impelled to do all manner of strange
and inconsequent things for reasons which to us are
at once obscure and unreasonable. It is not that
the motives are not amply sufficient, according to the
notions of the man who acts upon them, but merely

that we, who cannot get inside the creature's mind, find it hard to credit that any sane human being can really regard them as things of enough importance to serve as a guide to him in the shaping of his conduct. This story is an instance in point, and I tell it because, to my thinking, it has an interest altogether its own, in that it throws some light upon the workings of the mind of one of the lowest specimens of our human stock.

Those who know the Chinese cooly, as he is when he is first imported from Southern China, will probably not dispute the statement that he is intellectually as debased a type of man as any in existence. It is this that so largely helps the more unscrupulous employers of labour, in the schemes which they are accustomed to devise for his undoing, for they can feel quite secure that it will never occur to the cooly that he can complain to the authorities if he is defrauded or ill-treated. His ideas play around rice, and the messes he is accustomed to eat with his rice; around opium, when he can get it, and even more when he cannot, for the want of the drug sometimes makes him desperate. His pleasures are unspeakable things, into the nature of which it is best not to inquire too closely; he has an innate love of money, which he very rarely sees, for more often than not he is deeply in debt to his employer for food and opium supplied to him, even after he has served him as long as Jacob served for Rachel. When he is very angry, when he considers that he has been put upon past all bearing, when he has an undying grudge against some one, upon whom it is impossible to retaliate in kind, or when he goes to gaol, and his supply of opium is knocked off, the Chinese cooly not infrequently commits suicide. At such times, he will hang himself at a height of two feet from the ground, with a foot-long rope fashioned from a few twisted strands of his ragged garments. He will show marvellous resolution, holding his ankles firmly with his hands, to prevent his feet from touching the floor and so taking some of the strain off his neck. He is quite determined to die, and the actual manner in which he brings about his self-inflicted death does not appear to be an affair of much importance in his eyes. He dies to spite some one, as a rule, and his last moments are made beautiful to him by the thought that his spirit will return from the Land of Shadows, and will haunt his enemies in such a manner as to render the remainder of their lives upon earth well-nigh unbearable. It is well that he should have some compensations to comfort him, for such a very amateurish piece of hangman's work, as I have described, must be an exceedingly unpleasant thing to endure.

Sometimes, however, the Chinese cooly prefers murder to suicide, and it is then that one really sees what a strange creature he is, and what a very thin coating of humanity overlies the animal part of his nature. He occasionally shows some faint traces of courage when he makes one of a crowd ; but as soon as the inevitable panic sets in, he treads his best friend ruthlessly under foot in his frantic eagerness to save himself. Often he kills his *Mandor*, after talking over the advisability of doing so, calmly and dispassionately, with his fellows, in the *kong-si* house, during the long, quiet nights. As soon as the plan has been finally approved, the *Mandor* is beaten to death from behind, and most of the coolies have a share in the killing. But occasionally, and far more rarely, a cooly does murder alone and unaided, and since, in these cases, one is enabled to mark the workings of an individual mind, much may be learned concerning the mental arrangements of the Chinese cooly, from a study of the emotions and motives that prompted him to take a life. Such an instance is that of Lim Teng Wah, a mining cooly who worked at Kuantan, in Pahang, during the Year of Grace 1896.

Lim Teng Wah had drifted from China on the labour-stream, that sets so strongly towards the Malay Peninsula, and indeed to any part of the World where the Justice of the White Man,—'Red-Headed Devil' though he be,—makes life and property secure, and money easy to win, for the Celestial finds nothing romantic in unnecessary risk. He had left his home because his father required him to do so, for in China they hold the eminently sound doctrine that parents should be supported by their children, not children by their parents. He had been shipped to the Peninsula as an indentured cooly, and a *Tau-keh*, who chanced to be in need of labour, took him over on his arrival, after signing certain documents at the Chinese Protectorate which were duly read over to Lim Teng Wah and a batch of fellow-coolies, by a gabbling native clerk. It was nobody's fault that the strangeness of the scene in which they found themselves, and the mysterious nature of these proceedings, which were quite beyond the grasp of the cooly mind, prevented Lim and his companions from understanding a single word of the paper which set forth the terms of their agreement with their new employer. As matters turned out, this affected Lim Teng Wah very little, for he was a steady worker, a man of good physique, who was never on the sick-list, and since he did not smoke opium, he soon succeeded in paying off his advances, and becoming a *lau-keh*, or 'old cooly,' who can make his own contract, and work where, with whom, and how he likes.

It was now that he was a free man, that the troubles of Lim Teng Wah began. There are always numerous contractors living in a large mining camp, who have not the necessary capital to enable them to undertake big jobs on their own account, but who subcontract for little bits of work, here and there, under the holders of the main contracts. They are usually coolies who are too idle to work themselves, if they can by any means avoid doing so, upon whom Fortune has smiled in the gambling-houses, thus placing them in the temporary possession of a little capital. The big contractors have to make their profit, so the rates at which job-work is let to these men are not very remunerative, and as money gained in the gambling-houses has a knack of returning whence it came, it frequently happens that the sub-contractor is unable to meet the calls made upon him when pay-day arrives, and the coolies, like the Daughters of the Horse-Leech, cry 'Give! Give!' These petty jobsters are more practised in lying and fawning to those to whom they owe money, in bluffing the stupid, and in bullying the timid, than are any other people with whom I am acquainted. When they have been dunned for weeks and months, and their starving coolies can bear the delay no longer, a sum sufficient to pay the cost of a summons is scraped together, and proceedings are taken in the nearest Court. But, unfortunately, their debtor has usually by this time got rid of any property of which he may once have been possessed, and the defrauded coolies get little or nothing for their pains.

Ah Sun was a man of this stamp, and it was into his clutches that Lim Teng Wah fell, as soon as he became a free cooly. He worked with Ah Sun for a month only, and at the end of that time no wages were forthcoming. Lim Teng Wah was much exercised in mind. He thought of his father in distant China, who would be looking for a remittance from his son, and would surely impute unfilial conduct to him when no money arrived. The sum due amounted to $ 7.68, which, at the present wholly ridiculous rate of exchange, is equivalent to about fourteen shillings and sixpence, but to Lim Teng Wah this was a by no means insignificant amount. Moreover it was the first real ready money that he had ever earned, and our earliest earnings are always things of enormous value in our eyes, of far more importance than much larger sums gained at any future time. It was very bitter to Lim Teng Wah to find himself defrauded of this money, and he became most persistent in his attentions to Ah Sun, following him about constantly, and claiming his money in season and out of season, to the no little confusion and discomfort of his debtor. Lim Teng Wah procured employment elsewhere, in the same mining camp, however, and he now drew his wages regularly, for the contractor with whom he

worked was well-to-do. But the thought of the
seven odd dollars out of which Ah Sun was keeping
him continued to rankle, and whenever an opportunity
offered, he renewed his application for payment. Ah
Sun, meanwhile, would seem to have taken a strong
dislike to Lim Teng Wah, which is not perhaps to
be wondered at. Did any one ever endear himself
to another by constantly dunning him for money?
Ah Sun was at his old game of sub-contracting
now, and Lim had good reason to believe that his
enemy was fairly flush of cash. And it was thus
that the trouble began.

One day Lim Teng Wah paid his usual visit to
Ah Sun's *kong-si* house, with the object of dunning
him, and it so chanced that he found Ah Sun, with
a bag of jingling dollars in his hands, in the act of
paying his men. Lim at once claimed to be paid too,
and Ah Sun thereupon gathered up his money, tied
the string of the bag, with great deliberation, and, to
paraphrase his untranslatable Chinese monosyllables,
told Lim Teng Wah to go to the Devil. He then
smiled sweetly upon the infuriated Lim, put the bag
containing the money into his hat, for greater convenience in carrying it, and bowed himself out of the
kong-si house.

This was only one of many occasions upon which
Ah Sun treated Lim Teng Wah with scorn and
derision when he came to claim his just dues. Once
he told him that the Magistrate of the District had
specially decreed that no money should be paid to so
unworthy a person, and when on inquiry this proved
to be an impudent fabrication, Ah Sun was in no way

abashed, and told Lim that the debt should be liqui-
dated when next he chanced to be in funds.

'You had better make shift to pay me,' said Lim,
and Ah Sun entered his *kong-si* house without deigning
to answer a word.

Next day, when Lim Teng Wah arose from
sleep, his heart, as he subsequently stated, felt very
angry. I have said that in his new employment he
was receiving regular pay, but the memory of the
money due to him by Ah Sun wiped out all thought
of the good treatment he was now receiving from his
present employer. He said to himself [I am giving—*tceh*
his own account of the thoughts that passed through his
mind], 'Other folk labour and are paid for their toil,
I alone of all men work and receive no guerdon. To-
day, therefore, I will not go minewards with the other
coolies.'

He had a slight sore on his foot, which he showed
to the *Mandor*, making it his excuse for refusing to
work, though, in his heart, he had determined never
to labour any more. He was too angry and too
dissatisfied with the present, to have any care for the
future, or it would have occurred to him that a cooly
who will not work is very likely to starve. He had
no intention of retaliating upon Ah Sun ; he had had
many and ample opportunities of doing so, and he
had not availed himself of any of them ; all he felt
was that he was the victim of oppression, and that he
would therefore do no work for the future, as a protest
against things as they are. He did not put his feelings —*tzlh*
before himself quite so clearly as this, nor in the words
which I have used, but, none the less, these were the

trend and shape of the thoughts that passed through his mind, as he sat swinging his legs on the edge of his bunk, and watched his fellow-coolies troop off to their work through the early morning mist.

Then, when they were all gone, Lim Teng Wah lay down again, under his musty mosquito-curtain, and slept peacefully for a few hours. At about eleven o'clock, he got up, bathed, cooked his rice, ate a hearty meal, and sat down to smoke reeking Chinese tobacco, in his long bamboo pipe. He was still very angry. The extreme injustice of Ah Sun's treatment of him, and the unfairness of the fact that he was defrauded of his pay, while other coolies received their wages regularly, appealed to him with fresh force, as he sat ruminating over his tobacco. It never occurred to him that there was anything to be done. Ah Sun was paying his way now, and was therefore a person of far greater consideration in the mining camp than was the unfortunate Lim. The debt due to him, of which his friends had heard so much during the last few months, was fast becoming a sort of joke among them, and poor Lim Teng Wah knew that he was powerless to do anything to force Ah Sun to comply with his just demands. All this seemed to him to be very hard, but it was with Fate that he felt that his real quarrel lay. Had he not been the impotent creature he was, Ah Sun would never have dared to treat him as he had done, and yet this was a matter which, from the very nature of things, poor Lim was quite unable to control.

The sore upon his foot was causing him some inconvenience, and as there can be no possible object in neglecting the body because the mind chances to be ill at ease, Lim sallied out at about one o'clock to search for herbs, such as Chinese coolies are wont to use for the preparation of the loathsome concoctions with which they smear and doctor themselves as occasion requires. He carried a native *párang*, or chopper, in his hand, to cut the boughs and twigs which bore medicinal leaves, and to aid him in rooting up the herbs. He went into the jungle and succeeded in collecting a quantity of rubbish, which he considered suitable for his purpose, and, as the afternoon was beginning to decline, he turned his face once more towards the mining camp. His way chanced to lead past the *kong-si* house in which Ah Sun was then living, and the coolies had just returned from work. Ah Sun, himself, chanced to be coming up from the wattled hut on the river bank, where he had been bathing, as Lim Teng Wah walked by. He wore a pair of short drawers, and a limp, damp loin-cloth, that he had used while bathing, was clinging closely about his shoulders. In his left hand he carried the bark water-can with which he had sluiced the water over his dusty body.

It had become a sort of instinct with Lim Teng Wah to ask Ah Sun for the seven dollars and sixty-eight cents wherever and whenever they chanced to meet, so he at once rushed at him, all undraped though he was, and angrily demanded payment.

Ah Sun stood quite still, and bent his gaze upon Lim, as though the latter was some strange and unclean animal, whose presence had just attracted his attention. He continued to look steadily at his creditor in this manner for a considerable time, without uttering a word, and Lim, writhing under the cool contempt of the glance, felt the cup of his bitterness was full to overflowing. The quarrel he had with Fate, and the dispute with Ah Sun concerning the seven dollars and sixty-eight cents began to be welded into one, and a fiery longing to be even with his enemies sprang into being in his breast.

The pause was a long one, and never once did Ah Sun remove his gaze from Lim's face. Then very slowly and deliberately he said, in a kind of monotonous sing-song, 'I will not pay thee one single tiny cent!' As he spoke, he made a motion with his right arm, as though he were sweeping some unpleasant insect from before him, and to Lim Teng Wah, standing angry and ashamed in his path, it seemed as if Ah Sun was attempting to add blows to the other injuries and insults that he had heaped upon him. The *párang* was ready in his hand, and Lim, almost blind with fury, raised his arm and brought the heavy iron blade crashing down upon the naked shoulder of his enemy. The force and the unexpectedness of the blow felled Ah Sun to the ground, and Lim Teng Wah threw himself upon him, and hacked again and again at the writhing body. Presently Ah Sun's feeble struggles grew fainter, and then ceased, and now the animal part of Lim Teng Wah broke through what there was of humanity in his composition. He let his *párang* fall from his grip, and began literally to bathe in the blood of the murdered man. With cries of horrible satisfaction, he rubbed the blood, which still ran warm from the gaping wounds that the *párang* had made, over his face and chest; he scooped up a

double handful in his reddened palms and drank of it ;
he grovelled about the dead body in a hideous revel of
satisfied revenge ; and perhaps, in those wild moments
of incomprehensible delight, he got what he considered
a fair return for the sum of seven dollars and sixty-
eight cents, which was still due to him when a couple
of months later he stood upon the gallows.

All this happened in the broad daylight, in front of
Ah Sun's *kong-si* house, and in the sight of several eye-
witnesses, yet no one attempted to interfere, to aid
Ah Sun, or to prevent the escape of his murderer.
But Lim Teng Wah, as the madness of his fury
began to cool, experienced no desire to save himself by
flight. He went straight to the Police Station, which
stood only a quarter of a mile away, and asked to be
suffered to enter. He was smeared with blood from
head to foot, he was panting and out of breath, for he
had come quickly from the scene of the murder, and
the charge-taker naturally supposed that he had been
the victim of an assault which he had come hither to
report. The Policemen pressed round him, plying
him eagerly with questions as to what had befallen
him, but he waved them aside, and seating himself
upon a stool, said that he would tell them all about it
when he had recovered his breath sufficiently to speak.
It is said that he expressed considerable surprise and
dissatisfaction when, his tale having been told, he was
promptly clapped into the Station lock-up, for he
appeared to have imagined that now that he had stated
his case,—the injustice of which he had been a victim,
and the unpremeditated nature of the murder that he
had committed,—he would meet with nothing but

F

sympathy and commiseration.   So poor Lim Teng Wah carried his quarrel with Fate and injustice with him to the grave, but as he never expressed any regret for the murder of Ah Sun, and as he took an evident pleasure in recalling that wild moment when he had found himself struggling above the prostrate body of his enemy, I fancy that he derived some solid satisfaction from the recollection that he had succeeded in paying off a portion of the score that lay betwixt them.

Incidentally, the story of Lim Teng Wah throws some lurid side-lights upon the psychology of the Chinese cooly.

THE SCHOONER WITH A PAST

The Ghosts of the West are laid, are laid,
    The Spirits, and Elves, and Sprites ;
The steam-whistle's scream hath made them afraid,—
    Too clear are the White Men's nights.
The gas-jet's flare, and the lamp-light's glare,
    The clamour, the rush, the roar,
Have driven them forth from the lands of the North
    To roam on an alien shore.

But the Ghosts of the East wax strong, wax strong,
    For the land is spent and old,
And the corpse-lights whisper a tale of wrong
    To dead men under the mould,
While the *Hantus* cry 'neath the starless sky,
    And the Weird-Hags laugh and yell,
When the night shuts down o'er village and town,
    And opens the gates of Hell.

I CANNOT pretend to explain this story, nor do I ask any one to believe it; that is entirely a matter for private judgment. But those who know the East intimately will hesitate to assert that anything, no matter how unlikely, is impossible in the lands where man's body is bathed in eternal splendour, while his mind remains hopelessly steeped in unending night and gloom. I can only tell the tale as I heard it; first from a white man, who knew me well enough to trust

me not to laugh at him, and later from a Malay boatswain, who did not realise that, by telling a plain
story simply and by relating facts exactly as they
occurred, he was running any risk of becoming an
object of ridicule.   I have not attempted to use the
words of either of my informants, for the eyes of the
East and the eyes of the West are of different focus,
the one seeing clearly where the other is almost blind.
No given circumstances have precisely the same value
when they are related by a Native or by a European,
yet each may speak truly according to his vision ; and
who shall say which of the twain attains the more
nearly to the abstract truth ?

The islands of the Eastern Seas, where life is too
indolent for a man to do more than dream over the
marvellous grouping of the treasures, and the lavish
use of light and colour and shade wherewith Nature
paints her pictures for lazy eyes to look upon ; where
the sad, soft winds lull you gently with their spicy
breath ; where the air comes to you heavy with
memories of the cool sleeping forest ; where action is
folly, and all effort seems a madness ; and where the
drowsy people, taking the true spirit of their surroundings, seem to be given over to slumber and to
dreamy rest,—these islands of the Eastern Seas have
the power to bind a man to them for all his days.   It
needs an effort, for one who has drunk deeply of the
intoxication of these sleepy-places, to break away from
them, and effort has become repugnant to his very
being.   But if, as happens now and again, a man
grows weary of the islands, he must turn his back alike

upon them and upon the rising sun, for if he goes towards the East he only increases his trouble. Almost before he is aware of it he will slip into the archipelagoes of the Pacific, and there life is still so entrancing, in spite of the Germans and the Missionaries, that he will soon find himself bound hand and foot by ties stronger even than those from which he seeks to free himself.

If, however, he turns resolutely to the West, he may push his way through any one of the hundred gaps that are to be found in that long fringe of forest-clad islands which skirts the edge of the Malay Archipelago. Then, peeping through the gates of the strait, he may see once more the open, restless sea, throbbing and heaving to the horizon, beyond which, separated from him by more than a thousand leagues of storm-swept ocean, lies the east coast of Africa. The little Straits of Sunda are the favourite track for such wayfarers, and as you near the western outlet, the point where the calm seas of the Archipelago join issue with the fierce waters of the Indian Ocean, you look your last upon Malayan lands. However insensible you may be to beauty, however impervious to the influence of your surroundings, if you have sojourned long enough among the islands, or in the Malay Peninsula, the fascination of this corner of the earth will have eaten into your heart, and a keen pang of regret will be yours as you turn your back upon the land and beat out to the open sea.

On your right hand lies a broad tract of forest, broken here and there by little dainty villages, the bright patches of green marking the cultivated land.

The jungle, fading away in the distance, colours the earth it cloaks an even greenish blue, softer than any hue for which man has a name; and behind that, very far and faint and dim, rise the white and azure mountains of the interior. The fleecy clouds appear to float around them, casting broad belts of shadow on the plain beneath, and all the land slumbers peacefully under its green coverlet. This is Sumatra; and on your left the coast of Java smiles at you through the evening light. The villages cluster closely along the shore, the ordered fields, gay with the splendours of the standing crops, spreading inland almost as far as the eye can carry. Here and there a dark patch of forest breaks the brighter green of the rice-fields, and the hills are seen dimly, blushing faintly in the glow of the setting sun.

Ahead of you lies the ocean, restless and hungry, a strange contrast to the sleepy shore; and in the very portals of the strait, grim and hard and awful, without a blade of grass to soften its harsh outlines, Krakatau, rising sheer from the sea, stands blackly outlined against the ruddy sky.

This wild mountain of roughly-hewn volcanic rock, so black in colour and so strong and harsh in outline, so rudely unlike the smiling land on either side, resembles some fearful monster that stands on guard before the gates of Paradise. In 1883 Krakatau belched forth fire and lava, destroying thousands of human beings and laying whole districts waste. Ships far out of sight of land were licked up, and burned like chaff, by the floating fire that covered the sea for miles. Reefs rose clear from out the deep sea-bottom where formerly the waters had been unfathomed, while islands disappeared, dragged down into the bowels of the ocean. The deafening reports of the eruption's thousand explosions carried far and wide, filling distant Malayan lands with strange rumours of battle. But to-day Krakatau rears its sullen crest skywards, silent, grim, and terrible, like a destroying angel that has the power to strike, but itself is indestructible.

It was lying close under the lee of Krakatau that my friend the White Man chanced to find the schooner, which he bought so cheaply from the *adipâti*, or headman, of the coast near Java Head. She was a dainty little craft, and in first-rate condition. The price asked and given for her was absurdly small, and the White Man was full of his luck at having fallen in with her. He had no very high opinion of the morals of the Râjas, or headmen, who dwell in Malayan lands, and he told himself that the *adipâti* had probably come in possession of the schooner by means which would hardly bear scrutiny. That, however, he considered was no affair of his, for men who roam about the Archipelago are not apt to be over scrupulous, nor do they usually ask awkward questions about such gifts as the gods send them.

All went well until my friend set about seeking for a crew to man his schooner. Then he found that no living soul upon the coast of Java, nor yet among the villages on the Sumatran shore, would set foot aboard her. He wasted weeks in vainly trying to persuade and bribe the people to lend him a hand to sail the ship up to Tanjong Priuk, which is the port for Batavia, but at length he was forced to abandon the

attempt. Not without difficulty he succeeded in
forcing the *adipâti* to refund one-half of the purchase
money, as a guarantee that the ship should not be re-
sold until he returned to fetch her. Then he set off
for Sûlu, where he had a large connection among the
divers and fisher-folk. A couple of months later he
returned to Krakatau, with a gang of yelling Sûlu boys
crowding a tiny native craft, and took formal charge
of the schooner.

The money was paid, and the ship began to beat
up the Straits before a gentle breeze; and, after putting in at Tanjong Prîuk to refit, and lying for a
week or two under the shadow of the great Dutch
guard-ships inside the breakwater, the White Man
and his crew set sail for an oyster-bed of which the
former alone knew the situation. I cannot tell you
exactly where this fishing-ground is, for the White
Man hugged his secret closely. (Among the islands
men pride themselves upon having exclusive knowledge of some out-of-the-way corner that no one else
is supposed to have visited.) It not infrequently
happens that a dozen men plume themselves upon
possession of such knowledge in regard to one and the
same spot, and until two of them meet there all goes
happily enough.

The White Man spoke to me of his schooner, in
after days, with tears in his voice. She was 'a daisy
to sail, and as pretty as a picture,' he said; and even
the Malay boatswain, who had his own sufficient
reasons for hating her very name, told me that at first
he loved her like the youngest of his daughters.

Now the custom of the Malay pearl-fishers is this :

the ship is anchored on the oyster-beds, or as near to
them as is possible, and the diving takes place twice
daily, at morning and evening. All the boats are
manned at these hours, and the Sûlu boys row them
out to the point selected for the day's operations.
The white man in charge always goes with them in
order to keep an eye upon the shells, to physic exhausted divers with brandy or gin, and generally to
look after his own interests.

Presently a man lowers himself slowly over the
side, takes a long deep breath, and then, turning head
downwards, swims into the depths, his limbs showing
dimly in frog-like motions, until, if the water be very
deep, he is completely lost to sight. In a few minutes
he again comes into view, his face straining upwards,
yearning with extended neck for the air that he now
needs so sorely. His hands cleave the water in strong,
downward strokes ; his form grows momentarily more
distinct, until the fixed, tense expression of his staring
face is plainly visible. Then the quiet surface of the
sea splashes in a thousand drops of sun-steeped light,
as his head tears through it, and his bursting lungs,
expelling the imprisoned air, draw in the breath, for
which they crave, in long, hard gasps. If the dive has
been a deep one a little blood may be seen to trickle
from nose and mouth and ears ; at times even the
eye-sockets ooze blood, in token of the fearful pressure
to which the diver has been subjected. He brings
with him, from the depths of the sea, two oyster-
shells, never more and very rarely less, and when these
have been secured, he is helped back into the boat,
from which another diver is now lowering himself.

These men can on occasions dive to the depth of twenty fathoms, one hundred and twenty feet; and though the strain kills them early, they are a cheery, devil-may-care set of ruffians till such time as their lungs and hearts give way.

The shells are the property of the white man, for the divers dive for a wage, and it is the mother-of pearl to which the European looks for his sure profit, the pearls themselves forming the plums which may or may not fall to his lot. My friend always opened his shells himself; and, indeed, it is a fascinating employment, when each closed bivalve may contain within it a treasure on the proceeds of which a man may live in comfort for the best half of a year. The Malay boatswain sometimes helped him, but his interest in the matter, being vicarious, was less keen.

The White Man and his schooner reached the oyster-bed in safety, and work was begun on the following morning, each of the divers making two trips to the bottom during the day. The shells were lying 'as thick as mites in a cheese,' my friend told me, and he got three fine pearls on the first day, which is more than any pearl-fisher living has a right to hope for. Therefore he turned into his bunk, and dreamed of great wealth and an honoured old age. He was just shaking hands warmly with Queen Victoria, to whom a moment earlier he had presented a necklace of pearls as big as plover's eggs, when he awoke to find the Malay boatswain standing over him.

'What thing ails thee?' asked the White Man in Malay.

'The order hath come to Abu,' was the reply.

'When did he die?' asked the White Man, who understood the Malay idiom.

'I know not, *Túan*,'[1] said the boatswain. 'I found him lying face downwards on the deck a little abaft the mainmast. He died startled (suddenly) and no man was at hand to watch him at his death.'

'Come, let us see,' said the White Man, rolling off his bunk, and together they went to view the body by the light of a ship's lantern.

Abu lay dead, naked to the waist, with outstretched arms extended and the palms lying flat upon the deck. Half a dozen of the Sûlu boys stood in a frightened group at a little distance from him, talking together in low, uneasy whispers.

The White Man turned the body over on its back, and put his hand upon the dead man's breast. He noted that the face had been badly bruised by the boards of the deck, against which it had struck when Abu fell. Apparently the man, who in his lifetime had always appeared to be a strong, healthy fellow enough, had had a weak heart, and the diving had proved too great a strain for him. The White Man said so to the boatswain, but the latter did not seem to be convinced.

'Has the *Túan* noted this?' he asked, turning the body over as he spoke, and pointing to a minute black stain on the skin below the left shoulder-blade.

The White Man examined the spot carefully. 'It is a birth-mark,' he said.

'Perhaps,' said the boatswain doubtfully; 'but in

---

[1] *Túan* is the word commonly used in addressing Europeans in the Malay Peninsula.

all the years that I have seen Abu stripped for the diving never have I remarked the said birth-mark.'

'Nor I,' said the White Man; 'but if it is not a birth-mark, what then may it be?'

'God alone knows, *Túan*,' said the boatswain piously; ' but I have heard tell of spirits who scar their victims, leaving such a mark as that we see.'

The White Man was righteously indignant. He felt that he did well to be angry, for superstition is an unseemly thing, more especially when it tends to prevent a man from working one of the best oyster-beds in the whole of the Malay Archipelago. The boatswain took all the hard things that the White Man said to him with the utmost composure; but it was not difficult to see that the Sûlu boys, who had stood listening to all that passed, felt that reason lay upon his side.

Diving was resumed on the morrow, but my friend noticed that some of the younger men failed to reach the bottom, apparently lacking the nerve required for the violent effort, while both old and young seemed to be somewhat sullen and uneasy. The White Man did not like these symptoms at all, for every wise pearl-fisher knows that much depends upon his divers being kept in good spirits. Accordingly when night had fallen, and after the evening rice had been devoured in silence, he did his best to rouse his people by organising a dance on the open space abaft the mainmast. Drums and gongs were produced, and the Sûlu boys thumped and clanged them vigorously, while one of their number blew the shrill *sěrûnai*, whose note resembles that of a demented bagpipe. Then some stood up and danced nimbly, and all lifted up their voices in discordant song.

Men of the Malayan race are gifted with volatile natures, easily cast down and easily lifted up again ; and soon the people on the deck of the schooner were singing and laughing, bandying jests, each man competing eagerly for his turn to rise up and dance. Their faces, with flashing eyes and teeth showing white through gums stained dark red with areca-nut, looked as merry and as happy in the flare of the ship's lanterns as though death and the fear of death were thoughts to which they were utter strangers. The White Man heaved a sigh of relief, and shortly before midnight he stole away to his cabin, and set about the task of opening the oyster-shells which had been taken during the day.

Suddenly a bewildering hubbub broke out upon the deck. The drums and gongs were silenced, and the sound of the *sĕrúnai* died away in one expiring wail. The lusty song ceased, and the noises which replaced it were yells and screams of fear, mingled with the pattering sound of naked feet scurrying along the deck. The White Man seized a pistol and rushed out of his cabin. He found the boatswain cowering against the bulwarks, his teeth chattering like castanets and his body bathed in a cold sweat. He was too spent with fear to do more than moan, but at last the White Man succeeded in shaking him into articulate speech.

'Behold!' said the boatswain, and with a hand that shook violently he pointed to an object a little abaft the mainmast. The White Man walked up to it, and found that it was the body of one of his people, a youngster named Intan. He lay quite dead in the same attitude as that in which Abu's body had lain upon the previous night, and on his back, a little below the left shoulder-blade, was a small, dark stain upon the skin.

The White Man picked up the body and carried it to his cabin, where he laid it gently down upon his bunk. In the bright light of the lamp he could see Intan's face clearly for the first time. The nose and forehead had been bruised and cut by the fall upon the deck, but the face still wore fixed upon it the expression which it had borne at the moment of death. The eyes were starting from their sockets, the mouth seemed open to scream, and the whole face told a tale of abject, masterless terror—fear such as it is given to few to experience and to fewer still to survive. The White Man tried to tell himself that Intan's heart had been rotten, and that death was due to natural causes ; but with that strange mark below the shoulder-blade before his eyes, he failed to convince even himself.

While he still stood pondering upon the mystery, the boatswain, and the *Mandor*, or headman, of the Sûlu divers, came to the cabin door and begged to have speech with him. They spoke in the name of all on board, and entreated the White Man to set sail that very night, and shape a course for the nearest land.

'This ship is the abode of devils,' said the boatswain ; 'of evil spirits that war with man, and in the name of Allah we pray thee to depart from this place, and to abandon this woful ship. Behold, as we sat singing, but an hour ago, singing and dancing with our hearts at ease, of a sudden it was laid upon us to gaze upwards, and lo, we spied an aged man climbing out of the rigging of the mainmast. Out of the black darkness, above the reach of the lantern light, he came, climbing slowly, after the manner of the aged, and indeed he was far stricken in years. His hair was white as the plumage of the *pâdi* crane, and his beard also was white and fell to his waist. His body from the belt upwards was naked and bare, and the skin was creased and wrinkled like the inner seed of a *dúrian*. He was clad in a. yellow waist-skirt looped about his middle, and his fighting-drawers were also yellow. It is the colour of the Spirits, as the *Túan* knows. He had a long dagger, a *kris chèrita*, of many tens of waves to its blade, and he carried it cross-wise in his mouth as he climbed. We who looked upon him were stricken with a great fear, so that we might not stir hand or foot, and presently he descended on to the deck. Then we fled screaming, but He of the Long Dagger pursued Intan, and smote him on the back as he ran, so that he died. Thereafter the spirit swarmed back up the mast, and disappeared into the darkness. Many beheld this thing, *Túan;* it is not the talk of a child; and we that saw the evil one cannot endure to dwell longer within this haunted ship.'

The White Man did not know what to make of it, for he was not himself inclined to superstition. His influence with his people was great, and their faith in him was as the faith of little children in their parents. Therefore he made a pact with his crew, by which he promised to sail for the nearest land if anything untoward should happen on the following night, and he further promised to watch with them, and protect them from the spirit, should it again descend among them.

The crew were in a state of abject fear, but they at last agreed to accept the White Man's terms. No diving was done on the morrow, for the men had no heart for the effort, and though an attempt was made it was speedily abandoned as useless. Night found the crew huddled together on the deck, a little forward the mainmast, with the White Man sitting nearest to that dreaded spot. He tried to induce them to keep up their hearts by thumping the drums and gongs, as on the previous night ; but the songs died down in the singers' throats, the *sěrúnai* wailed discordantly, then ceased, and as the hour of danger approached, a dead silence of fear fell upon the crowd of men, huddled one against another for the sake of company on the dimly lighted deck.

Shortly after midnight a tremor ran through the crew, and half a dozen men started to their feet. All were gazing upwards with craning necks to the rigging of the mainmast. The White Man could hear the sighing of the wind through the cordage, the creaking of a rope against the mast, and the hard breathing of the frightened crew ; but though he strained his eyes to peer eagerly through the darkness, nothing could he see. It made his flesh creep queerly, he told me, as he stood there, while the night wind sighed gently overhead and the little lazy ripple broke against the ship's side, to watch the frightened faces of the Malays, gazing with protruding eyes at something that he could not see, something in the rigging of the mainmast, whose descent towards the deck they seemed to watch.

' It is He of the Long Dagger ! ' whispered a voice behind that sounded harsh and strange. The White Man would never have recognised it as that of the boatswain, had he not seen the man's lips moving. ' Where, where ? ' he cried eagerly, glancing from one terrified face to another ; but no one heeded him, all seeming spellbound by the creeping, invisible thing they watched in agony. The harsh tones of the White Man's voice died down, and the little quiet noises of the night. alone broke the stillness of the heavy air. The sea and the sky seemed alike to wait for a catastrophe, and the fear of death, and worse than death, lay heavy on the watchers.

Presently the awful silence was broken rudely by yells and screams, such sounds as the human voice alone can produce when men wax mad with panic. The groups behind the White Man broke like a herd of frightened deer, the Malays flying in every direction, shrieking their terror of some unseen pursuer.

And still the White Man could see nothing. He turned to watch his people in their flight, and as he did so a chill breath, such as often whispers over the surface of the tropic sea during the quiet night-time, seemed to fan his cheek and pass him by. As he watched, the headman of the divers, who was running up the deck, his breath coming in hard, short gasps, suddenly threw up his arms, his hands extended widely, and with a fearful yell fell prone upon the deck, his

G

face striking the planks with a heavy, sickening thud. The White Man ran to him, and lifted him across his knee ; but the headman was dead, and below the left shoulder-blade the strange, dark stain that the boatswain had called the scar of the Spirits was plainly to be seen.

Before dawn the schooner was under way, heading bravely for the nearest land. The Sûlu boys slunk about the deck, or sat huddled up against the bulwarks, talking together in scared whispers. The sun shone down brightly on the dancing waves, and the schooner leaped joyously through them to the song of the wind in the rigging and the ripple of the forefoot through the water ; but Nature alone was gay and well pleased that day, for the schooner carried none but heavy hearts, and souls on which lay the fear of an awful dread.

Early in the afternoon land was sighted, and when the white trunks of the cocoanut-trees could be clearly distinguished below the dancing palm-fronds, first one and then another of the Sûlu boys leaped upon the bulwarks and plunged headlong into the sea. The White Man could do naught to stay them, for they were mad with fear, so he stood despairingly gazing at the black heads bobbing on the waves as the swimmers made for the shore. Only the old Malay boatswain remained by his side, but even his fidelity could not look the prospect of another night spent aboard that devil's ship steadily in the face. The White Man aiding, they made shift to lower a boat, and taking such articles of value as were capable of being removed, they too turned their faces shorewards.

During the night a wind from off the land sprang up, and carried the schooner away with it. By dawn she had vanished, and so far as I am aware, she has never been heard of since.

I have said that I cannot pretend to explain this story, nor do I know anything of the former history of the schooner, before the White Man chanced upon her at Krakatau. Perhaps, if we knew the whole of the facts, an explanation might be found ; but, for the present, you must content yourselves with a fragment, as I have had to do.

IN ARCADIA

When Ambition lies stricken and dying,
  And can rowel Mankind no more ;
When there's nought worth the labour of trying
  To strive for and grip, as of yore ;
When no grapes may be pressed for the drinking,
  When money's unknown in the Land ;
When we've done with all knowing and thinking,
  All struggles to understand ;
When men shall live tamely together,
  And all be, as kine, fat fed,
When the Passions are bound with a tether,
  And the Deadlier Sins are dead,
There will still be some laughing Daughter
  Of Men, to rekindle our strife,
And that—God be thanked—will mean slaughter,
  And later more full-blooded Life !

                                    The Millennium.

ARCADIA is situated some five days' journey by
steamer from the Sunda Straits,—the main exit by
which a man may make his way out of the maze
of islands that together form the Malay Archipelago,
—and about a fortnight's hard steaming due east of
the island of Madagascar. Arcadia lies well off the
track of any recognised trade route, and no vessel visits
it unless the fierce winds, which rage and roar across

the wide expanse of the Indian Ocean, have taken
charge of her, for the time, and will not suffer the
men on board her to have a say in the selection
of her course. Naturally, if this were not so, Arcadia
would very soon cease to be the quiet, peaceful, un-
sophisticated spot we know it to be, and indeed the
revolutionary tendencies of the shipwrecked mariners
who have from time to time been cast ashore here, have
too often endangered the tranquillity of the island. In
fact, if you go deep enough into the thing, you will
find that the excellent Arcadians differ from the rest of
humanity, not so much in their love of virtue, and
hatred of vice, as in a greater lack of opportunities of
doing evil. Year after year, the Special Commissioners,
who visit the island in the little wallowing gunboats,
state in their official reports that there is 'no crime,'
and everybody who reads the blue - books holds up
astonished hands in admiration, and feels dimly that
they, and every one else connected with the rule of
Great Britain in Asia, are deserving of much credit
for this high standard of morality. They altogether
overlook the fact that, even if we accept the statement
that there is no crime, the credit is chiefly due to the
geographical position of the islands, with which even
the all-powerful Great Britain itself can have had
nothing to do.

The Cocos Keeling Islands, for this is Arcadia's
official name, are inhabited by some six hundred
cross - bred Malays, the descendants of the slaves
brought thither, from the Archipelago, by the
founder of the Scotch family to which the islands still
belong. The men and the women are about equally

numerous, and as a consequence polygamy has died out, though the people still profess a bastard form of Muhammadanism. The *sârong*, or waist - cloth, the national garment, without which no self-respecting Malay ever willingly allows himself to be seen, has been abandoned in favour of white duck trousers, and a coloured flannel or linen shirt, while a broad-brimmed straw hat crowns the whole, in open defiance of the Prophet's Law, which forbids the Faithful to wear any head-gear that shall prevent the forehead from touching the ground when the wearer prostrates himself in prayer.

The islands, which are some twenty in number, rise up out of the Indian Ocean in such a manner as to form a complete circle, the centre of which is a broad, land-locked lagoon. At the northern edge of the circle, the islands do not quite join, and thus a portal is left, by means of which a fairly large steamer can make its way into the lagoon. The other islands so very nearly touch hands, that a man can wade from one to another without difficulty. All the Arcadians live on Settlement Island, as it is called, but on every side of the lagoon the vast groves of cocoanut-trees stand up against the sky, shielding the anchorage from the wild onslaught of the tireless winds which rip ceaselessly up and down these seas. Cocoanuts are practically the only things that grow with comfort in Arcadia, and every one of them has been planted by the hand of man. Yearly a ship, specially chartered for the purpose by the Scotch owners of the islands, puts into the lagoon, and after discharging her cargo of ' Europe goods,' is loaded up with copra, which is beaten down with stampers, until her hull is a solid mass of whitish stuff, with a wooden casing enclosing it. It is sad to have to add that, whenever the Arcadians can elude the vigilance of their masters, they tap the palms for toddy, and thereafter wax exceedingly intoxicated on the stolen spirits.

As you enter the lagoon, leaving behind you the throbbing, leaping, excited seas which have been your companions ever since you slipped out of the Straits of Sunda, and left the black bulk of Krakatau, the fearful volcanic mountain that rises abruptly from the ocean, standing awful and threatening in your wake, it seems as though a strange silence and peace had fallen upon the earth. The beating of the hungry waves upon the outer edge of the circle of rock-bound islands comes to you in a faint murmur, softened by distance into a dreamy hush ; around you the intensely blue waters of the lagoon lie calm and smooth, with scarcely a ripple to roughen their even, sunlit surface ; and gazing downwards over the ship's side, the white coral of the bottom makes the deep, clear water look incredibly shallow, so that every branching spray of plant-like rock, every waving tassel of strange seaweed, every tiny shell of dainty shape and colour, every fish that glides hither and thither in this marine Fairyland, is seen with marvellous distinctness of detail. A fantastic-looking sea-bird or two float around the ship, searching for food, or wing their way across the lagoon, dipping now and again to seize some object floating on the surface of the water ; far away, on the shores of Settlement Island, the roofs of a house or twain may be seen, showing

indistinctly among the palm-trees on the beach ; a few
fishing boats lie rocking at anchor near the houses ;
but over all is an air of lazy, dreamful peace, in such
sharp contrast to the busy, hurrying life of the world
you have left behind you, that no man needs to be told
that this is in truth Arcadia.

Hàri was an Arcadian born, and he was proud of
the fact when he met any of the Bantamese coolies,
who were periodically imported from the Malay Archipelago to help the owners of the islands to work the
copra.   While he was still little, he had been through
the course of education that is prescribed by the owners
of the island for every child in the place.   This was
before the days of Special Commissioners, so reading
and writing, and sums in pounds, shillings, and pence,
—the latter a study of doubtful utility, seeing that the
Arcadians are not allowed to handle money fashioned
from anything more precious than sheep-skin, and
seeing also that their arithmetic is done for them by
the Scotch Family aforesaid,—found no place in the
curriculum.   He had, however, been through the
carpenter's and blacksmith's shops, and could use
tools of either trade as well and as skilfully as any
man need desire.   This, according to the custom
of the islands, is a necessary step in the development
of one who wishes to become the father of a family,
for until a boy has, so to speak, won his spurs in the
shops, he is not permitted to marry.   If you come to
think of it, this is a fairly sound arrangement.   Hàri
—his name was a corruption of a corruption of 'Henry'
—had raced hard to pass through the shops more

quickly than any of his fellows, for it so chanced that, at that time, there was only one marriageable girl upon the island who was still unwedded, and the first comer would in all probability be served first. This girl was named ̲M̲ê̲r̲i̲, a mispronunciation of Mary, for on the islands the natives always give their children European names, which is yet one more sign of how ragged is the coating of Muhammadanism that their long intercourse with the White Men has left them. Hâri had known Mêri all her life, for they had lived always on the islands, and this means seeing more of your neighbours than is likely even in a secluded village, for it is impossible to get away from Arcadia, whereas in the most out-of-the-way places on the mainland, an absence of a day or two must occur, for one or the other, during the years while two young people are coming to maturity. He was under no illusions as to this young woman's character, such as may be entertained by one upon whom his lady-love comes suddenly in all the wonder of her beauty and full-fledged charms, turning a commonplace existence to the likeness of a fairy-tale, until such time as the said illusions wear off. He knew her to be very much like other young women, such as men on the island were accustomed to take to wife. She had pulled his short, black hair, any time these ten years past, when he chanced to anger her, she had used her nails too, with good effect, as the tiny white scars on his nose still bore witness, but everybody on the islands knew that women always treated men roughly, domineering over them, so that even the bravest sailors and strongest rowers were often sent weeping from their own houses, to tell a woful tale of all they had endured at the hands of their wives, to the sympathetic crowd of loafers on the beach. Old men said that things had been otherwise in the good half-forgotten days, before the present ruler of the islands came back from the White Men's country with fantastic notions anent the wickedness of wife-beating; but since the punishment that was dealt out to Jan the son of Charli, for stripping the hide off his woman's back with a piece of rattan, no man had dared to lift his hand against the women-folk, and these, realising their immunity from physical harm, had taken to bullying the men most mercilessly. Hâri found it difficult to believe that things had ever really been different from what they had been, in this respect, ever since he could remember anything; and anyway, a man was better off with a woman to wash and cook for him, than as a bachelor in a land where a wife could not be picked up for the asking whenever a young man's fancy 'lightly turned to thoughts of love.' Regarded in this light, Mêri was exceedingly desirable, and as far as the thin blood of the Arcadian is capable of the emotion, Hâri may be said to have been in love with the girl. She was a big, strapping wench, round-faced, and full-busted, as are most of the sturdy Arcadian women, and her eye was as bright, and her ready tongue as saucy, as her fists and nails were quick to act when she happened to be annoyed. On the whole, Hâri told himself, Mêri was about as attractive a girl as a man had any right to expect to win for a wife; and he was therefore all the more anxious that no one else should step in to take her from him, before such time as he was in a position to start a household on his own account.

Unfortunately for Hàri's peace of mind, precisely the same thoughts had occurred to Sam, a youth who was passing through the shops at the same time as Hâri, and who was equally well aware that if, by any chance, he was to fail to secure Mêri for his wife he would have to wait in single cursedness until some of the half-naked little girls, now playing about the beach, had attained to a marriageable age. Sam was also a Cocos-born native, and he therefore had known Mêri quite as long, and quite as intimately, as Hâri had done. His hair had been pulled quite as often, and if it came to counting the marks left by the young lady's nails, Sam had two to show for every one on Hâri's nose. The Fates, being like every one else in Arcadia, considerably bored by the monotony of the drearily peaceful and uneventful life, decreed that both Hâri and Sam should earn their discharge from the shops upon one and the same day. They both, therefore, became entitled to marry at the same time, and since Mêri was the only maiden on the island who had attained to a ripe age, one or the other of them was obviously destined to remain celibate. It is to meet the requirements of such communities as those of Arcadia, that polyandry is adopted in some parts of the world, but the enlightened owner of the island had at least as strong a prejudice against that much misunderstood system, as he had against the more common one of wife-beating. That they both should wed Mêri was, therefore, out of the question ; and it merely re-

mained to be seen which of the two suitors was to
be the happy man.

All other things being equal, it fell to Mêri and
to Mêri's mamma,—for of course Mêri's papa, being
only a mere man, was not to be suffered to have any
say in so important a matter,—to select the youth who
was most to their taste.

Mêri's choice inclined towards Hâri ; for she remembered how, a week or so before, when she went
to the factory to draw the family ration of flour, Hâri
had thrown his arm about her and had *chium'd*
('smelt') her cheeks and lips.   She had cuffed him
soundly at the time for his audacity, but the memory
of his warm lips against her cheek seemed, somehow,
to make him nearer and dearer to her than any one
else in all the world.   For even in Arcadia, it must be
noted, old Human Nature is apt to be very much like
itself.

Mêri's mamma, on the other hand, was a hot partisan
of Sam ; for she had had a warm flirtation with Sam's
father, in the days when both of them were young,
and she cherished a sentimental affection for the son
of her old lover.   She had viewed with keen suspicion
the disappearance of Mêri and Hâri behind the big
factory-chimney, on that occasion when she and her
daughter had gone to fetch the flour, and even when
Hâri reappeared rubbing his bruised cheeks ruefully,
she had not felt completely reassured.   Now that by
the blessing of the God, whose name for the moment
she forgot,—Allah, was it not ?—both Sam and Hâri
were placed on an equal footing, and the choice had
passed from the hands of Fate to those of herself and

Mêri, she had very little doubt, in her own mind, as to which of the twain should be condemned to a life of celibacy.

As the days wore on, it became more and more apparent to every one concerned that the choice of the mother would also be the choice of the daughter. Sam took to himself a swaggering strut and an arrogant bearing which Hâri found it very difficult to bear with equanimity. The traditional scrap of comfort, which is always offered to the unlucky lover, that there are as good fish in the sea as ever came out of it, was powerless to console Hâri in his affliction, for unless some other islander was so obliging as to die, and leave an attractive widow behind him,—and in Arcadia people are terribly long-lived,—there was no possibility of Hâri finding another wife if he had to stand aside and watch Sam carrying off Mêri from before his eyes. This thought seemed to fill Hâri's cup of bitterness to the brim, and from being a cheery, light-hearted little fellow enough, he gradually became very glum, taciturn, and surly. None the less, how-ever, it was observed that he evinced no desire to avoid his rival, and on the frequent occasions when chance threw them together, the two youths appeared to be, if anything, more friendly than of old. Sam 'came' the favoured lover over poor Hâri, in season and out of season, and never wearied of descanting upon the charms of the lady whom he was about to wed, when Hâri was at hand to listen. Even in Arcadia, people are not always careful to avoid hurting the feelings of their neighbours.

The older men, who watched the two youths

going about together, marvelled exceedingly at Hâri's choice of a companion, and even more at the good temper he displayed when Sam waxed most jubilant and offensive. Though they had come to Forty Year, and had long ago learned 'the worth of a lass,' they had been young in their day, and they felt that had they been in Hâri's place the peace of Arcadia had like to have been broken. He was evidently a poor-spirited fellow, and perhaps Mêri was well out of a marriage with such a poltroon.

Things went on in this way for several weeks, and at last the day for Sam's marriage with Mêri was fixed. On the Saturday before the great event, Hâri invited Sam to go out fishing with him on the lagoon.

'Thou wilt need much fish for thy Wedding Feast,' he said.

'When will *thy* Wedding Feast be, Bachelor?' asked Sam with a maddening laugh.

'God alone knows!' replied Hâri piously; 'but say, Brother, wilt thou go a-fishing, for my lines are ready, and if thou art unwilling I go single-handed.'

'As thou art like to go through life!' jeered Sam; 'but for once thou shalt not be lonely in thy boat, as thou wilt surely be hereafter in thy bed. Come let us be gone.'

The two friends made their way down to the shore, through the fenced enclosures in which the houses of the Cocos people stand. They could see the women hard at work at their weekly task of washing the household clothes, and scrubbing the plank floors of their dwellings, for the Scotch owners of the islands have brought the tradition of a Saturday Washing from

the far-off Hebrides to these remote atolls in the
Indian Ocean. The men were loafing wearily about
the beach, for they knew better than to cross the
thresholds of their homes when the women-folk were
'redding up.' Some of them were out fishing on the
lagoon, Saturday being a half-holiday on the island,—
yet another imported tradition from a land to which
the Cocos natives are strangers,—but others sat about
doing nothing in particular, with the listless air that
is peculiar to the Arcadians. If you do away with
money, and substitute sheepskin; if the hardest
worker and the most skilful mechanic fares no better
and no worse than other men of ordinary proficiency;
when polygamy has disappeared, and a man, no matter
what he may do, is bound in marriage to the same
woman for all his days; every possible incentive to
struggle for an improvement in his lot, every source
of ambition, every reason for competition vanishes,
and as a result life becomes a very insipid, dull, and
dreary business, in which no man can be expected to
take any particularly vivid interest. The wise men
in Europe and America, who are anxious to see things
reduced to this dead level, in the interests of Humanity,
and are of opinion that their theories and ideas are
the one new thing under the sun, might study with
advantage the effect of a precisely similar system on
the people of distant Arcadia. On the whole, the
results are not encouraging. Humanity is 'no great
shakes' as it is, but if we were all Arcadians! Heaven
help us!

The great *kôlek* which belonged to Hâri's father,
and was the fishing boat of the family, lay rocking at

anchor, some twenty yards from the shore, and the two Cocos men waded out to her and stepped aboard.

'Is no other man joining our party?' asked Sam, as he threw his leg over the side.

'We twain go a-fishing this tide. Art thou afraid to do so?' answered Hâri.

Sam got on board without a word. Then they put to sea, each holding an oar.

'Is it fitting that the future husband of Mêri should fear aught?' Sam asked after a pause.

'Indeed the future husband of Mêri fears nothing in Heaven or Earth, and nothing in this life nor in the life that is to come!' said Hâri very quietly.

Those who know the lagoon of the Cocos Islands are aware that though to the new-comer it looks so peaceful and delightful, it is in reality a most dangerous place. All manner of unexpected and unaccountable currents run around it, and about it, and across. Some years ago two or three men from one of the visiting men-of-war fell victims to the treacherous under-swirls; but the Cocos folk, born and bred upon the islands, know the safe and the dangerous places fairly well, and when they go a-fishing no one feels any anxiety as to their safety.

Hâri and Sam put out towards the centre of the lagoon, dancing across the little playful waves, upon as joyous a day as can well be imagined by the poor people whose eyes have never feasted upon the wonders of an Eastern land. The sun, burning overhead, threw up the vivid blue of the sea, and the glistening waters reflected the blazing sun-glare in a myriad dazzling shimmering flecks of shifting, leaping, frolicsome light. The murmur of the breakers on the rocks beyond the cocoanut-trees came to the rowers' ears in a distant, sleepy whisper ; the harsh cry of an occasional sea-bird served only to emphasise the great stillness that lay heavily upon the sea and shore ; and the profound and dreamy peace of Arcadia hallowed all the world. The two men in the boat probably felt the influence of the hush which marked Nature's quiet, even breathing, as she took her *siesta*, for they too were silent, as they rowed on and on over the glistening surface of the lagoon.

Sam, as he pulled mechanically at his oar, thought lazily of Mêri, and of the life that he was soon to live in her company. She was a good girl, and a comely, he thought, and worthy in every way to be his wife. Also, the very fact that Hâri desired her in vain, added a zest which his own love for her might have lacked, had no other man sought her for a wife. Sam felt very contented with himself, and with the world as he found it, so much so in fact that his mind was too absorbed in the recollection of his own wellbeing for a thought to be spared for the direction in which Hâri was guiding the boat.

Suddenly he looked up, and in a moment all memory of Mêri and the rest was lost to mind in a wild access of fear.

' Have a care, Hâri,' he cried ; ' have a care !   Dost thou not know that this is the belly of the great sub-eddy ?   Pull, Brother, pull, or we shall be sucked down into the under-world, and fall screaming into the grip of the Water Demon ! '

' *Biar-lah !*   So be it, Bachelor ! ' said Hâri quietly,

H

as he deliberately shipped his oar. 'In the dwelling of the Water Demon thou mayest find much fish wherewith to deck the table at thy bridal feast, for now surely thou shalt wed the daughter of the said Demon !' Then for the first time for some weeks Hâri laughed heartily, but his laughter was not pleasant to listen to.

The surface of the water, in that part of the lagoon over which they were now drifting, seemed to have become suddenly strangely smooth and oily, and the boat seemed to be drawn forward by some invisible force, which also appeared to be pulling the sheet of water bodily along with it, much as a fisherman draws a sail, which he is spreading to dry, along the ground. Sam was straining every nerve, tugging desperately at his oar, striving with might and main to check the progress of the boat. The single oar caused the light craft to spin slowly round and round, and seeing this, Sam made a clutch at its fellow, which Hâri had shipped when first the undertow began to grip them. Before he could reach it, however, Hâri, who was watching him intently, leaned quickly forward, seized the oar in both hands, and threw it over the side, far out of reach of either of the men in the boat. The slimy, oily current caught the lighter object at once, and the oar drew quickly away from the boat, running swiftly ahead in the course in which the men knew that they must presently follow. Sam gave an inarticulate howl, half curse, half lamentation, and redoubled his efforts at the rowing, causing the boat to spin giddily. Hâri leaned back in the stern and watched Sam keenly, with a very genuine satisfaction.

The hard-held resentment against this man, the firm grip over his rebellious temper which Hâri had so often found it difficult to maintain in the face of Sam's constant jibes and jeers, the fierce hatred that during the last few weeks had been eating into his heart,—the memory of all these things made the sight of Sam's agonised face, and wild struggles to avert the destruction that threatened them both, very sweet to watch and linger over to the man who sat gloating over the other's misery from his seat in the stern of the boat.

Sam's eyes seemed to be starting out of his head ; his face was convulsed with his rending efforts to delay the onrush of the whirling boat, and it was lined and drawn with the agony of terror that was marked in his wildly roving eyes, in his parted, parched lips, in the hard, cruel puckers and bruise-like discolorations which had suddenly sprung into being on his brown forehead. The sweat of fear and exertion was streaming down his face and chest, and his breath came in short, tearing, hard-drawn gasps and gulps, while the apple in his throat leaped up and down ceaselessly like a ball balanced on a dancing jet of water.

Presently Hâri leaned forward, with his elbows on his knees, and began to speak in a strangely calm and even voice.

'The men of ancient days,' he began, 'have left us a saying, that it is not good to straighten the legs, stretching them before thee, until the buttocks have reached the floor in sitting. It is a good saying, and a true. What thinkest thou, Bachelor ? '

Sam, still labouring convulsively at his useless toil,

while the boat spun round and round, drifting certainly, slowly to destruction, groaned aloud, and Hâri laughed discordantly.

'Who thinkest thou will now have Mèri to wife? If I chance to win through she will be mine,—fairly won. But as for thee, Bachelor, thou wilt not pass the rocks alive, for I will be at hand to see that the Water Demon's Daughter is not robbed of a husband as thou wilt be of a wife! Row, Brother, row! Row for Mèri, and for me, while I sit here, like a *Túan*, beholding thy labour!'

The boat was travelling at an increased rate of speed now, and at last, in despair, Sam ceased his useless rowing, and stood erect in the bows, facing Hâri, his breath coming hissingly through his parted lips. He raised the oar he held high above his head and brought it down in an ill-aimed blow at Hâri's jeering face. He was desperately out of breath with his hard rowing, and his limbs felt weak and spent, so when the oar lay clattering on the boat's side, Hâri had no difficulty in wresting it from his feeble grasp, and hurling it overboard after its fellow.

Sam glared furiously at the man who had led him into this terrible position, and whom he seemed to be powerless to harm.

'Thou hast seemingly forgotten thy knack of husking cocoanuts, Brother,' laughed Hâri, and then, with a roar of rage, Sam was upon him, and the two stood locked in the death-grapple. From side to side they swayed, reeling this way and that, balancing themselves as best they might on the thwarts of the rocking boat. At any time Hâri could outmatch

Sam in strength, and now the latter was sore spent with the furious efforts he had made to save himself from the grip of the sucking eddy, and, with the fear of death, which, more than any other emotion, draws the virtue from a man's bones. For a second or two they clutched one another in their fierce wrestling match, and then Hâri partially freed himself from the hands of his adversary, and hurled him over the boat's side. But Hâri had had to put forth all his strength to gain the advantage over his maddened victim, and before he could save himself, he too had lost his balance, and was struggling aimlessly in the fast-running oily sea. A rush of salt water into his gullet, a tugging at his heels, which seemed as though it would draw him down into the depths, then a slow upward motion, and a blue-white light overhead showed him that he was coming to the surface. His lungs expelled the imprisoned air, which felt as though it must burst them to atoms, and Hâri, dashing the water from his eyes, looked round him over the face of the waters. Sam's straw hat he could see floating at some distance to his left, and the boat was lurching along at a great pace farther to the left still, but no sign of Sam was visible. Hâri noticed with surprise that both the hat and the boat were moving much faster than he appeared to be doing, and eventually it was borne in upon his mind that by some marvellous chance the undertow, which had dragged him down into the depths, had cast him up again beyond the reach of the swirling eddy, towards which the boat was still hurrying wildly. Hâri had so completely made up his mind to die, and during the last half hour had become so entirely reconciled to the idea, provided always that he could arrange a similar fate for Sam, that at first he hardly grasped the possibility of escape. Then in a whelming rush the love of life, and the instinct of self-preservation, which will cause even a suicide to struggle to undo his own work, if he have but the time to make the effort, awoke in Hâri, goading him to agonised struggles. All the people of Arcadia can swim rather better than any otter in Great Britain, for they are in and out of the sea all day long, from the time when they first learn to crawl, and many of them can make headway in the water long before they can walk erect upon the dry land. So Hâri was not really so much out of his natural element during the fight for life in which he now engaged. The current still tugged at his toes, and made it hard to win away, little by little, and yard by yard, from the hungry eddy which was not more than a mile distant across the smooth water. Gradually the current grew slacker, and a quarter of an hour later, Hâri dragged himself dead-beat from the sea, and sank exhausted on the sandy shore.

When he awoke it was already night, and Hâri found the darkness very unattractive. There was a dim moon, looking sleepy and woebegone behind her trailing bed-curtains of cloud, and now and again the water at his feet broke into blue and silver streaks of phosphorescence, in token of the disturbance caused by some fish floating close to the surface. Hâri fancied that he could see the strained face of Sam, distorted and prominent-eyed as he had seen it last, peering at him, out of the shadows, from half a dozen directions at once, and the fancy displeased him mightily. He was very stiff with his late exertions, and he was chilled to the bone. Moreover he had got rid of his shirt and pants, during his long swim, and now stood mother-naked on the shore, with all Nature standing still to gaze at him. All at once he was filled with a great sense of failure. He had worked very hard in order that Mêri might be his, and now in this shivering moment of reaction, when his mind was suddenly released from the keen tension of the last few hours, life seemed suddenly flat, insipid, unalluring, and Mêri herself, for whom he had schemed and sinned, no longer specially desirable.

He made his way back to Settlement Island, shivering and depressed, a draggled, miserable object, starting, like a shying horse, at every shadow on his path. The usual night-guard of watchmen was snoring peacefully, as though its members had but a single nose, when Hâri staggered into the hut, and having borrowed a pair of pants from one of the rudely awakened guards, was duly led before the Scotchman, in the big bungalow among the fruit-trees. The owner of the island promptly dosed Hâri with a brimming tot of very choice old Scotch Whisky, thirty years in cask, and thus encouraged, the victim or the disaster told a moving story of the treacherous whirlpool which had dragged down Sam and the boat, while only he was left to tell the tale. The whisky danced through his veins and made him feel that, after all, life was not so flat, stale, and unprofitable a thing as he had at one time imagined.

There was nothing to point to Hâri as having caused Sam's death, indeed all could testify to the friendship which had subsisted between the twain, so in due time Sam was forgotten, and Hâri took Mêri to wife.

It was a week or two after this, one night, as it chanced to be Hâri's turn to take his share of the guard duty in the watch-house, that old Sandi, the headman of the watch, crept close to Hâri, when the other men were sleeping, and asked him if he was still awake. Sandi wriggled up closer still, and peered into Hâri's face.

'Little Brother,' he said, 'I have long desired to have private speech with thee, for on that day when thou didst go a-fishing with Sam I too was fishing on the lagoon.'

He looked at Hâri meaningly, but the latter made no sign of comprehension.

'Have no fear of me, Little Brother,' the old man went on, 'I have no desire to harm thee, but, from afar, I beheld Sam arise and strive to strike thee with his oar, and thereafter ye twain were locked in a wrestling match, and I saw how both fell into the sea. I held my peace then and later, for I am an old man, and I have learned that little good comes to him who sees too much, and thereafter blabs of what his eyes have beheld ; but, Little Brother, tell me of that which befell that day, for it did my old heart good to see once more two youths acting as men should act, fighting to the death for the love of a maiden.'

There was such a genuine ring of real feeling and appreciation in Sandi's voice, that Hâri had no further doubts as to his good faith, and he at once launched out into a boastful, swaggering account of his great deed, cheered and encouraged in the recital by the vivid appreciation evinced by his audience.

'It was well done,' commented the old man, when at last the tale was ended, 'and, in truth, my liver waxes warm when I remember that there be still MEN left to us in this land of cowards; for, Little Brother, in the far-off days when I also was young, *Ya Allah!* we took but little thought for the value of a life when the man who owned it stood between us and our heart's desire! *Ya Allah!* I too, in my time, have seen the red blood gush out, and have smelt its reek, more sweet than the cheek of maiden! But now these dull islands from which we may not depart into the great world, beyond the leaping waves, are no longer utterly without light, for they have bred at least two Men,—thee and me, Little Brother,—who knew how to fashion our actions into the mould that befits our sex!'

And thereafter Hàri felt that he had acted as became a MAN, and a bond of sympathy bound him and Sandi together with a tie which nothing might sever.

Varro says that even the ancient Arcadians, chosen by lot (which is another name for Fate), swam across a certain pool, and henceforth were transformed into wolves, living in the desert places with wild beasts like unto themselves; and in this modern Arcadia of the Indian Ocean, Destiny still beckons to a few of the people, bidding them put off the miserable tameness of their fellows, and break, be it only for a little space, the dead and dreary monotony of the island life. For even in these sheltered and secluded spots, where there is 'no crime,' old Human Nature, as I have already said, is very much like itself.

THE SPIRIT OF THE TREE

Ere the dank Earth sank 'neath the tread of Man,
  Ere huts were built in the dell ;
Ere the streams were girt with the bamboo span,
  When none save the Winds dared fell ;
When the Fairies and Sprites, through the soft, sad nights,
  Played unscared by the voices of men,
The Old One, whose arm fends the great trees from harm,
  Was guarding them even then !

Then Man came creeping with halting feet,
  O'er the ground, which to him was strange,
But still he worshipped, with service meet,
  The trees where he late did range ;
And as feet grew strong, while the years wax'd long,
  Till the tree-tops were foreign land,
The Ancient One's ban was respected of Man,
  Though he saw not the Ancient One's hand !

IT was during the first few years of my service in the
East, that I forgathered with poor Trimlett. He
was a Cornishman by birth, and his father was the
manager or purser of one of the largest tin-mines in
the Duchy. This father of Trimlett's was a man who
held strong views as to the virtue of hard work, and
its salutary effect upon the young ; and since we are
all, up to a certain point, dependent upon our parents

for the moulding of our characters, Trimlett owed many things to the training which his father had ordained for him. After he left school, Trimlett had been sent 'underground,' to work for a year as a common mining hand. He had acquired thereby a very sound knowledge of sinking and driving and stopping ; a network of hard knotty muscles ; an elaborate vocabulary, in the use of which, however, he was very economical ; and an extraordinary fund of Old-World superstitions, all of which he accepted as Gospel.

People who only know the Cornish Miner in his later developments, since Mining Acts have relieved his body, and Board Schools have made gallant efforts to expand his mind, can have little conception of what he was wont to be, and of what he was called upon to endure, in the bad old days before any one had learned to concern himself with the sorrows of the working classes. In those times, a Cornish boy began life 'underground' at the age of nine, or ten. The poor little shivering mite would often be called from the bed, that in winter was never too warm, at three or four o'clock in the morning, and with a thin mess of porridge, or gruel pap, to warm his half-starved body, would have to trudge through the black darkness,— which to his imagination was peopled by a thousand horrors,—to the mine, that lay perhaps a mile or two away from the hovel he called Home. Then his real miseries began. There was only one job of which a child in a big mine was capable, namely the turning of an air-fan, to force a current of less impure breathing-matter into the stifling depths of the drives and stopes,

in which the men worked, nude and sweating.
Though most of miners had endured, in their time,
the agonies through which the poor little brat at the
air-fan was going, no one had a thought to save him,
or to help him. Economy is an excellent virtue,
which was much practised in the mines of Cornwall,
even in the days before the Chinese coolies of the
Peninsula flooded the World's markets with tin, and
since no light was necessary to enable a child to turn
the crank of an air-fan, candles were not served out to
the poor brat, when his turn came to be lowered into
the bowels of the mine. Thus for a shift of many
hours, which to him seemed as years, the miserable little
Cornish boy would stand quaking with fear, in total
darkness. Any one who, as a child, has endured the
agony of terror, that is to be experienced when fear
falls upon one in the dark, will be able to picture to
himself something of what the little Cornish boy felt,
day after day, as he toiled at turning the air-fan. But
it is at best only dimly that an educated man can
realise the full measure of the child's sufferings, for
while we are taught to disbelieve in all the things that
are not apparent to the senses, even the grown men in
Cornwall are steeped in every kind of superstition, and
from their earliest infancy, the children of the Duchy
hear tales of ghosts, and goblins, and 'pixies,' told
gravely by their elders, whose words they naturally are
not accustomed to doubt. It was in a world of
horrible, malignant beings,—usually invisible, but
sometimes, so men said, terrifically apparent to human
eyes,—that the poorly fed, ill-nurtured Cornish child
began his days, with the hours of darkness, in which

Evil Spirits chiefly have power, lengthened exceedingly by the awful blackness of the mine.

I have seen Cornishmen tremble with fear at the bare recollection of the heavy things they suffered as children, in the perpetual darkness in which they worked. Often and often, one man told me, he had ceased turning the crank of the fan, so that the miners in the drives and stopes below would begin to suffer from the foulness of the air, and would promptly climb up the ladder-way, very full of wrath, and bubbling over with strange oaths, and 'Put the buckle-strap in about 'un,'—which means a very complete licking. He said that he did this 'for the sake of company,' and it needs little proving how acute the mental sufferings of the unhappy little urchin must have been, before he voluntarily exchanged it for the physical pain of a sound thrashing, administered by the hand of one who had spent all his life smashing rocks.

It is not difficult to understand what the effect of such a youth as this was upon the mind of many Cornish miners. The prolonged and intense strain upon the child's nerves, combined with the agony of fear, which had gradually become an almost chronic condition of his mind, too often rendered him, in after years, a man of poor courage in an emergency, and a weak-charactered individual, possessed of little power of self-control. I must be understood as generalising widely, for of course there are many and brilliant exceptions to the broad rule which I am laying down, —men who have acted gallantly, saving life, when no one save their God was at hand to blame them if they played the coward ; and others, scattered up and down the World, who have 'broken their birth's invidious bars' and have risen to positions of great trust and responsibility, and to the attainment of as much wealth as is good for any man. But such men as these cannot be regarded as in any way typical of the class from which they spring. They would probably have come to the fore under any circumstances, no matter what the conditions in which they chanced to be born, and they must be regarded as having done so in spite of their surroundings, rather than as owing anything to their early training.

YOUNG Trimlett's first experience in the mine to which his father elected to send him, was a severe clout on the side of the head, administered whole-heartedly by an irate miner, whose susceptibilities the lad had unwittingly offended. Trimlett could not for the life of him understand what he had done to call for this summary punishment, and as the angry miner was a far older man than himself, and was, moreover, several sizes larger, the youngster saw that retaliation was out of the question, and with a view to showing that he did not mind, began to whistle unconcernedly. Thereupon the brawny miner promptly knocked him down. When he began to recover from the effects of this new outrage, some one explained to him the cause of the assault. 'Tha' must na' whustle ondergroond,' he said ; 'if tha' do tha'll carl the Pixies, sure 'nuff, an' the 'ands'll vair slay thee ! ' That was the beginning of young Trimlett's training among the men of the Cornish mine. He was only a lad of sixteen or seventeen at the time, and that is perhaps the most im-pressionable of all ages. Gradually, and imperceptibly,

Trimlett began to absorb the strange beliefs and superstitions of the men among whom all his days were spent. He was as credulous concerning things supernatural as Mrs. Crow herself could have desired, and when I knew him, a dozen years ago, his mental attitude, in regard to such matters, was the most extraordinary, for an educated man, that can well be conceived.

All that has been written above is designed to enable the reader to form his own opinion as to the probability or otherwise of the story I have to tell. Personally, I know Trimlett to have been a very truthful individual, and though I am altogether unable to find a working explanation that will fit the facts, that does not shake my faith in the tale as he told it to me.

At the time of which I write, TRIMLETT was stationed in Pêrak, at an out-of-the-way little place called Sĕpûteh, trying to teach the intractable Chinese miner not to mine on his neighbour's land, and to refrain from misappropriating his friends' pay-dirt. The life was a very lonely one, and there was nothing to be had in the nature of amusements, such as Englishmen conjure up all over the World from out the ground, wherever a few of them are gathered together. This it was that drove Trimlett to tree-felling as an occupation, during his leisure hours. It is a healthy form of exercise, and it kept Trimlett's muscles in good trim for the occasional rough-and-tumbles in which he was called upon to engage with refractory Chinese coolies. The Malays put it down to drunkenness, that useful explanation, which, to the native

mind, accounts for ninety per cent of the incomprehensible eccentricities of the White Men,—the Chinese
imagined that Trimlett hoped to make a fortune in the
timber trade, and the Englishman, quite undisturbed
by the opinions of those about him, went on hacking
away at all the finest trees in the vicinity of his hut.
For this was in the very early days, before such things
as forest-conservancy were dreamed of in Pêrak.

I had occasion to visit Trimlett in his camp among
the tin-mines once or twice every month, and I must
own that his surroundings were the reverse of cheering.
His hut, which was composed of a single room, stood
on a spot that had been flattened out, from the
side of a hill, and the jungle around it had been partially cleared, the felled trees lying in all directions, a
confused mass of dying trunks and boughs. In the
valley below, the paddocks of the Chinese alluvial
mines were plainly visible, the coolies swarming up
and down the ladders, and round and about the brink,
like ants near their nest. The unsightly heaps of
earth, of an ugly yellow colour, sparsely grown upon
with scant and weedy green-stuff, made the whole
scene hideous, and even the queerly-shaped palm-
leaf coolie-lines, on the left, were powerless to impart
an air of picturesqueness to the place. About half
way up the hill, to the right of the hut in which
Trimlett lived, there stood a gigantic *mêrbau* tree,
running up sheer into the sky, without branch or
fork, to a height of more than a hundred feet. At its
foot, in the spaces between the spreading, knotty roots,
half a dozen handfuls of Chinese joss-sticks were
stuck into the ground, the tips smouldering sulkily,

I

and emitting an unpleasantly 'Chinese' smell. The charred ashes of tinsel paper, lying all about, marked the spots where paper money, which is piously supposed to satisfy the financial desires of the Spirits, had been burned by some devout Chinamen. On projections of the bark, and from wands fixed in the ground, depended the strips of foul rag which both the Malays and the Chinese furnish to the Beings of the other World, with a view to supplying their strangely incomprehensible wants. When we remember that, in the first instance, the idea of what things were most likely to prove acceptable to the Spirits must have been evolved by human beings, a contemplation of the extraordinary uselessness of the offerings selected fills one with wonder. The charred tinsel, which is designed to represent money, may be explained by the belief entertained by men, in all parts of the World, that the Spirits are very easily deceived by counterfeit of any kind. But when ·we come to such things as rags, which even a scavenger might despise, an ex-·planation is less easy to find. Perhaps these gifts had their origin in the far-off days, when garments of any sort were things of price, and a man was accounted rich who could go abroad among his fellows lightly garbed in a wisp of coarse stuff bound about his head. In those times, conceivably, a rag given to the gods represented a large part of a man's possessions, the sacrifice of which meant some real high-mindedness on the part of the giver ; and though, in these days of Birmingham and Manchester goods, any man can spare a handful of rotting calico, if thereby he may please the Spirits, the practice has survived, though the

original meaning of the gifts has long ago been forgotten. Of course such speculations as these must
necessarily be the purest guess-work, though, for my
own part, I regard the above as being at least as good
an explanation as any other.

Trimlett pointed the *mérbau* tree out to me, as we
sat smoking in front of his hut.

'I mean to have a try at him, one of these days,'
he said.

'How do you mean?' I asked him.

'Oh, I mean to try and fell him,' he said. 'He is an
awful monster, and he will give me a hard job of it, I
expect, but I will get him down none the less, sooner
or later, sure enough.'

'I do not fancy that the natives will like it much
if you do,' I said. 'The tree is supposed to be *kramat*
—sacred—by the Malays, and it is a Joss of the
CHINAMEN's also. You had far better leave it alone.'

'Rubbish!' said TRIMLETT; 'they won't care;
besides, he is a splendid fellow to axe, and I have
promised myself the treat of bringing him down for a
long time past.'

'Well, if I had anything to do with it I would
stop you,' I said; 'I do not believe in hurting the feelings of the natives on these sort of subjects.'

'But you see you have *not* got anything to do with
it, Old Man!' Trimlett replied; and as I knew that
quite well, without Trimlett going out of his way to
tell me, I said nothing more about it, which was
possibly Trimlett's object in making the remark.

I did not see Trimlett again for a week, or more,
and then he was brought in to Kuâla Kangsar, where

I then lived, swearing horribly at each jolt of the stretcher upon which he lay.

I put him to bed, and sent for the Dresser, to bind him up, and it was while he lay propped against the pillows, that he told me of what had befallen him.

He had been very busy, after I had left him at Sĕpûteh, and had not had time to give the *mĕrbau* tree another thought, until the work slackened. Then he had recalled our conversation about the tree, and since I had strongly advised him not to touch it, he, of course, determined to cut it down, with as little delay as possible.

He stated his intention to his Malay followers, who, one and all, entreated him to forgo his purpose, and, when they found that they could not prevail upon him, lost no time in reporting the matter to the Malay Headman at Enggor. This worthy hastened to the spot, and added his prayers to those of the other Malays, and the *Mandors* of the Chinese miners joined their voices to the clamour of general protest.

'What possible harm can come of it?' Trimlett asked.

'God alone knows,' replied the Malay Headman. 'The tree is said to be sacred to the Spirits. The men of ancient days bade us have a care how we tampered with aught that the Spirits hold dear, and such an one is the said tree.'

'But any risk there may be I take; no other man will suffer, is that not so, *Pĕnghulu?*' asked Trimlett.

'I know not,' was the reply. 'Who shall say what the Spirits may do if they wax wrathful? And if indeed, *Tûan*, thou only shouldst suffer, will not the

"Company" be angry with me, the Headman, in that I did not deter thee from a so foolish enterprise?'

TRIMLETT was not pleased with the *Pénghúlu* for presuming to stigmatise as foolish any project upon which his mind was set; and he let the Malay know his opinion in a manner which was unmistakable. Eventually both the Malays and the Chinese took themselves off, for every wise native is aware that an angry White Man is an ill creature to deal with, and their visit left Trimlett more set upon felling the tree than ever.

It was at about five o'clock in the afternoon that Trimlett strolled across from his hut to the foot of the *mérbau* tree. He stood there, for a moment or two, gazing with upturned face at the great gray trunk, running in a sheer unbroken line, from the knotted roots below, to the spreading boughs, silhouetted against the clear evening sky. It seemed a veritable tower of strength, 'that stood four square to all the winds that blew,' and the knowledge that he could fell it to the ground gave Trimlett a strange sense of power. He had no compunction, for in common with a large class of Englishmen, Trimlett took a keen pleasure in any act of destruction, and the enjoyment to be experienced was in direct proportion to the size of the object of his attack. He peeled off his coat, rolled up his shirt-sleeves, and prepared for action.

There was one thing that Trimlett, when he told me the story, was particularly anxious that I should clearly understand. The warnings and protests of the natives had not, so he averred, left any sort of impression on his mind. As he stood before the tree, prior to beginning his attack upon it, no thought of its supposed sanctity, no memory of the Spirits to whom the Headman had said that the tree was dear, was in Trimlett's mind. He felt no greater measure of excitement than he was accustomed to experience when his axe was in his hand, and a new forest giant, of rather more than the ordinary dimensions, was marked for the felling. Trimlett was very clear upon this point, and was wont to resent any insinuation to the effect that the strange thing that happened to him, was due to a preconceived opinion upon his part, that the felling of the Spirits' tree was likely to be accompanied by some supernatural event. (It is, of course, a matter of some doubt, how far a man can be trusted to know what is, and what is not in his mind, at any given time, or to judge how much, or how little he has been influenced by any trivial, or even important occurrence ; for most of us are so put together that we can never be quite sure what functions are being performed by the various parts of our complicated mental machinery.) Anyhow, to the best of his belief, Trimlett's thoughts were wholly occupied with considerations as to the best manner in which he might fell the tree, and with the triumph which would be his when the great feat was at length accomplished.

He planted his feet firmly on the ground, rather far apart, weighed his axe lightly, poising it in his hands, then, clasping it tightly, raised it high above his right shoulder, and brought it down, with all his force, upon the gnarled bark of the tree. The clear, crisp ring of the steel upon the wood, as the blow told loudly, floated out on the still air, and the awakened echoes called

to one another, from hill to hill, through the forest-
clad uplands. The thousand noises which, taken
together, make the heavy stillness of the afternoon,
were lost for a moment, drowned by the sound of the
axe. Then the jungle-songs broke out once more, as
the echoes died away, on the scented, slow-breathing
wind. A couple of *bârau-bârau* thrushes were warb-
ling liquidly ; the clear, far - carrying note of the
sélanting mixed with their swift trilling ; and the
shriek of the great noisy earth - worm, that cries
sullenly from its burrow, a foot beneath the ground,
strove manfully to drown the sweeter music of the
birds. An odd dozen of *cicada* were chirping and ticking
in the forest, and very far away the moaning hoot of
the *siâmang* monkeys could be faintly heard. All these
voices of bird, and beast, and insect made the quiet
evening hour alive with sound, as, in jungle places, it
always must be ; but though the chorus went on with
unabated vigour, after that first blow of Trimlett's axe,
somehow it seemed to the Englishman as though a
kind of hush had fallen upon the land. He had some
difficulty in explaining precisely what he meant, when
he told me the story, but it seemed, he said, as though
there were two spheres of sound,—one in which he
heard the chorus of birds and insects, as clearly as ever,
and another, totally different, in which the stillness
seemed to be suddenly intensified and deepened, to an
awful pitch of tension, that had something terrifying in
it. It was this other, stranger region of sound, however,
that seemed for the moment to be the more real. The
other, in which the songs of bird and insect had part,
appeared to be indescribably remote and distant. It

was a curious sensation to have experienced, and afterwards, when he came to recall it, Trimlett felt surprised that he had not been more impressed by it at the time. As it was, however, he read no warning in the strange prank that his ears appeared to be playing upon him; and once more he swung the axe back, high above his shoulder, preparatory to bringing it down for another blow, slightly advancing his left foot as he did so.

It was at this moment that he became aware of a weird object at his feet. It had no particular size, or shape, or colour ; it bore no sort of resemblance to any object that Trimlett had ever seen. It simply forced the fact of its horrible, revolting, repulsive presence upon Trimlett, without the Englishman being able clearly to distinguish through which of his senses the unearthly impression was conveyed. It seemed to seize his attention in a grip that was an agony ; to rivet every function of his mind ; to possess him utterly with overwhelming aversion, and uncontrollable fear. Trimlett's axe was uplifted for a stroke, and, almost before he was aware what he was doing, he brought it crashing down upon the Unspeakable Uncleanliness at his feet. It was not till he was apprised of the fact, by an agony of pain, that Trimlett became aware that the object at which he had smitten so fiercely was his own left foot. Even then, the idea of that revolting, disgusting Presence was so firmly fixed in his mind that, as he fell over, he tried with all his might to throw himself down on the side farthest from that upon which he believed it to be lying. The earth, for many yards around the tree, was worn smooth and hard, by the passing to and fro of countless generations of horny-footed worshippers, so there was not sufficient cover to effectually conceal a beetle, yet Trimlett could see nothing unusual, except the red glouts of blood that had leaped from the wide wound in his foot. Then and after, he maintained stoutly that it was wholly impossible that anything, which had really been there, could have evaded his scrutiny ; and since a sane man is not generally scared out of his senses by the sight of one of his own limbs, Trimlett accounted for the besetment that had seized him by the theory that the Spirit of the Tree had hypnotised him into mistaking his foot for the weird denizen of some mysterious unknown World. If, in truth, the tree, as the Headman said, was dear to the Spirits, this mode of protecting their property was certainly as effectual as any that could have been devised, for Trimlett never tried to fell the *mérbau*, and no one else had any desire to make the attempt.

It is no part of my business to offer any explanation of this affair, for the story is not mine, but Trimlett's ; but since he, poor fellow, is no longer amongst us to tell the tale himself, I have thought it perhaps worth while to place the facts, such as they are, on record.

We Fettered Folk have felt your yoke,
  For heavy years and long;
We've learned to sight where tortuous Right
  Breaks loose from tangled Wrong.
To us the twain, 'tis all too plain,
  Be like as pea to pea,
But ye be wise, and so our eyes
  Must see as White Men see.

Your rule is just, and since we must,
  We learn to kiss the yoke;
You we'll obey, by night and day,
  But not your dark-skin'd Folk!
The bearded Sikh, and Tamil sleek,
  With them we will not deal,
Nor with the throng that crowds along
  Close to the White Man's heel!

To begin to understand anything at all about the Malay, you must realise, from the first, that he is intensely self-respecting. He possesses, in a high degree, one of the most characteristic qualities of the English gentleman,—he is absolutely and supremely sure of himself. It does not occur to him to assume airs of equality or superiority, for the very simple reason that he is quite satisfied with himself as he is,—as it has pleased God to fashion him,—and this, instead of making him unbearably conceited, as might well be the case, causes him to take his place in any society quite naturally with comfort to both himself and his neighbours, since he is not for ever mentally comparing his own position with that of others. Thus one may make an intimate friend of a Malay, may share the same hut with him for long periods at a time, and may talk to him of all things within his comprehension, without there being any risk of familiarity breeding contempt, or of the Malay taking advantage of his position to dig you in the ribs, or to call you by your Christian name. He respects himself far too much to dream of taking liberties, or to be otherwise than courteous and respectful towards those with whom he has to deal. And this, be it remembered, is a national characteristic ; for everything that I have said applies with equal force to the humblest Malay villager, and to the most courtly Native Chief. There are, of course, many lamentable instances of Malays who have been educated out of this self-respecting reserve, and who have become almost as offensive and familiar as a low-caste European, but the existence of these unfortunates must be placed to the credit of the White Men, whose presence has produced them, and not debited against the Malay, with whom they have nothing in common. Any way you look at them, these abnormal developments are a subject for tears.

We English have an immense deal to answer for, and it will be interesting to see exactly how our account stands when the good and the bad that we have done,—both with the most excellent intentions, —face one another, in double columns, on the pages of the Recording Angel's Day-Book. We come into a country which is racked with war and rapine, and after making a little war of our own, to help to set things straight, we reduce the land to a dead monotony of order and peace. We find vile misrule, and a government which is so incompetent and impotent that it is incapable of even oppressing its subjects completely, or upon any organised system, and we replace it by a high - class, triple - action, automatic, revenue-producing administration that presses equally upon all alike. We give the poor and hitherto undefended rights, of the very existence of which they had never formerly dreamed ; we free the slaves, who have for generations been made to labour sorely against their will, and who celebrate their emancipation by declining to engage in any toil more arduous than *betel* - chewing, with an occasional theft thrown in, when the children cry for rice ; we lop his power from the Chief, who, it must be confessed, has always consistently abused it, but finds little to comfort him in the recollection ; we open up the most inaccessible places ; we bring Trade, and Money, and Prosperity, and Material Comfort, and Sanitation, and Drains, and a thousand other blessings of Civilisation in our wake. We educate ; we vaccinate ; we physic ; we punish the Wicked, and we reward the Good. We administer the native till we make him almost giddy, and he begins to forget that he is an absurd anachronism in the Nineteenth Century, and must surely lose his way most utterly if he tries to stay there. We sweep away the horrible gaol-cages of Independent Malaya, and replace them by model prisons of so excellent a type that a native comes to regard them as places where, should the Fates so decree, he may lodge with considerable convenience to himself. You can never instil into a Malay of the lower classes the idea that going to gaol is something which disgraces a man for all his days. From his point of view, the whole thing is purely a matter of capricious chance. He 'gets' imprisonment, just as he catches fever ; and separation from his women-folk and abstinence from tobacco are the unfortunate accessories of the former, much as chills and burnings are the accompaniments of the latter. All these things, and many others also, we do for the native when we take over the administration of a barbarous land, and on the whole we do it all very well indeed. That the sudden introduction to an elaborate civilisation, which is itself the result of long and slow evolution from very primitive beginnings, should not always tend to immediately improve the moral character of the bulk of the native population is unfortunate but inevitable. The fault obviously lies with the moral nature of the native, for which no man can hold us responsible ; and, as I have already said, we do our part of the business very well indeed, for we are a great and peculiar people, and the majority of us are quite ready to wear our souls out in the struggle to realise what we believe to be for the ultimate good of the folk we try to rule and serve. And this, be it said, is neither a light nor an easy task.

Unfortunately we cannot do everything ourselves, and it is here that the weak part of our administration comes in. White Men are most expensive creatures in the World. The schooling fees of an average

English boy would be a sufficient sum to pay for the restocking of an old-world *râja's* harem, and we all know what sinful waste goes on in that department ot the State. If all our understrappers were Europeans the revenue of even the richest lands would be inadequate to defray the cost of our administration, and realising this, we are obliged to bring a host of aliens at our heels, when we enter a new country for the purpose of converting things as they are, into things as they ought to be. When we first make our appearance we are not particularly loved by anybody. The Chiefs know that, cloak it as we will, we are there to wrest the power they have misused from their unwilling grasp. Naturally the notion is not one which inspires them with any particular enthusiasm for us. To the peasants we are strange new Beings, whom their masters, the Chiefs, abhor. If half the tales men tell them of us are true, our coming is indeed a calamity hard to be borne. The oppression of the Chiefs is, in the eyes of the peasant, a thing of course. Since ever Time was, the ill things which a man must suffer at the hands of one more powerful than himself have formed the impassable horizon of the peasant's life. But when the White Men come, no one can say what new horrors will now be added to the heavy lot of the people. The Chiefs are at some pains to confirm this fear, and so the newly arrived European finds every man's hand against him. If the work is to be done at all, during the weary years that must pass before their new rulers can hope to win the trust and confidence of the people of the land, aliens must be brought in, to help the White

Men in their work. And it is thus that the strangers, who sell our names for a song, win a foothold from the very inception of our rule.

They are a miscellaneous crew, of almost any shade of colour, from coal black to olive, dressed in all manner of nondescript garments, a weird compound of the costumes of half a dozen different races. Some are very dark - complexioned gentry indeed, who wear excessively European clothes,—collars that once, in some forgotten age, were white, and neck-ties which, from much wear, show patches of yellow through their dingy blackness. Others there are who are obviously European from their necks to their waists, and as evidently Oriental from their belts downwards. And there are other some who wear English shoes, and their hair in a chignon. They are a strange collection of different races and classes of human beings ; from the burly Sikh, in his coiled turban, to the little Malay from the Colony, or from some well - settled District of a neighbouring State ; from the fluent, educated Tamil, to the black and naked cooly of the same race, whom the Malays name ' *Búkit Pĕkan*,'—the Hill-Tribes of the town,—because they also go abroad among men uncumbered with any garment save a narrow wisp of dirty loin-cloth twisted about their middles.

The Malays loathe and detest the men of their own race who flock into a newly protected State at the heels of their white masters. In the villages, where the people are ignorant, and therefore are the natural prey of any one who stands possessed of a little cunning, the Malay Policeman is treated with elaborate courtesy. They call him 'Che' Sarjin,'—which means Mr. Sergeant,—defer to him on almost every point, give him their daughters to wife, if he so wills it, and do all they can to propitiate him. At the King's Court men hate him more, and fear him less. They are aware that he is not the bravest person of their acquaintance, and they find it hard to resist the very natural temptation to beat him whenever the opportunity offers. He is better educated than are the youths of the Capital, and since he has a pretty knack of turning a love verse, he is constantly the object of some lady's attentions. This has a great deal to do with the hatred he inspires in the men, and it is because of his love affairs that the opportunity for beating him so frequently occurs, and always proves so irresistible.

But perhaps it is the Sikh who is most abhorrent to the Malay of all the followers of the White Men. He is possessed of as absolute a conviction of his own superiority to the men of any other race—Europeans alone excepted—as is the White Man himself. He is quite frank about this opinion, and he is accustomed to act upon it at all times. To other Asiatics he is as arrogant and overbearing as can well be conceived, and he displays none of the tact which helps to make a European less hated for his airs of superiority than he might be. The noisy, loud-mouthed, awkward, familiar-mannered, bullying Sikh is as unlike the courteous, soft-tongued Malay as one human being can well be from another, and his conduct and behaviour to the people of the land hurts the latter's self-respect at every turn.

No man needs to be told that the Sikh is a splendid soldier. His powers of endurance, especially his marching capabilities, would astonish a man whose experience of troops was confined to European soldiers; but the Sikh, partly perhaps because the discipline to which he is accustomed has become an inseparable portion of his nature, seems to be altogether incapable of thinking rationally for himself, and he is altogether lost unless he has a White Man at his shoulder to tell him what to be at.

'Why do you not go inside your sentry-box?' a friend of mine cried from his verandah to a Sikh who was solemnly marching up and down upon his beat in rain such as the Malays say prevents one from even opening one's eyes.

'There is no order!' was the reply, and this is typical of the race to which the sentry belonged. So long as there is some one at hand to give an order, the Sikh will obey it as few other men will do. He never counts the cost, he never hesitates, though he be commanded to attempt the obviously impossible. There is an order, and the wisdom and the folly of the said order does not concern him in the least. The Malay, on the other hand, is utterly incapable of being disciplined into a machine. He has, and always retains, his own ideas—usually wrong ones, be it said—of how any given thing ought to be done, and no amount of training will teach him to jump to the word of command, while wholly abandoning his own opinion as to its wisdom. This makes the Malay altogether hopeless as a regular, but fairly useful as an irregular, for he can think for himself and does not need to be told how, when, and where to do any given thing. But it is when the Malay and the Sikh are set to work together, and there is no White Man at hand to direct either of them, that the contrast between the two races comes out at its best. Here is an instance :—

Alang Abdollah, the Headman, squatted, flustered and dejected, upon the matted verandah of my house, and spat, with disgusted emphasis, when he mentioned the name of Ram Singh, the Sikh sergeant of Police. He was of a full habit of body, and the sun had enforced payment of a heavy tribute as he trudged along in the heat, so his features were caked with dust, which clung to each wrinkle, and cracked oddly as his face worked with anger. For the heart of Alang Abdollah was full of wrath. He had already expended most of his available stock of bad language while limping along the fifteen miles of glaring, aching, white-hot road, which separated his village from the place in which I lived, and for a space, he could do little more than pant, and puff, and blow, expressing his fury with the Sikh by dumb-show, and an occasional meaningless expletive.

I saw that he had come to unburden himself to me, and I gathered that he needed rest before he would be fit to tell his tale, so I pushed the wooden *sirih*-box across the verandah, and spoke fluently of the crops, while he prepared his quid, and began to regain his self-possession.

Presently he secreted the folded quid in his cheek, pushed a large round wad of finely-shredded tobacco under his upper lip, after carefully wiping his gums with it, and began to speak, in a voice that seemed to come from behind the thickest part of a baked potato.

' *Túan*, I come to thee wailing and weeping,' he said, ' because of the shame which has been put upon me, and upon the sons of my village, by reason of the so great folly and wickedness of Ram Singh, the Sikh ! '

' How is that ? ' I asked. ' Relate the matter to me from the beginning even to the end.'

' Good, *Túan;* be pleased to listen to my words, the words of one who is not skilled in lying.

''The *Túan* knows the little Police Station at Changkat Medang ? Well it is of that station that Ram Singh hath charge ; and many times he hath come to me, the Headman, praying that I will give him knowledge of all untoward things which may from time to time occur within the limits of my District.

' Now it chanced upon the afternoon of Friday, when the Congregational Prayers had been chanted in the Mosque, that Ngah Seman, a man of my village, while searching for a buffalo which had gone astraying, espied some twenty Chinamen camping in the jungle about one mile-stone distant from the village of Batu Nering. Ngah Seman was astonished at the sight of these men, and he squatted in the brushwood watching them. Then he beheld that they had swords, and many weapons, and the knowledge came to him that they were gang-robbers. Therefore, being filled with a great fear, he retired quietly and with caution, and ran to me at Changkat Medang, to make known that which he had seen.

'Thereafter did I, with much haste, get me to the Police Station, and make *raport* to the Sikh Ram Singh.

'For a long time did we sit consulting one with another, and cunningly did we devise a plan. Thou knowest the nature of the village of Batu Nering. The road runs through it, and the shops are built adjoining one unto another on each side of the way. Behind the row of shops, upon the side on which the sun comes to life, there is a deep swamp through which no man may pass; and on the other hand, where the sun dieth daily, there riseth a steep hill. The house of the Opium Farmer is on the edge of the swamp, in the centre of the village, and well I knew that no other house would be sought by the gang-robbers, for in no other is there much property, the folk of that village being an indigent and pauper-like people. Therefore I said to Ram Singh, "When the night hath fallen, we will go quietly to the village of Batu Nering, and we will hide in the shadow of the five-foot way, so that no man may see us. Thou, O Brother, shalt hide thee and thy Sikh men near the far entrance to the village, and I with all my folk will hide near the other end of the road. Now, when the gang-robbers come to pillage the Farm we will suffer them to pass, and then they will be like unto fish in a trap, having no means of egress. So shall we slay them or capture them, and our names shall be much praised by the Government of the White Men."

'What sayest thou, *Tüan*, was not my stratagem a clever one?

'Ram Singh said "It is good!" and when the

evening had fallen, we betook ourselves to Batu
Nering, and ordered all things as I had arranged.
The night was dark, for the moon was not alight,
and no man could see those who sat in the shadow
of the five-foot way.

'We sat there waiting for as long as it would take
to cook a pot of rice, and thereafter to chew a quid of
betel-nut ; and presently the robbers came. They
entered the village by the end which Ram Singh
guarded, directing their steps straight to the door of
the Farmer's House, and the Sikhs suffered them to
pass, as had been agreed between us. The robbers
were some twenty men, ill-looking, and of a fierce
and tyrannical mien, and they began forthwith to
break open the door of the Farm.

'Then I cried "*Amok ! Amok !*" and my people
sounded the *sorak*, as we rushed out of the shadow, and
began to advance upon the robbers up the centre of
the road. Ram Singh and his men also made a great
shouting, and spread themselves in a line across their
end of the roadway. Then again I cried "Charge !
Charge ! *Amok ! Amok !*" and my people following me,
we began to make shift to throw ourselves upon the
robbers, who stood stricken with fear in the middle of
the village, seeing no means of escape.

'Then above the tumult, and the noise, and the
shouting, I heard the voice of Ram Singh, the Sikh,
calling to his men, "*Porisint arrrums ! Pire !*" and
at the word, all the Sikh men did fire their rifles down
the road, so that the bullets made sharp sounds about
my ears. Thereupon I and all my people were overcome with a great fear, and we fell flat upon the

ground thus to avoid the bullets of the Sikhs. Once again their rifles sounded, and the bullets went *ting*, *ting*, above my head, and *pat*, *pat*, in the dust of the road, but no one of the gang-robbers was hit, for these folk have great skill in charms against bullets.

'Now when the gang-robbers beheld that we were overcome with fear, by reason of the so great folly and wickedness of the Sikhs, they made haste to escape, their bare feet treading on our bodies where we lay hiding from the bullets. One man placed his foot upon my head' (Alang Abdollah paused to spit at the recollection), 'and my heart was hot in my breast, so I rose to my knees, seizing his pig-tail as it flew behind him. I grasped it very tightly, and, *Túan*—it came off! It was a false pig-tail that the robber wore in order to deceive his enemies, and it was charged with very sharp fish-hooks, so that my hand was lacerated by them, even as thou seest. Then as I still gazed at him in astonishment, he turned towards me, and threw a little parcel of paper in my face. *Túan*, it contained much black pepper, and the paper becoming torn, my eyes were filled with the burning thereof, so that I was blinded, and fell to the ground screaming in pain. Accursed be these Chinese gang-robbers, who are so fierce, and cruel, and tyrannical, and withal so very cunning and full of wiles!

'Thus these robbers escaped from our hands one and all; and as I sat upon the dust of the road, in pain and blindness, lamenting my fate, Ram Singh, the Sikh, came to me, and gave abuse, very keen and pungent, so that a greater shame was put upon me, and in my agony, I could find but few words to reply.

Moreover, I fear that Ram Singh will make *raport* to his *Tūan*, saying evil things of me and mine, whereas it was through his sin that the Chinese escaped. How can a man stand up and fight in the face of the much shooting of his friends ? Let our enemies and our friends be known, then may a man fight with a willing heart, but how can he bear it when his friends also war against him ? My face is stained with soot because of this thing, and I come hither wailing and weeping that thou mayest aid me in the cleansing thereof. O cause some very heavy punishment to fall upon Ram Singh, the Sikh, as a return for his wickedness and sin. Then only will my heart know satisfaction ! '

At the back of his soul, if you could only probe so deep, the Malay has the firm belief that all non-Muhammadan people are equally despicable, equally outcast. He may admire the wisdom and ingenuity of the White Man, the physical strength and the skill in athletic exercises displayed by the Sikh, or the cunning and deft trading of the Chinaman, but, though he will express his admiration quite freely, he daily thanks God that he is not as others,—such as these Publicans. Not that he is in any way a Pharisee, in the ordinary sense of the term, for he has very little spiritual pride. All he does think is that he professes the True Faith, while other folk are hapless Infidels ; and that consequently he will be saved (no matter what his deeds in this life may be) while the rest of the world will be damned, as they deserve to be. In this belief, which he holds with an unquestioning faith, he not unnaturally finds considerable comfort. All the same, the Malays are less fanatical than any other Muhammadans in Asia, and a man of this race will tolerate, and even take pleasure in your society in this world, secure in the knowledge that he will not be called upon to continue the intimacy in the next.

For himself this is in his own eyes quite right and fitting, but in the East what is sauce for the goose is by no means necessarily sauce for the gander. Native women, to do them justice, though they are ready enough to forgive their fellows for lapses from virtue if the man be a Muhammadan, have very little mercy on a girl who so far forgets herself as to become entangled in an intrigue with an Infidel; and since standards of morality are chiefly set by Public Opinion, it is rare for a Malay woman of birth or social standing to war against the prejudices of her people in this respect. To the male Malay, however, it is horrible to think that any exceptions to this rule should exist, and in the in-rush of aliens of all sorts and conditions he sees a danger which he cannot pretend to view with any sort of equanimity.

Quite apart from any considerations of this sort, the inability of the White Man to do his own great work unaided carries with it its only too obvious drawbacks. Our motto is Justice, and from end to end of Asia our name is a proverb for that virtue in its highest expressions; but, alas! our understrappers' reputation is a byword in quite another sense. If a native can win to the presence of the European he is satisfied that he will get a fair hearing, and a fair unbiassed decision, with which, though he may very heartily disagree with it, he will rest content, feeling absolutely secure that no personal prejudice has influenced it by a hair's breadth. The more sophisticated natives are not by any means to be bluffed out of seeing and laying their cases before the White Men, but the poor villager and the more ignorant classes generally dare not brave the anger of the subordinate who would keep them from ' wearying the *Túan* with many words,' and such as these are very apt to have the rank injustice of the native policeman, or the peon, or the punkah-wallah palmed off upon them as the order of the White Man. You must remember that to natives of this class the ways and works of the Europeans and their Government are wholly obscure and incomprehensible, and therefore, no matter how preposterous the ruling they obtain from the subordinate, these poor people have nothing against which to scale it with a view to gauging its propriety or authenticity. It is thus that an incalculable amount of harm, the greater proportion of which never reaches our ears, is daily done in the name of the White Man's government.

Every one living in Asia knows all this, and, alas! of remedy there is none. Perhaps,

Far off in Summers that we may not see,

in the days that we are taught to look for, 'When nobody works for money, and nobody works for fame,' the White Men will do all their work for themselves, or, more unlikely still, will have embued their Oriental subordinates with an exalted spirit of honour and truthfulness, and devotion to duty even higher than their own. But until all this comes to pass, we must worry along as we are, and can only trust to Europeans trying honestly and untiringly to learn the character, and the requirements, and above all the language of the people whose destinies are in their hands. If interpreters are to be used at all, they should be highly-paid officials, of standing and position, but this is, perhaps, as Utopian a proposal as any of the other impossible changes which must take place before the White Man's rule can cease to be marred by the many things which now do so much to disfigure it.

In the meantime, it is worth considering how far we are morally responsible for the evil that is daily done in our name by those that follow at our heels.

TÛKANG BÛROK'S STORY

Though my bones be old, yet my soul within
    Is wrung with the old Desire ;
Though my limbs wax cold, though my blood runs thin,
    Yet my Heart it is still afire !
And ever I long, as the night shuts down,
    For my Love that was lost to me,
And pray to the Gods of the White and the Brown
That the villain who robbed me,—that base-born clown,
Unworthy to finger the hem of her gown,—
    May be blighted utterly !

OLD Tûkang Bûrok, the fashioner of wooden dagger-
hilts and sheaths, sat cróss-legged on the narrow
verandah of his hut, which, perched upon the top of
the high bank, overlooked the Pârit River. I squatted,
smoking, at his side, watching him at his work, and
listening to the tales of the days of long ago, which
were for ever on his lips.

Forty feet below us the red, peat-stained waters of
the Pàrit, banked up by the tide now flowing up the
Pahang River, crawled lazily back towards their source.
The thatched roofs of more than a score of rafts lay
under our feet, so that anything rolling off the verandah
would fall plump upon the nearest of them. Nozzling
one another, and rubbing sides with a mighty creak-

ing, lay twice as many large native boats, moored in
the red water that they might be out of the reach of
the borers, which honeycomb the bottoms of crafts left
to ride in purer rivers. A narrow fair-way opened
between the boats and rafts, and down and up this
passed a constant stream of tiny dug-outs shooting
swiftly in and out of the numerous obstructions. The
bright colours of the Malays' garments touched the
scene here and there with little splashes of red, or
green, or yellow; the flickering fronds of the cocoanut, sugar, betel, and sago palms, and the spreading
boughs of the clustering fruit-trees,—dividing among
them almost every conceivable shade of green,—
stretched friendly hands, which nearly met, from bank
to bank, casting a grateful, sun-flecked, shifting shade
upon the ruddy water of the stream. Above, seen
through the mass of fronds, and boughs, and leaves,
the intensely pure and vividly-blue Malayan sky arched
over us; and below us the dusty browns and yellows
of the thatching, and palm-leaf roofings of boats and
rafts relieved the even redness of the river. A gentle
wind, which had run up river from the sea, playing
catch as catch can with the flowing tide, sighed
dreamily about us; and the heavy silence was only
broken by the monotonous thud of a paddle-handle
against a boat's side, the faint bleat of a goat, the
whisper of a gust among the palm-fronds, and the
purring sound of old Tûkang Bûrok's polishing tools.

'*Tüan*, the maiden was passing fair, and the madness came upon me, and I loved her.' He held a
beautiful piece of *kĕmúning* wood between the toes of
his left foot, and sat polishing it lovingly with a mass

of rough *émpélas* leaves, held in both hands. ' Thy servant was a youth in those so long ago days, and when it comes to the young, the madness is very hot and burning, and the eyes will not sleep, and the belly will not eat rice, and the liver takes to itself the likeness of a live ember. And, in truth, old age changes a man but little, for his desire is as great, only his bones are stiff, and his limbs are turned traitor, and he sees the maidens playing the game of eye-play with the children, who deem themselves men, shooting their love-darts before his very face, and never casting a glance his way, like a bone to a hungry dog, unless they would seek his help to aid them in their courtings and their stolen meetings. *Ya Allah! Túan*, it is very evil to grow old, so that the eyes wax dim, and the ears are heavy of hearing, and only the liver within is unchanged in the fury of unsatisfied desire! Some there be who turn their thoughts to money, when the maidens will have nought of them, but what is the *clink-a-clunk* of the silver coins to the love-words whispered in the ear by a fair girl, and what profits the white face of a dollar if it be compared with the laughing lips and eyes of a lovely maiden! *Ambui! Túan*, it is verily hard to grow old! I, thy servant, sit here all the long day through, fashioning *kris* hilts and dagger sheaths for the youths, that they may make a brave show in the eyes of their loves, and the boys and maidens pass hither and thither, and I watch the glint in their eyes when they look one upon the other, and *Túan*, the tears of envy rise up in these old eyes of mine, when I know that never again will a maiden love me!

'Therefore, *Túan*, I sit here musing over the days of long ago, and tears once again gather in my eyes, so that I can barely see the wood to fashion it, for ever I think of the girl I loved better than any, and how in an evil hour she was lost to me, ere I had known her for my wife. In truth, *Túan*, my lot has been *chĕlâka*, accursed of Fate.

'Be pleased to listen to my tale, *Túan*, for it is passing strange ; though I suffered greatly, men made a mock of me because of my calamity.

'It was very long ago, far to the *úlu* (upper reaches of the river), in the places where, as men say, the folk call a bushel of water a deep pool, and I was wandering through the country, for I had incurred guilt owing to a trouble that arose concerning certain love passages betwixt me and a maiden of the palace ; and for a while my father deemed it prudent that I should leave the Capital, where the King was very wroth, and hide far away, among the little bustling, shallow streams, where the folk are peaceful, and foolish, and ready to do aught that they are bidden by a youth from the Court, since they fear such people greatly. It was here that I met the maiden, and forthwith the madness fell upon me and I loved her.

'She was a daughter of the village-folk, and such are ofttimes coarse, and big, and ill-favoured, tanned black, like the bottom of a cooking-pot, with working in the sunlight, so that no man may desire them ; but this maiden, *Túan*, was—in truth I cannot tell of the wonder of her beauty. Even now, when I am old, as I then was young, I feel my liver wax hot, and my love spring up anew when I think upon her !

For every man in all the World there is always One Woman. God knoweth that our loves be many, but the others are as the shadows of the real, while She, the Only One, is the Presence that casts the shades. So it was with me,—a son of the Court, born to mate with one bred gently in the towns, as I also had been, —for my liver was crumbled to atoms at the sight of this maid, and I sent my wedding portion to her parents, who were well pleased that their daughter should wed my father's son.

'At night-time I would creep beneath her house, and listen to the music of her words, as she spake with the woman, her mother, and all the folk who sat within the dwelling. Through the chinks in the wattled walls I would watch her, till I was hungry as one who thirsts for water, and thereafter sleep would not fall upon my eyes, so that in those days of waiting my body grew lean and dry as a fish that men have smoked above the leaping fire, and indeed, my liver was broiled over fierce flames that tide, by reason of my so great love and longing for this maiden.

'Now it was upon a day, about a Friday-span before that upon which the Feast of the Becoming One, as our folk name it, was to be held, that the calamity came upon me, utterly destroying me like the blight destroys the standing crops, making the ears empty things and vain. It was in this wise. Listen, *Tûan*, and say was ever trouble like unto mine, shame like unto the disgrace that ·fell upon me, or sorrow like unto the grief I suffered.

'Hôdoh was her name. Yes, *Tûan*, as thou sayest, she was ill-named, for in truth she was beautiful, not

ugly, as the word implies,—but it was thus that her
folk had called her when she was little, and in my ears
it was ever more lovely than the singing of the *thikir*
women, and that, thou knowest, is no mean music.
Hodôh chanced to be alone in her house, all her people
being gone to the fields, but she, being so near the
appointed time of her wedding, stayed at home. Thus
she only was at hand when a Sâkai man, named Pa'
Ah-Gap, the Rhinoceros, came to her house out of the
jungle, praying for rice and tobacco. Now these
Sâkai, as thou knowest, *Tuan*, be sorry animals, and
our people love not to suffer them to enter our dwellings, for they are of an evil odour, dirty, and covered
with skin disease, so that from afar they seem to be
white, like a fair woman. The villagers of the interior
bear little love to the Sâkai, and the women especially
cannot abide their presence near to them, so when
Hôdoh beheld the face of Pa' Ah-Gap, scarred with
tattoo-marks, grimed with soot, as are always the Sâkai
who sleep in the warm ashes of their fires, with hair
in locks like the ragged sago-palm yonder, she shrieked
aloud, cursing him for a filthy, unclean, mite-eaten
Sâkai, and bidding him begone, crying " Hinchit !
Hinchit ! " as men do when they drive away a dog.
Pa' Ah-Gap stood still gazing upon her, rubbing his
left leg slowly against his right shin-bone, and scratching his scalp with one claw-like hand hidden in his
frowsy hair, while Hôdoh abated not her railing, and
ceased not from heaping shame upon him with many
injurious words. Then he lifted up his voice and
spoke.

' " Daughter of the Gobs " (Malays), he said, " why

miscallest thou thy lover? In a little while thou shalt seek me in the forests, imploring me to take thee for my own, and in that day thou shalt be to me as a wife!" and so saying he laughed harshly as the frogs croak in the Winter-time, while she fled into the house, but ceased not from her railings and abuse.

'Then, when Hôdoh had entered into the house, Pa' Ah-Gap—Iblis has had him in Jehannam these fifty years, but not before we too had had our will of him—pattered a charm in the Sâkai tongue,—for these folk have great skill in magic, the gods of the ancient-days, whom we have deserted for Allah and Muhammad, abiding with them, as once they abode with us also,— and slowly, slowly he picked the bark of his loin-cloth into little ragged flecks, as he stood in the open space before the house. Then he cast seven pieces to the North and to the South, and towards the spot where the sun cometh to life, and towards the place where the sun dieth; then he shouted three times, so that the folk in the rice-fields fell awondering what manner of animal was crying from the jungles; and lastly he danced silent and alone, making a complete circuit of the house. When these things had been accomplished Pa' Ah-Gap slipped into the forest, making no sound in his going, as is the manner of the jungle people. And as he went, he let fall little pieces of his torn loin-cloth, leaving behind him such as a man makes who walks chewing sugar-cane, casting on the ground the sucked pith that he has robbed of its sweet juices.

'At the hour at which the kine go down to water, Hôdoh's parents and brethren returned from the rice-fields, and they were told all that had happened

L

concerning Pa' Ah-Gap, and Che' Mat, Hôdoh's father, swore that he would punish Pa' Ah-Gap for molesting his women-kind, and that with no sparing hand. There was much talk that night, in Hôdoh's house, and I, hiding beneath the flooring, heard all that passed, until the hour came for extinguishing the lights, and I went to my mat, sad at heart because I could no longer gaze upon the beauty of my Love.

'Now it was shortly after sleep had come to all within the house, save only Hôdoh, who lay wide-eyed and wakeful, that a strange burning came upon her, consuming her as it were in a fire, from her head even to her feet, and her heart, and her liver, and her spleen, and her lungs were like unto so many red-hot embers, scorching their way through her body, and at the same time her speech was wholly reft from her, so that she could by no means cry out or call any one to her aid. Then, too, a sudden knowledge came to her that the cool, dark jungles could alone abate the agony of her pain, and forthwith she arose, and making no sound, passed out of the house. The moon was at the full, very bright and vivid, so that Hôdoh found it an easy matter to pick her way into the forest, following the track marked by the shreds of Pa' Ah-Gap's loin-cloth, and each one of these she gathered up lovingly, kissing them, for the touch of the 'rough bark-cloth against her lips seemed to cool the burning pain within her. (All these things she told us later, as thou shalt hear, *Túan.*) Till the moonlight was wrestling with the yellow dawn, Hôdoh travelled on alone, though our folk fear greatly to thread the jungle single-foot, and the shreds of loin-cloth, which led her on and on,

grew few and few, as she wandered ever onwards into
the Sâkai people's country. The Sun had come to life
when her journey was at last accomplished, and she
came out of the jungle on to a vast Sâkai clearing, and
at the door of the first hut, facing the track by which
she had come, sat Pa' Ah-Gap,—waiting for her!
He sat still, looking at her, with eyes that mocked her
and, of a sudden, she was aware of a fierce love for
this man springing up in her breast, so that, lost to
shame, she ran forward and cast herself at his feet,
praying him to take her for his wife,—even as the so-
accursed animal had foretold that she would do!
Then, as she touched him, the burning pain departed
from her, and she was utterly at peace.

'Was not the magic of this Sâkai very great, and
strong, and marvellous? For, even among our own
folk, no maiden willingly throws herself into the arms
of her lover, though she love him dearly, for women
are fashioned in such wise that they feel shame like an
overwhelming burden, crushing them utterly, so that
they may not move hand or foot. Allah, in his
wisdom, has done well so to order, for otherwise, were
there no shame among women, their passions being ✓
more fierce than those of men, great trouble would
ensue, and verily there is enough already, even though
shame be not quite dead in the land. But now Hôdoh,
the Core of my Heart's Core, my Betrothed, my Loved
One, the sweetest and most virtuous of all the many
women I have known, ran to this so filthy and
diseased Sâkai,—a wild man of the woods, an Infidel,
—entreating for his love, and kissing his soot-begrimed
hide! *Ya Allah!* Verily I cannot think upon it!'

Old Tûkang Bûrok paused in his narrative, and
spat disgustedly, and with emphasis, into the stream
below. His lined and wrinkled face was working
queerly with the tumult of fierce emotions which were
brought to life by the memory of his balked desire for
Hôdoh, by the thought of his Love given over to a
despised jungle-dweller, by hatred, fury, and consuming
jealousy and envy. He spat once more, and then,
selecting one of his tools, he set to work to bevel a
piece of beautifully grained wood with great delicacy
and finish. The story he was telling me was one
which was evidently fraught with such painful re-
collections for the old man, that I could not find it in
my heart to urge him to finish what he had begun,
but seemingly he was glad to have for once a sympathetic listener, for I could well imagine how a
Malay audience would laugh and jeer at a man who
had been robbed of his lady-love by a despised Sàkai of
the jungles. Any way Tûkang Bûrok presently
resumed his narrative.

'She whom I loved had dwelt three full days and
nights with this accursed Sàkai,—may Allah blight
him utterly!—before we learned from some of his own
folk that she was among the jungle people. Then,
Che' Mat, her father, and her brethren, and her
relatives, men knowing the use of weapons, went, and
I with them, making great speed, to the Sàkai camp.
But, alas! we found her not, though, by means of the
túas,[1] we persuaded the men in the huts to show to us

---

[1] The *túas* is a very simple and effective torture in considerable favour
among the Malays. The victim is placed upon the ground, with his
legs extended in front of him, and a stout piece of wood is then laid

the path which Pa' Ah-Gap had taken, when he fled
into the forest, bearing my Love with him. Thereafter for many weary days we followed on his trail,
now close at his heels, now losing all traces of him and
of the maiden, for she went willingly with him, the
love-spell still working in her. On that terrible
journey I ate no food, though I drank deeply at the
springs, for my throat was rough and parched, and
sleep visited me not, for the madness of love was upon
me, and I hungered for the blood of the base-born
creature who had robbed me of my heart's desire !

'For how long a time we journeyed I cannot tell
thee, for day was night to me during our marches, but
in the fulness of the appointed hour we found Pa' Ah-
Gap sleeping, with her I loved lying, clothed in the
scant garments of the Sâkai women, at his side among
the warm embers of their fire. *Tûan*, it was with
difficulty that I could recognise her, whose every
feature was well known to me, for, in truth, I had
loved her. The vile Sâkai had tattooed her sweet
face, as is the custom of these so animal-like people,
and moreover she was very thin and worn, and aged,
and grimed with the dirt of the Sâkai lairs. We
caught him alive, for he slept heavily, being wearied
by his long marches, and I and one other, her brother,
crept very cautiously upon him. Also I think, Allah,
whom he had offended, for he was an Infidel while

across his knees. A second piece of wood is then passed over the first,
and under the buttocks of the sitting man. Next, using the second piece
of wood as a lever, and the first piece as the fulcrum, great pressure is
exerted, in such a manner that the thighs of the victim are crushed down
towards the ground, while the buttocks are pushed violently upwards,
causing terrible pain.

the woman was of the Faith, gave him that day to our hands, for mostly the jungle folk sleep with one ear cocked and one eye agape.

'We bound him hand and foot, the cords of rattan eating into his flesh as this chisel eats into the *kĕmŭning* wood, so that he screamed aloud with the pain ; and she who had been Hôdoh fought and bit at us, like a wild-cat newly caught in the woods, so that she too we were forced to bind, but gently, with the cloth of our *sârongs*, doing her no hurt.   Then we bore them back to our village, whence Hôdoh had fled that night, and thereafter we put Pa' Ah-Gap to the torture of the bamboo.'

'What is that ?' I asked.

Tûkang Bûrok smiled grimly, his old eyes lighting up with a thrill of pleasurable recollection.

'It is not fitting, *Tûan*, that I should tell thee much concerning it,' he replied.   'There be certain methods by means of which the quick-growing shoot of the bamboo can be taught to grow into a man's flesh, causing him such agony as even the Shetans in Jehannam have scarce dreamed of.   When first we bound him to the seat on which he was to die, he glared upon us out of angry eyes, saying no word, and I was sorry that he did not plead for mercy, that I might mock him and refuse him ; later he prayed to be spared till I, even I, was nearly satisfied, watching his pain, long-drawn, slow, and very keen ; later again and he implored for death, as a lover entreats his mistress to give him her love ; then for a space he went mad, throwing his body from side to side, so far as the cords which bound him made possible, and again I was angry, and sad withal, for when the madness comes to a man he no longer *feels*, as I had a mind that that man should feel, even to the very brink of the hour in which Death came to set him free. *Tûan*, for three days the life endured within him, and for all that time I sat beside him, mocking him when his ears could hear, and his brain could understand, and praying to Allah that his agony might endure for ever.

'In the hour that he died, Hôdoh came back to us out of the enchantment which had held her captive, for the spell laid upon her was broken ; but her memory held the recollection of all that had befallen her, so that she was wellnigh distraught with shame. Also her body was weakened with the life in the jungle, and she was racked with fever and many aches and pains, and, so she said, the burning of her skin was that which had been laid upon her by Pa' Ah-Gap that evening when she miscalled him. In a fortnight my Love was dead ; and I was left here mourning for all my days over the loss of the sweetest maiden born of woman, she for whom above all others my soul has been consumed with a wild fire of desire, which the years have never quenched! And, alas! alas! how bitter is the thought that she was wasted upon a Sâkai dog,— the vilest of our kind ! Wherefore, *Tûan*, when, as occasion requires, thou prayest to thy Christian God, bid Him join with Allah in the utter blighting and destruction of the soul of Pa' Ah-Gap, the Sâkai ! '

ON MALAYAN RIVERS.

Onward o'er sunken sands, through a wilderness sombre with forest,
Day after day they glided adown the turbulent river ;
Night after night, by their blazing fires encamped on its borders.
Now through rushing chutes, among green islands where plumelike
Cotton-trees nodded their shadowy crests, they swept with the current.

Evangeline.

In the Jungles of the Peninsula, where the soil under foot is a rich, black loam, composed of decayed vegetation, and the damp earth is littered with brown and sodden leaves, newly shed, or partially decomposed, one may often chance upon a pale, ghost-like object, white or gray in colour, and delicately fine in its texture as a piece of fairy lace. This is the complete skeleton of a giant leaf, which once was fair, and green, and sappy, but now has rotted away, little by little, until nothing remains save the midrib, from which the spines branch off, and a mazy network of tiny veins.

If you could strip any river basin, in the Peninsula, of its forests, and could then lay bare its water-system, you would find that it presented, on a gigantic scale, an appearance very similar to that of the skeleton leaf. The main river would represent the midrib ; the principal tributaries falling into it would supply the place of the branching spines ; and the myriad tiny streams and rivulets, which babble and trickle through the jungles, or worm their way, slowly and painfully, through the low-lying tracts of swampy country, would be the numberless delicate veins of the leaf. All the spaces and interstices, which in the skeleton are found between midrib and spine, and spine and vein, are, in the river basin, wide tracts of forest-clad country, intersected, and cut up, across, and through and through, by the rivers and streams of the most lavish water-system in the world.

The dense jungles present a barrier which has very effectually resisted the encroachments of primitive men. In the valleys of the large rivers, the Malay villages cluster along the banks, and the rice-fields spread behind the groves of palm and fruit trees, but half a mile inland, the forest shuts down around the cultivated patches, like a wall about a kitchen-garden. Up-country, where the rivers are smaller, man has won an even more insecure foothold, and the tiny plots of tilled land peep from out of the masses of jungle that surround them like a bird from out of a field of standing rice. Further up river still, you will find the camps of the Sâkai and Sĕmang, but even these forest-dwelling people make their homes on the edges of the streams, and thread their way through the jungles, in which they roam, by wading up and down the water-courses. Thus, it is not too much to say that only an insignificant fraction of the Peninsula has ever been trodden by the foot of man in all the long days since this old world was young. There are thousands of miles of river, in the Peninsula, whose banks have never even been camped upon by human beings, and, in country which is comparatively thickly populated, the vast tracts of jungle, lying between river and river, and between stream and stream, are as unexplored and untrodden as are the distant polar regions of the South. Thus it comes to pass, that one who would here study native life must learn his lessons, and seek his knowledge, on the banks of the rivers, and upon the waterways of the Malay Peninsula.

On the West Coast, where the roads and railways of the White Men have partially annihilated distance, and have made travelling and transport easy, even through the densest jungle, the waterways are fast becoming deserted. The enterprising Chinese hawker still makes his way from village to village, in his patched and rotting *sampan,* for the people on the river banks need dried sea-fish, sugar, that is more than half sand, and salt, that is three-parts dirt. Also little bits of jungle produce that have escaped duty may be bought and smuggled, if a man works carefully and with cunning. Now and again, a half-empty boat sags and lolls adown the long reaches, or an old-world Chief, who prefers the cool recesses of his *prâhu* to the heat and dust of a railway carriage, is punted up stream by half a dozen straining boatmen. For the rest, the river is no longer alive with crafts, as it was in the days of old, and the sleepy villager, whose patient eyes watch life indolently from the water's brink, wonders why the land has fallen to sleep since the coming of the noisy, energetic White Men.

But in Pahang, Trĕnggânu, and Kĕlantan, where men still punt and paddle and wade, as of old, the rivers are the chief, if not the only highways, and, sitting in the shade of the palm-trees on the· bank, a man may watch all the world gliding to and fro. There he may see the King's boat — gay with the bright silks of swaggering youths and nobles, with men sitting on the palm-leaf roofing, and dangling their legs at the bow, to mark that their Master is aboard—steam past him, with its waving flag, amid a wild tumult of drums and yells. There he may see the heavily - laden craft, banked high with freight to the very bow, propelled up river by a dozen punters, whose clattering poles drip streams of sun-steeped water; or the yellow face of a Chinese trader, peering from under the shelter at the stern, shows for a moment as a trading boat glides by. As he sits watching, the villager sees the tiny dug-out, bearing the wrinkled midwives, paddled down-stream by a sweating man, who works as he has never worked before, that relief and aid may come speedily to the woman he holds dear. Or, amid the rhythmical thud of the drums, the droning of verses from the Kurân, and wild bursts of the *sôrak*, another *sampan*, bright with gorgeous silks and glittering with tinsel, passes by, bearing the bridegroom and his relations to the hut where the little frightened bride awaits their coming. Or·perhaps, when the heavens are bright, lying there stark in his graveclothes, carefully covered from head to foot, and surrounded by a cluster of sad-faced relations, who shield his head lovingly from the fierce sun's rays, another villager may be seen, gliding gently towards the little, shady graveyard, making his last journey on the bosom of the river by which his days have been spent. The birth, the marriage, the death, all the comings and the goings, all the sorrows and the labour, and the rest, may be seen hinted at or exemplified, if a man watch long enough on the banks of a Malayan river ; for the running water, which bears them to and fro, enters more closely into the everyday life of the people, than do any of the other natural objects with which the Malays are surrounded.

The large river boats, which ply on the rivers of Kĕlantan, Trĕnggànu, and Pahang, are of different builds, each one of which is in some measure peculiar to the State in which it is used. In Kĕlantan the favourite craft is one which, for some obscure reason, is called by the natives *kĕpala bĕlàlang*—or the grasshopper's head. Needless to say, it resembles anything in the world more closely than it does the head of any known insect. It is long and narrow, with a short tilted punting-platform at the bow, and the cabin consists of a bark or wooden erection, like a low, square tunnel. The decking is sunk below the water-level, so that the occupants of the cabin sit or lie in a deep hollow with only an inch of bamboo flooring between them and the boat's bottom. If the calking be sound, this is cool and fairly comfortable—though a man might as well lie in his coffin for all he can see of the world around him—but, if the boat leaks, as it usually does, this arrangement means wet bedding, and thereafter lumbago and rheumatism. The long narrow tunnel has no windows, and the only means of egress or entrance is by the open space at each end of the cabin. Malays of other States, who do not love the Kĕlantan people, say that this form of boat is the only one which can be used in their country, because a window would enable thieves to possess themselves of the entire property of the occupant of the cabin with too great ease and convenience. It is due to the people of Kĕlantan, however, that I should state that their ingenuity is not baffled by such a trifle as the absence of windows, for two young Saiyids, whom I once sent from the interior to Kôta Bharu—the King's capital —had most of their raiment removed from between them, as they lay sleeping on board one of these boats, during the quiet night-time. This, when they awoke, seemed to them to be almost as miraculous as it was annoying, for they would certainly have been roused had the thief entered the boat, nor was the mystery explained until they found that one of their own boat-poles had been fashioned into a hook, while they slept, and that the thief had successfully fished for their property, with this cunning instrument, over their recumbent bodies. Fortunately, however, they had been provided with a professional thief by the courtesy and forethought of my good friend Dâto' Lêla Dĕrja, and he quickly restored their missing property, by the simple expedient of robbing the original thief, who was now lapped in peaceful slumber. For such is the custom of the land.

The boat-poles used in Kĕlantan are furnished with large crutch-handles, and, when the punters have walked up the steep incline of the forward platform, and have found bottom with their poles, they suddenly double up their bodies, from the waist, and throw the whole of their weight on to the crutch, which they wedge into the hollow of their shoulders. They rarely touch their poles with their hands, during this part of the operation, and their arms wave about, clawing the air aimlessly, as the punters step slowly down the incline, doing all the pushing with their shoulders, and deriving the power from the weight of their great, fleshy bodies. They give a melancholy, discordant, inarticulate howl each time that they take the strain, and, with their bent backs, quivering legs, and groping arms, they present the appearance of some strange quadrupeds, impaled upon spears, vainly striving to fight their way to the earth on which their forefeet cannot win a grip.

In the Trĕnggànu Valley—which in some ways is one of the most curious places in the Peninsula—the river boats are inferior to those found elsewhere. This is to be explained by the fact that the great Trĕnggànu River is only navigable for fifty miles from its mouth, and this waterway is therefore of less importance to the natives than are most of the wide rivers of the East Coast. In 1895, only some five hundred Malays were living in the broad tracts of country that lie above the Kĕlĕmang Falls. The rest of the population of the Trĕnggànu Valley was wedged into the space between the rapids and the sea. To this is mainly attributable the great ingenuity and industry of the Trĕnggànu Malays, for, in a land where men are very thick upon the ground, a lack of these qualities will surely result in a want of anything to eat. The banks of the Trĕnggànu, from Kĕlĕmang to the mouth, are cultivated and inhabited, as are only a very few regions in the Peninsula. No produce of a bulky nature can be brought from the interior, for the slender footpath, which runs round

the Falls, is the only means of communication, and all
things must be carried on men's shoulders. Therefore, such things as bamboos, from which the walls,
and flooring of houses, and the fences round the standing crops, are constructed, must be *planted* by the
people who need them, since there is no possibility of
cutting them in the neighbouring jungles, as may be
done in more comfortable lands. Accordingly there
are vast areas under cultivation, and a man may travel
on foot from Kĕlĕmang to Kuàla Trĕnggànu without
once leaving the string of villages that line the bank.

There is one form of boat, however, which is to be
met on the Trĕnggànu River, that would make a
stranger fancy that this valley, which was never visited
by White Men until 1895, had long been under the
influence of Europeans. Clinker-built boats, beautifully fashioned from Siamese teak, and constructed
with a finish and a grace of line which excel anything
that the dockyards of Singapore can produce, look
somewhat incongruous on the rivers of an Independent
Malay State; and but for the palms upon the banks,
and the paddles with which the gaily dressed natives
propel these boats in lieu of oars, one might almost
fancy one's self once more upon the brown waters
around Chertsey.

But it is in Pahang, where the current of the river
is stronger than that of any other on the East Coast,
and where a boat may travel up stream two hundred
and twenty miles from the mouth without let or
hindrance, that the large river-craft approaches most
nearly to perfection. The best constructed boats are
nearly eight fathoms long, and the poling platform

occupies much space forward, so as to give the punters plenty of room as they step aft, leaning heavily on their poles. At the bow and the stern, a square sheet of meshed woodwork is fixed in such a manner as to give the deck of the boat an almost rectangular surface, without diminishing the speed-power by widening her lines. The cabins are usually two in number—the *kûrong* or main apartment, and *kûrong ânak* or after cabin. They are roofed in with thatch, overlaid with sheets of dried *mĕngkûang* leaves, kept firmly in place by long lathes of split bamboo, lashed securely with rattan. The line of the roof forms a bold, sweeping curve, from the peak at the extreme stern to the middle of the boat. There is a slight flattening of this curve near the centre, and an even slighter rise near the forward end of the cabin ; the effect being exceedingly graceful, the more so since the long sloping line is broken by a tiny, thatched perch, in which the steersman has his seat.

The Pahang Malay punts with an air, a swagger,— as he does everything,—and the clatter and the clash of the poles, the single recurring thud against the side, which results from the excellent time the men keep, the loud complaining creak of the rudder-rod, as the boat lurches along up stream, make a lilting, rhythmic cadence not unpleasant to listen to. And descending the river, also, when punting-poles are laid aside, and the men grasp their paddles, the splash and the beat of the even strokes, the song of the steersman in his perch, and the crashing chorus of the crew, combined with the cool current of air which the pace of the gliding boat sends rushing through the cabin, make as soothing

and lazy a lullaby as a man need desire to listen to.
The boatmen take a pride in displaying their skill in
all kinds of 'fancy' paddling, which, while it has a
pretty and graceful effect, serves also to ease their
muscles by employing them in a constantly changing
motion. The bow paddler sets the stroke ; first, one
long sweep of the blade, quickly followed by three
short ones ; or later, three long strokes with a short
one in between. There are hundreds of combinations
of long and short, each of which has its own well-
known name in the vernacular, and a properly trained
crew will travel all day long without rowing in precisely
the same manner for half an hour together. It is
marvellous how long a time Malays will sit at their
paddles, without ever pausing in their rowing, and yet
experience no especial fatigue or exhaustion. I remember, on one occasion, in 1894, setting a crew of
five-and-twenty men to paddle down river at four
o'clock in the morning. They had never worked with
me before, they were not a picked crowd, and they were
not men who were accustomed to row together. Yet
these Malays paddled down river to Pĕkan, a distance
of a hundred miles, in twenty-six hours. They never
quitted their work all that long and weary time except
twice, when half their number ate rice while the other
half continued rowing. Once in an hour, or so, they
would shift from one side of the boat to the other ;
but that was all the relief that they sought for their
aching limbs. The time in which we did the journey
was not particularly good, for the river chanced to be
somewhat shrunken by drought, and we frequently
ran aground. During the night, which was intensely

M

dark, we more than once found ourselves straying from the main stream into a backwater, or *cul de sac*, and so had to paddle up river again, the way we had come, with all the weary work to do once more. Yet, in spite of all these trials to body and temper, no word of complaint, no whispered murmur of remonstrance, came from the men at the paddles. That they suffered to some extent I do not doubt, for I, who was awake all night to see that they kept at it, was dropping with fatigue long before the dawn showed grayly in the East. Towards morning, their *sôrak* grew very thin and weedy and faint, and their eyes were dull and heavy, but this did not prevent them from making half a dozen spurts in the last three or four miles. To appreciate to the full the achievement of these men, you must realise what paddling is like. Personally I know of no more tiring occupation. The rower sits cross-legged on the hard decking of the boat, with nothing to support his back, and with nothing in the nature of a stretcher against which to gain a purchase for his feet. The cross-piece at the top of the paddle shaft is gripped in one hand, the other holding the shaft firmly an inch or two above its point of junction with the blade. Then the body of the rower is bent forward from the hips, the arms extended to their full length, as the paddle-blade takes the water. The arm which is uppermost is held rather stiffly, the whole strain of the stroke being taken by the hand and arm that grips the paddle near the base of the blade. When this motion has been repeated half a dozen times the lower arm begins to complain, and presently its fellow joins in the protest. Continue paddling for an hour or two, and not only your arms, but your shoulders, your back, your legs, almost every muscle in your body, will begin to ache as they have never ached before, and, though practice is half the battle, you may thus come by a sound working knowledge of what the sensations of a man must be who has laboured for more than five-and-twenty hours at the paddles. After this, it is probable that you will hesitate to join in the loud-mouthed chorus of those who tell you that the Malays are the laziest people that inhabit God's Earth.

Those people who, nowadays, rush through Perak and Sĕlàngor in railway carriages can have but a poor conception of what a lovely land it is through which they are hurrying. The narrow lines, cut through the forest, are only broken, here and there, by patches of coffee-gardens, and other ranker cultivation. Here, there is nothing really distinctive of the Peninsula, and if you would see the country in its full glory and beauty, you must still keep to the river routes, which are the highways proper to the Land of the Malays. Travelling up and down the Peninsula, for a dozen years and more, one chances upon so many lovely scenes that it is not easy to decide which among them all is the most good to look upon. A hundred spots come before my mind's eye as, in spirit, I pass once more up and down the streams I love best ; but just as, among a collection of beautiful pictures, there must always be some which appeal to one more strongly than do the others, so, in this galaxy of Malayan scenes, I have my favourites. One is very far away, on a river called the Pĕrtang, a tiny stream of the

interior, that falls into the Tĕkai, which falls into
the Tĕmbĕling, which falls into the Pahang, which
flows into the China Sea.   The reach of river is
not wide, but it is very long for an up-country
stream, flowing, straight as an arrow, for a distance of nearly a mile.   The bed of this river is
shallow, its water running riot down long stretches of
shingle, forming a succession of miniature rapids.
Little sun-flecked splashes of water are thrown up by
the fiery dashing of the hurrying current against the
obstructions in its path, and the whole surface of the
stream seems to dance, and glitter, and shimmer, as
you look at it.   But the distinctive feature of this
reach of river, that marks it out from its fellows, is
to be looked for on its jungle-covered banks.   The
shelving earth at the water's edge is lined with magnificent specimens of the *ngĕram* tree,—a jungle giant
which is probably but little known to any White
Men whose work has not chanced to take them into
the far interior of the Malay Peninsula.   The peculiar
form in which these trees grow renders them specially
suitable for the river banks on which they are always
found.   Their trunks, which are several yards in circumference at their base, grow erect for only a few
feet.   Then they gradually trend outwards, leaning
lovingly over the stream ; and, when two of these trees
grow on the opposite banks of a river facing one
another, their branches not infrequently become inter-
laced, forming a natural arch of living greenery overhead.   In this reach of the Pĕrtang, of which I speak,
the banks from end to end are lined with *ngĕram* trees,
and with *ngĕram* trees only.   The effect is, therefore,

that of a splendid arch of foliage a mile in length, like a long green tent spread above a line of dancing, joyous river. Overhead, the network of graceful, slender boughs, with their trailing wealth of gorgeous leaves, sways gently in the faint, soft breeze that seems to be for ever sweeping swooningly over the still forests of the remote interior. On either hand, the massive trunks of the *ngĕram* trees show gray, save where the vivid flecks of sunlight paint them a whiter hue, and form the sides of the avenue through which the leaping waters run. The surface of the stream itself is alive with motion and colour. The brilliant sunshine struggles through the heavy masses of inter-woven boughs, and twigs, and leaves, forcing its way amid the thick clusters of creepers and trailing orchids with which the branches of these trees are draped, throughout their entire length. Here, for near a mile, there is cool, deep shade, that would almost be gloom, were it not that the fierce Eastern sun will not suffer himself to be altogether defeated, and still finds means to dust and powder the running water with little shifting flecks of light and colour, and, here and there, to cast broad belts of glimmering brilliancy on the surface of the stream. As you glide slowly down this reach upon your raft, a great brown kite, disturbed by your approach, flaps heavily away from you, between the long avenue of the *ngĕram* trees ; a brilliantly painted butterfly catches your eye, a tiny point of colour quickly fading into nothingness, as it flits adown the reach ; or, perhaps, a troop of monkeys passes scurryingly across the river, from tree to tree, and, in a moment, is swallowed up in the forest.

Your pleasure in gazing on the beauties of this scene
will not be diminished by the recollection that they
have only once before been looked upon by the eyes
of a White Man, and that the place is too far removed
from the beaten track for even the most energetic
globe-trotter to visit it, and defile it with his unappre-
ciative presence.

There is another spot on a river in Pahang that
will always have a place in my memory ; but, though
a few years ago it was almost as remote from the
paths of the European as is the *ngéram* tree-reach to-
day, the trunk-road across the Peninsula now skirts it
closely, so that every passer-by may see it. This is
the Jĕram Bĕsu, the great rapid on the Lipis River.
At this point the waters of the Lipis, which have
hitherto meandered through a broad green valley,
dotted with nestling villages, and gay with the vivid
colouring of the standing rice, suddenly become pent,
in a narrow bed, between grim walls of granite. The
stream above the rapid runs smooth and even, growing
more oily to look upon, as it combs over, in a great
curved wave, at the head of the fall. Then, in an
instant, the gliding water is broken up into a leaping,
whirling, tearing, fighting, roaring torrent, that dashes
madly against the rocky walls that hem it in, and seem
to lash it into a frenzy of rage. The rapid is only
about thirty yards long, and the drop is probably about
half as many feet, but the volume of pent water, that
strives to force itself through this narrow channel,
makes the pace furious, and gives a strength to the
leaping flood which is altogether irresistible. The
combing wave, at the rapid's head, first dashes itself

upon a prominent, outstanding wedge of rock on the left, which the natives of the place name 'The Wall,' and when the dangers of a capsize at this point have been avoided, 'The Toad' is found waiting, near the exit from the gorge, to pick up the bits. The rock which bears this name is set in mid-stream, leaning slightly towards the hurrying current, for the rush of water upon this side of it, during countless ages, has worn away the stone. This is really the only great danger to be encountered in shooting this rapid, for the offset of the water from the other rocks is sufficient to prevent a man being dashed with any great violence against them. But with 'The Frog' this is not the case. The whole run of the current tends to drive a man into the hollow in the rock, and once there, with the weight of that mighty torrent to keep him in place, he has but a poor chance of ever getting out again. Old Khatib Jafar, who lives in the little village above the rapid, and has spent all the best years of his life in ferrying men's rafts down the fall, boasts that he has, at different times, had every rib on his right side smashed between the rafts and 'The Frog,' but he says that he has always escaped being forced under it, or he would not be there to tell of his manifold experiences.

Before long, no doubt, some energetic White Man will utilise the power of Jĕram Bĕsu for the generation of electricity, and the place will be rendered unsightly by rusty iron piping, and cunningly constructed machinery. Then, incidentally, Khatib Jafar and his brethren will lose their means of livelihood, as, by the way, they are already doing as one of the first effects of the new road. I fear that they will

not be greatly comforted by the recollection that
their individual loss is for the good of the greater
number, or by the thought that they may in future
earn their rice and fish in a manner that carries with
it less risk than did their former occupation.

There is yet another place upon the banks of a
Malay river,—in Trĕnggánu, this time,—of which
I shall always retain a grateful recollection. At the
foot of the Kĕlĕmang Falls, a little stream flows into
the wide Trĕnggánu River on its left bank. It comes
straight down from the hills, which, at this point, rise
almost precipitously from within a few yards of the
river's edge. They mount up skywards, in a series of
steep ascents, and on the summit of the first of these
there stands a very ancient grave, in which, tradition
says, there repose the mouldering bones of a hermit of
old time, who dwelt here in solitude, during his days
of life, and elected to lie here through the ages, awaiting
his summons before the Judgment Seat. The still forest
spreads around him, the note of bird, and beast, and
insect comes to lull him in his long slumbers, and the
monotonous sound of the neighbouring waterfall cries
'Hush!' to the noisy world. Once in a long while
the Sultán of Trĕnggánu comes hither, with all his
Court, to do honour to the dead Sage ; now and again,
villagers visit the spot in pursuance of some vow, made
in their hour of need; but, for the rest, the place where
the hermit lies is undisturbed by the passing to and fro
of man.

From the natural terrace in the hill, upon which
the grave stands, the little stream of which I speak
falls in a series of cataracts to the valley below. Its

source must be at a spot far up the mountain side, for its waters, when they reach the plain, are as fresh and cold as those of a highland stream in Scotland. They come dashing and leaping along, from point to point, down the steep hillside, and fall in a body upon the broad, smooth surface of an immense granite boulder, which lies at the base of the rising land.

I, and the Pahang Malays who were my companions, reached this place one morning, just when the dew had dried, after travelling without rest, during all the long hours that should have been passed in sleep. We were weary and tired to the last degree, and our eyes had that curious feverish, burning sensation in their sockets, which ever comes to one who looks out at the blazing tropic sunshine after a sleepless night. We halted to cook our rice, and we were all, I think, pretty sorry for ourselves. I longed for champagne, even at that early hour in the morning, or for any pick-me-up to make me feel equal to the long journey which we should have to make between that hour and the dawn of the next day. My Malays, too, squatted about disconsolately by the river, where they were washing their rice, and by the fires, upon which the cooking-pots were humming. One or two of their number went off into the jungle, that lay round and about us, to search for fuel, and presently one of them returned, and said that he had found a capital place for a bath. He looked so fresh and comfortable, as he stood there with the beads of water still glistening in his hair, that several of our people went in search of the place of which he spoke. They all came back in tearing spirits, loudly extolling the marvels of the bath, and at last I, too, went to try what it was like.

When I arrived, I found two or three of my people lying sprawling on the large smooth boulder at the foot of the fall, and, when they presently made room for me, I crept cautiously on to the great stone upon which the stream of water from above was thudding heavily. The fall was about twenty feet in height, and the first blow of the icy water laid me flat upon the rock, and held me there breathless. It was like the most splendid combination of cold shower-bath and vigorous *massage* imaginable, and though it was not to be borne for more than a minute or two at a time, I stretched myself on the boulder, again and again, until my skin was turned to goose-flesh. Never was there a more splendid tonic, and though we did not rest again till the Eastern sky waxed red next morning, I, for one, felt no more fatigue of mind or body, after that marvellous bath.

When once a man falls a-thinking of the thousand scenes in the Malay Peninsula, any one of which it is a keen delight to look upon, it is difficult to quit the subject, and to make an end of vain attempts to picture to others some few of the things which have filled him with a pleasure that was an ample reward for the hardships of many a long and arduous journey. But the end must come, sooner or later, and perhaps, the sooner the better, for how can one hope to paint in words, things that, even as one looked upon them, seem too full of varied beauty for the sight to really comprehend them? On Malayan rivers, at any rate, the eye *is* abundantly filled with seeing.

A MALAY OTHELLO

Downward, in a flash, I swing,
   Hissing like a snake,
Make the bones about me ring,
   Splinter, chip, and break !
See the blood leap up to meet
   My hungry lover's kiss,
Ho ! Our meeting is most sweet,—
   I was born for this !

See the rent skin gape and start !
   Hear the spent lungs gasp !
See me red in every part,
   Handle, blade, and hasp !
Hear the dying moan his moan !
   Hear me swish and *hough !*
Rip through flesh, and shriek through bone !
   I ne'er lived till now !

               The Song of the Spear.

UP country, in the remote interior, where the words and manners of men are coarse and unseemly, honey is called *âyer lèbah*, — which means 'bees' water,'— but in more civilised parts of the Peninsula, where people pride themselves upon their exceeding culture and gentility, the vernacular term in use is *mâdu*. Malays, however, love to make a word do double duty, and, if possible, force it to bear at least one obscure and recondite meaning, in addition to its simple and obvious one. This it is which tends to make their beautiful, liquid tongue such a network of traps and pitfalls for the stranger ; and, verily, in speaking the Malay Language, a little knowledge is an excessively dangerous thing.

'*Hamba Túan bĕr-mádu*,— Thy servant possesses honey !' cries the indignant and infuriated native.

The European finds it difficult to conceive why the possession of honey should excite its owner to such a wild state of emotion ; but he has often found natives strange and unaccountable, and, perhaps, has never made any real effort to understand them, so he merely says :—

'Bring the said honey hither that I may eat thereof, for I love it greatly !' and everybody present, with the exception of the first speaker, titters furtively.

For *mádu*, in this instance, — though there is nothing in the wide World to show it,—has no connection whatever with bees, or with any of their works. Instead it means the lover of a man's wife, or the rival of a woman in her man's affections ; and to those who use it, the fact has nothing sweet about it, such as its original meaning would lead you to expect.

But the term is also applied to the injured husband. He is the 'Old Honey,' while his rival is 'Honey the Young,' and the only respectable and self-respecting thing for the former to do when he becomes aware of the existence of the latter, is, according to Malay ideas, to slay him as quickly as may be, and to thereafter send the faithless wife shrieking at his heels into the Land of Shadows. To kill one and not the other, is murder, and punishable as such, in the cross-eyed, squinting vision of Malay Law and Custom. To slaughter both offenders, no matter with what deliberation and precautions, is a meritorious deed deserving praise, the honour of men, and the love of other fair women to crown the slayer's happiness.

In the Native State of Pahang, before the White Men came, whenever you desired to lay your hand upon the most glaring instances of things as they ought not to be, it was generally safe to seek for them in the Tĕmbĕling Valley. Many miles of streaming river separate this district from Pĕkan,—the King's Capital,—and an attempt to supervise the outlying provinces of his country does not enter into the scheme of a Malay Râja's system of government. Occasionally he may learn of the existence of a man of wealth, living in some remote village, and the royal coffers are then not unlikely to be the richer by the amount of the fine, which the King will inflict upon his prosperous subject, on purely general principles. Once in a while, some grossly exaggerated *ex parte* statement will filter its way down stream, and swift punishment will forthwith be meted out, for unless the accused is a *persona grata* at Court, neither the King nor his Ministers dream of troubling themselves to hear anything which he may have to say in his defence. This is the Malay Ruler's method of 'larnin'' his people to be 'toads'; and how else should he be feared, or the treasury become stocked?

Unfortunately, all this does but little towards making the distant corners of the Land peaceful or orderly, for under the Malay system of government, the innocent suffer more frequently than the guilty, and a ready tongue, unhampered by feckless scruples, profits a man more than does the cleanest of consciences. Moreover there is truth in the somewhat coarse vernacular Proverb, which illustrates the fact that the pupil will out-do his teacher if the latter set him an ugly example. Therefore the District Chiefs act after the manner of their King with trimmings and additions.

In the Tĕmbĕling Valley, a dozen years or so ago, things were peculiarly bad, because the nominal Chief, Penghulu Râja, was an indolent creature, who cared only for his women and his opium-pipe, while the large clan of *Wans*—men of the royal stock—who had their homes there, preyed unchecked upon the peasants. When the Chief is a strong man, he is sure to quarrel violently with the distant connections of his King, who chance to dwell in his District; and since he is of more importance to his Master than they can hope to be, their complaints meet with small encouragement at Court. So the *Wans* fight him, as best they may, and in the struggle, the peasants sometimes are inadvertently suffered to come by their rights. 'When the junks are in collision,' says the Malay Proverb, 'the fishes have full bellies,' and this truth, like all the old wise-saws of the people, is constantly exemplified in the everyday experiences of the natives.

The Chief of the Tĕmbĕling *Wans*, whom I will call Wan Teh, was an exceedingly unpleasant person. He was rather deaf, had a harsh, discordant voice, a wicked eye, a shifty manner, and a cruel mouth ever gaping, as though seeking whom it might devour. It was more than whispered, even in his own District, that his courage was not of the highest quality ; and, with the possible exception of his only son, who was one of the most truculent young scoundrels living, no man or woman, in all the land, had a good word or a kind thought for him. He had one peculiar habit, which used to annoy me excessively every time I met him. A man, named Imâm Bakar, was once slain at Pasir Tambang, at the mouth of the Tĕmbĕling River. He incautiously touched hands in greeting with a Chief, called To' Gajah, and the latter, seizing him in an iron grip, held him fast, while he was stabbed to death with spears. The memory of this event was always present in the mind of Wan Teh, and his method of shaking hands was the result of the recollection. Accordingly, whenever a hand was extended to him in salutation, he was wont to grip it firmly by the thumb, and his victim needed no man to tell him that the brittle bones, so seized, were ready to break, almost at a touch. I have seen men fence with Wan Teh, for some seconds at a time, like wrestlers trying for a grip, but when their hands at length met, that of Wan Teh always held the thumb of his friend in a steely grasp.

Such then was the man who, in 1884, slew his wife and a reputed 'Young Honey,' under circumstances of more than ordinary atrocity.

That year the King was celebrating the marriage of his eldest daughter with the Ruler of a neighbouring State, and all the Chiefs, from one end of Pahang to the other, were, by his orders, gathered together at the Capital. The festivities lasted for nearly a twelve-month; gambling of all kinds, varied by cock-fighting, bull-matches, and top-spinning, engrossing the attention of the Court, while banquets and State Processions served to fill up the chinks. In the vernacular, when these Court Functions are going on, the King is said to be 'working,' but when you come to look into the matter, you will find that the labour of the King is strangely like the play of less privileged mortals.

During all the long months which are required to make the celebration of the event complete, the King keeps open house, to all his subjects, in the true feudal manner. The richly spiced viands, the fat rice, the sickening sweetmeats, which seem to be always lying in wait for you, are cooked in the palaces, and served without stint to the well-born guests in the Balai, or Hall of State, and to the people crowding the sheds, scattered up and down the King's compound. To all appearances, he spares money as little as he economises time, but experience will teach you that even the most generous of Malay Kings has an uncommonly keen eye to the main chance; and if you observe things closely, you will presently see that, in spite of the lavish expenditure, and the brave show, which are designed to attract the attention of the spectators, the months, during which the Court ceremonies last, are to be counted as the great revenue-producing periods of the King's reign.

In a Malay land, where all are at the mercy of a single individual, whose early training has been carefully calculated to strengthen the passions, which he has been taught to leave uncontrolled, it is expedient

to make unto yourself a friend of the occupant of the
Throne. The Chiefs know this, and the peasants
are accordingly ground down more thoroughly than
usual, in order that their immediate superiors may not
come to Court with empty hands. Where all bring
gifts to the King, something more striking than
ordinary must be produced, if a man is to win the royal
notice; so the Chiefs vie one with another, till the
serpentine lines of tribute-bearers trail over miles of
country, as they wind through the fruit groves to the
palace of the King. So the Monarch waxes rich in
gear and coin, and the bulging storehouses hide from
his sight the faces of the plundered peasantry. Also,
at many Malay Courts, the King takes a percentage
on every coin staked on the gambling-mats, and thus
makes a pleasant profit out of the sins of his people.

Wan Teh went to Pĕkan with the other Princes
and Chiefs, leaving his house in the Tĕmbĕling, and
all that it contained, under the charge of his cousin
Wan Kôming.

The King who reigns but a single day, the Malays
say, is ever a more tyrannical taskmaster than one
whose rule is permanent ; and Wan Kôming set himself to make his hay merrily while the sun shone in
the sky above his head. He knew that whenever his
cousin returned from the Capital, he would be forthwith stripped of his garb of brief authority, so he felt
that he had no time to waste. Therefore the hapless
folk in the Tĕmbĕling found life, for the moment,
more than usually unlovely.

Wan Kôming's rule was sufficiently unpopular
with all who had the ill fortune to live under it,—if

possible, it was even more disliked than that of Wan
Teh himself,—but there was one man in the Tĕmbĕling
who found the bare sight of Wan Kôming's temporary
power and greatness an insult to himself, and an outrage upon the District.   This was Wan Beh, another
cousin of the Chief, who held very strongly the view
that he, and not Wan Kôming, should have been
selected by Wan Teh to keep watch and ward over
the Tĕmbĕling during the absence of the latter at the
Capital.   He found it impossible to resist Wan
Kôming, for the latter was a strong man who had no
mind to brook interference from any man during the
term of his power, and as Wan Beh dared not slay him,
—which was of course the obvious thing to do, in
those days, to one who had earned your dislike,—he
asked himself in what manner he could most cunningly
and surely compass his downfall, and obtain authority
and sanction to deprive him of his life.

Having thought the whole matter out with considerable care, Wan Beh set off for Pĕkan, leaving
Wan Kôming in undisturbed possession of the Tĕmbĕling.   On his arrival at the Capital, he at once
sought out his kinsman, Wan Teh, and with many
tears, much well-assumed indignation, and a great
show of that keen shame, which was to be expected,
under the circumstances, in Wan Teh's near relative,
this Malay Iago haltingly told a lying tale of Wan
Kôming, and of the manner in which he was fulfill-
ing the trust reposed in him by his absent Chief and
kinsman.

Wan Teh's principal wife, Wan Po', had been left
by her husband in Wan Kôming's charge, a younger

and more favoured woman having been chosen to
accompany the Chief to Court; and, at the request
of the husband, Wan Kôming had taken up his
quarters in the big house at Mâchang Râja, which
had been given to Wan Po' for her dwelling-place.
This had been done in order that the lady's virtue and
her husband's honour might be guarded the more
securely; for marital confidence is not a strong point
in the Malay character, and the women, in whom no
trust is placed, only consider themselves bound to be
faithful so long as the precautions taken render it
impossible for them to be otherwise.

These facts all tended to aid Wan Beh, and to give
vraisemblance to his tale. Wan Teh was such an evil
person himself that he naturally found little difficulty
in crediting the reported wickedness of his kinsfolk;
and it must be confessed that no Malay's experience
is such as to warrant a disbelief in the extreme probability of misconduct on the part of any given man and
woman who happen to have a sufficient opportunity
for misbehaving themselves. Wan Po's husband was
therefore soon convinced of her guilt; but the one
redeeming virtue of courage, which helps to save the
pitiful character of Othello, was lacking in Wan Teh.
He had no desire to slay his Desdemona with his own
hands, and thereby to risk a rough and tumble with
his kinsman, Wan Kôming, who was reputed to be a
handy man with his knife. If left to his own devices
Wan Teh would probably have contented himself with
divorcing the woman, and would have been content
to allow his wounded honour to nurse itself back into
convalescence as best it might. But Wan Beh was

determined that his Chief should not suffer the matter to drop, and he dinned the tale of his dishonour in Wan Teh's ears morning, noon, and night, till the injured husband began to fear that he would be forced, very much against his will, to fight Wan Kôming for the credit of the family. He had very little stomach for the fray, and when, of a sudden, Wan Beh volunteered to do the job for him, if he would grant him the required authority, he jumped at the offer with the frantic eagerness of a man who sees at last a safe way out of an uncommonly tight and unpleasant place.

So Wan Beh, armed with verbal authority from Wan Teh, punted up the Pahang River, on his return journey to the Tĕmbĕling, having very successfully accomplished all that he had desired to effect by a visit to the Capital. He pushed on quickly, for he was burning to be at Wan Kôming, and upon the evening of a certain day, he tied up his boat at Labu, a village which is situated about half a mile down stream from Màchang Ràja, where Wan Po' and Wan Kôming were living.

At this place Wan Beh and his people waited till the night had fallen ; and as the moon was rising slowly above the long black line of jungle on the eastern bank of the river, he began a cautious and noiseless ascent of the last half mile of running water that still separated him from his victims. The boatmen poled in the manner called by the Malays *tanjak*, standing still at their work, dropping their poles noiselessly into the water, till they felt them touch bottom, and then propelling the boat forward against the current by throwing the weight of their bodies on to the poles. Punting in this fashion, they reached Mâchang Râja in about twenty minutes.

Arrived at his destination, Wan Beh landed with about a dozen of his followers, bidding the remainder of his people surround the house as soon as he had effected an entrance. Wan Po's dwelling stood by itself in a large grove of fruit-trees, and was surrounded on three sides by open fields, no longer under cultivation, upon which the rank *lalang* grass grew six feet high. The house itself consisted of a large main building, with a door opening from it on to a narrow verandah, that ran along the front facing the river. This verandah was guarded by a low balustrade of wattled bamboo, and the stair-ladder leading from it, at the down-river end, was the only means of entrance to and exit from the house. In common with every other Malay dwelling in the Peninsula, the house was raised from the ground on piles, some five or six feet high.

Wan Beh halted his followers at a distance of a few yards from the house, and himself, accompanied by a youngster, named Mâmat, crept cautiously forward to the foot of the ladder. They moved as noiselessly as they knew how, when they reached the head of the stairway, but laths of bamboo make a flooring upon which it is not easy to tread without sound, and the creaking of their footsteps awoke Wan Kôming.

He was sleeping at the far end of the verandah, under a mosquito-net, and near his head stood a *dâmar* torch guttering dimly. He was alone.

When the sound of Wan Beh's approach disturbed him, he sat up, pulled back the bed-curtains with one hand, and peered into the gloom, asking who was at hand. The only answer was a spear-thrust from Wan Beh, which pinned him to his mat, while Mâmat ran in, and completed the business by a dozen fierce stabs at his twisting, writhing body.

Wan Kôming died without a sound, save for a rending gulp or two, but Malays cannot slay any creature in silence, and the angry, triumphant cries of Wan Beh and Mâmat speedily awoke those who slept within the house. The murderers yelled defiance to the dead body of their enemy, and dinned in ears, that had ceased to hear for ever, the nature of the crime of which they accused him,— a foul lie, as those who shouted it knew full well.

Wan Po', within the house, heard their words, and in a moment she realised that her life also was desired by the ruffians without. Escape by the door was impossible, for her enemies were already battering upon it, and wrestling eagerly with its stout fastenings. There was no other recognised means of exit, and her sole chance of life lay in slipping through the flooring on to the ground beneath. She seized a wood-knife, and hacked with trembling hands at the plaited rattans, which bound the floor-laths one to another. The house was comparatively speaking a new one, and the bamboos which formed the flooring were sound and hard. The frightened women-folk, who were only companions in the house, sat huddled together, too paralysed with terror to dream of affording their mistress the aid of which she stood so sorely in need. And all the while, as Wan Po' fought for her life with the bamboos, the curses and imprecations of those who sought her blood, mingled with the heavy blows under which the stout door was rapidly giving way. In her excitement Wan Po' used her knife with little skill, and when, at last, a hole had been made, she strove to crush her body through it, before it was large enough to well admit of the passage of a child. The intensity of her fear gave unnatural strength to her limbs, and she fought bravely with the cruel, rasping bamboos, between which she was soon tightly wedged. The door bent inwards with the pressure from without, creaked, groaned, and then fell from its hinges with a mighty crash. Wan Beh and Màmat, with half a dozen others at their heels, leaped eagerly through the breach, and as at last Wan Po' wriggled herself free, Wan Beh's spear-blade darted through the gap in the flooring, above her head, and struck home on the shoulder, near the base of the neck, the keen steel penetrating deep into the breast.

Wan Beh and Màmat turned about, ran on to the verandah, and thence leaped down the stair-ladder to the ground, yelling to their fellows without not to suffer the woman to escape. The men on guard, however, were loth to stab a woman, so they contented themselves with trying to head her back to the house, when she broke cover from under it. She was sorely wounded, and dazed with fear, so she ran despairingly from one to another of the men, trying to flee from all, weeping, entreating, screaming pitifully, until at last she broke away and plunged into the *lâlang* grass that fringed the compound. But Wan Beh's spear-stab had done its work, and in a moment she sank upon the ground, and thereafter lay moaning and panting while her life-blood ebbed from her.

Then they lifted her up, and bore her to the great
state bed within the house, upon which they laid her.
Next they fetched the body of Wan Kôming, and
placed it at her side. When all this was done, they
summoned the elders of the village, that they might
look upon the corpses, swearing lustily the while that
thus the false friend and the faithless wife had paid for
their crime, dying in their wickedness, side by side,
while sleep still held them.

After the elders had departed, unconvinced, but
wisely silent as to what was in their minds, Wan Beh
and his people set to work and rested not till they had
constructed an efficient stockade. In this they took
up their quarters, and awaited the attack of Wan Ngah
and Wan Jebah,—the brothers of the woman they had
murdered,—which, they thought, might be confidently
expected. But these *Wans*, when the news reached
them, were themselves in deadly fear, so they too
built stockades, some miles away from Màchang Ràja ;
—and there the matter rested.

The truth concerning these doings very soon
filtered out, and before long every soul in Pahang
knew the facts of the case ; but no efforts were made
to bring the murderers to justice. The only comment
made by the King, and repeated to me by one who
heard it, was rather characteristic of a Malay Ruler.

Some five years after these events transpired, a
number of Tĕmbĕling Chieftains brought presents of
varying value to their sovereign, and Wan Teh, our
Malay Othello, was seated in the royal audience-
chamber when these gifts were being examined.

' Hast thou brought me no yellow wood for dagger-hilts, no *gharu* of a sweet odour, and no precious gums, as these others have done?' the King inquired looking with very little favour at Wan Teh.

The latter broke out into a torrent of voluble protests and excuses; but he had only empty hands to lift up in homage to the King   His Master's brow darkened.

'Have a care, Wan Teh,' he said. 'It were well for thee to bring gifts, ay, and precious gifts, to me, for a heavy charge has been preferred against thee, and it were wiser to give of thy substance, than, perchance, to lose thy life!'

Wan Teh understood the King's meaning, and acted, I believe, upon the advice thus given to him; for though the tale is told, and the men who did the deed are still living amongst us, no action was taken during the days before the Protection of the British Government came to pacify the troubled land, and the White Men always suffer bygones to be bygones, and begin to rule a new country with a slate washed clean of all past records of crime.

SOME NOTES AND THEORIES
CONCERNING LÂTAH

The Present and Past yield their secrets at last,
  For we've mastered their scope and their plan;
Moon and Sun, as they pass, must lie under our glass;
  We've measured the Earth to a span;
Each hurrying star, that we marked from afar,
  We've assayed and weighed as it ran;
Round about, high and low, all Creation we know;
But, somehow, we never know MAN!

So much has been written, of late years, by scientific
and medical men on the subject of the strange affliction
called *lâtah*, that a mere untrained observer, like
myself, who has gained such knowledge of the matter
as he may possess from living among the Malays,—
often in constant daily intercourse with *lâtah* folk,—
instead of being carefully educated in some recognised
school of pathology, cannot but experience some
feelings of diffidence, when he ventures to approach
the disputed questions of its nature and causation, and
to advance his own unscientific theories. I should
feel this in an even greater degree, were it not for the
fact, that as regards all that they have written on the
subject of *âmok*-running, at any rate, the scientists

have, to my thinking, persistently made a radical
error from the beginning, starting with a false hypothesis which has ended by landing them nowhere in
particular.

It is doubtless difficult for a medical man to always
bear in mind that a patient is a human being, in the
first instance, and a 'case' purely incidentally. Of
course there are many learned people nowadays who
hold that all crime is the result of brain trouble, but
most of them, I fancy, have not had to sit on the
bench, and thence to watch the crude, naked, ugly
motives, which quite logically prompt men to commit
crimes, peeping out of the actions of perfectly sane
people, who have kept certain objects very clearly and
steadily in view, and have worked for them slowly,
patiently, and steadfastly. The scientific theory anent
brain trouble and the causation of crime is often made
to look remarkably foolish when we see human nature
from the bench, and are able to bring thither a
tolerably sound knowledge of the inside—*les coulisses*—
of native life and character. In the same way, when
one has come a great deal into personal contact with
Malays as *men*, the study of *âmok* as purely a question
of pathology begins to look almost equally foolish. In
a story called 'The Âmok of Dàto' Kâya Bĭji Dĕrja,'
I have explained at some length what I believe to be
the real causes of *âmok*-running, and I will not go
over this ground again, further than by saying that
these are to be looked for in events which tend to
produce very intelligible psychological conditions, in
the man who is affected by them, rather than in any
obscure disorders of the brain. Some may, perhaps,

say that the two are inseparable ; but this is a statement which I, for one, am not prepared to accept until far more convincing proofs of the entire dependence of the moral nature upon physical conditions, than any at present in our possession, have been furnished to us. No one of course denies that physical disorders often breed moral troubles, but the latter may result from causes quite distinct from anything connected with the health of the body, and, after very carefully studying the subject, I am convinced that the typical *âmok* comes under this latter category.

Lâtah is an affliction which cannot so easily be explained by psychology, and undoubtedly it is a matter which must largely be treated as a question of pathology.   None the less, it is possible that it too may have its psychological side, which may require to be examined and analysed if the nature of the affliction is to be thoroughly understood.

Everybody who is interested in the Malay Peninsula has heard of *lâtah*, and even those amongst us who have not gone very far afield are, many of them, familiar with its manifestations.   There are other some, however, who may possibly never have seen any one who is afflicted in this way, and for their benefit, and as illustrations, which I shall need to point the remarks I have to make on the subject, I will describe one or two cases which have come under my own notice, and which I have had opportunities of watching closely, and for extended periods of time. Before doing so, however, there are a few general remarks on the subject which will be necessary for the complete understanding of what follows, by those who have no previous experience of *lâtah* and *lâtah* people.

Lâtah is an affliction, a disease, one hardly knows what name to give it, which causes certain men and women to lose their self-control, for longer or shorter periods, as the case may be, whenever they are startled, or receive any sudden shock. While in this condition they appear to be unable to realise their own identity, or to employ any but imitative faculties, though they very frequently, nay, almost invariably, make use of villainously bad language, without any one prompting them to do so. Any person who chances to attract their attention, at such times, can make them do any action by simply feigning to do it himself by a gesture. A complete stranger, by startling a *lâtah* man or woman, can induce the condition, of which I speak, accidentally, and without exercising any effort of will. This should be borne in mind, for though *lâtah* resembles hypnotic suggestion in many respects, it differs from it in the important respect that it in no way depends upon an original voluntary surrender of the will-power.

The most typical case of *lâtah*, within my experience, was that of a Sĕlângor Malay named Sat, who, in 1887 and 1888, cooked the rice for me, and for the twenty or thirty Malays who were then living in my house at Pĕkan. He was a great, big, heavy-featured, large-boned, clumsily-built fellow, very stolid, very stupid, very phlegmatic, the last person in the world, one would have thought, to be the victim of any nervous disorder. To the lay mind

any abnormal degree of sensitiveness should be accompanied by a somewhat etherial physique, a delicate
skin, a blue-veined forehead, tiny hands and feet, and a
highly strung organisation. To none of these things
could poor Sat lay any sort of claim, and though no
doubt Doctors will say that these are by no means
invariable accompaniments of a highly nervous temperament, I must own that Sat looked vastly improbable as
the possessor of anything so rarefied. All the other
Malays in my household were accustomed to put upon
Sat most unmercifully, making him do almost the
whole of the work that should rightly have been
shared between them all. Sat never appeared to resent
this arrangement, and he never made any complaint to
me then, or at any later time, of the manner in which
his fellows treated him. He spent almost the whole
of his day in the great ramshackle room, built out
over the river on supporting piles of *nibong*, in which
the large wooden box filled with baked clay, which
served as our simple cooking-range, occupied the
chief place in the centre of the lath floor. When the
others were most noisy, Sat was still silent. When
some of my men boasted of the great deeds they had
performed in the old days in Sĕlăngor, Sat would
listen obediently to the thrice-told tales, stolidly but
without excitement. Most of the other men had
their own particular chums, but Sat was always solitary,
and he never appeared to have any ideas, in that great
bullet head of his, which he desired to exchange with
his neighbours.

He had been an inmate of my hut for nearly a year
before any one discovered that he was *làtah*. The fact

came to light quite accidentally, Sat being startled out of his self-possession by the sudden capsizing of a cooking-pot over which he was watching. A boy, who chanced to be alone in the cook-room with Sat, made an instinctive grab at the fallen rice-pot, and in an instant Sat's hand was in the fire, grasping the burning-hot metal. He withdrew his flayed fingers quickly, as the pain brought to him consciousness of what he had done, and he carried them at once to his head,—that queer, groping, scratching motion, which is an invariable accompaniment of *lâtah*,—and the boy at his side needed no man to tell him that Sat was a victim to that extraordinary affliction. With the wanton cruelty and mischief of his age, the boy once more made a feint at the smoking rice-pot, and again Sat's fingers glued themselves, for a moment, to the scalding metal, and then returned aimlessly to his head. I do not know how many times this was repeated, but Sat's fingers were in a terribly lacerated condition when, at last, some one chanced to enter the cook-room, and interfered to prevent the continuation of Sat's torture. After that, though I did all I could to protect him from molestation, Sat was never, I fancy, left in peace for long by the other men of my household. Gradually, in the course of a couple of months or so, this man, who for nearly a year had shown no signs of being the victim of any nervous disorder, was reduced to a really pitiable condition. The occasional *lâtah* seizures, which were at first induced by the persecutions of his fellows, ceased to be abnormal phases, and became the chronic condition of his mind. If one spoke to him, with no matter how much gentleness, he would repeat the words addressed to him over and over again, aimlessly, unintelligently, without apparently comprehending their meaning, and that wandering, groping hand of his would steal to his head, and scratch helplessly at his close-cropped hair. 'Sat! Listen, Sat!' I would say to him, as quietly and reassuringly as I knew how, 'Listen, no man is worrying thee. Try to listen to what I say to thee.' 'Listen to what I say to thee!' Sat would make answer, and then very low, in a whisper under his breath, 'Listen, listen, listen, listen, listen, what I say to thee.'

I instituted a fine for any one who was found annoying Sat, but it was almost impossible to get a conviction, for the unfortunate victim could never say who the man was who had teased him into a more than usually severe paroxysm of *lâtah*.

It was about this time that a number of other people in my household began to develop signs of the affliction. I must not be understood as suggesting that they became infected with *lâtah*, for on inquiry I found that they had one and all been subject to occasional seizures, when anything chanced to startle them badly, long before they joined my people, but the presence of so complete a slave to the affliction as poor Sat seemed to cause them to lose the control which they had hitherto contrived to exercise over themselves. One of the older men among my people,—Pa' Chim, we called him,—a Malay of birth, and of some standing with his fellows, came to me and begged that I would see that no one did anything to give him a sudden start, since, he said, only a very little was needed to

make him *látah* also. Yet this man neither then nor
later showed any signs of the affliction. He probably
exercised a considerable amount of self-control, but I
always knew that in a moment I could have broken
through his guard, and have startled him into as complete a seizure of *látah* as those of which Sat was the
victim.

One day a curious thing happened, which I will
relate as it occurred, though I only witnessed the end
of the incident. A Trĕnggânu Malay, who had a cousin
among my people, came in to visit his relative, and
chanced to find no one but Sat in the house. The latter
invited the Trĕnggânu man to partake of *sirih*, and they
squatted down on the *péntas*, or raised eating platform,
in the centre of the house, with the *sirih*-box between
them. The villainous small boy who had first discovered
Sat's weakness, was playing about in the room, and in
some unholy way he had learned that the Trĕnggânu
visitor was also a *látah* subject. He seized a long rattan,
which I think was kept in the room by one of the older
men for his occasional correction, and smote the *sirih*-
box, as it lay between the two betel-chewers, making the
wooden covering resound with the smart blow. The
sudden and unexpected noise at once deprived both
men of all power of self-restraint. Each gave a sharp
cry, and a 'jump,' to use the colloquial expression, and,
since there was nothing to distract their attention from
one another, they fell to imitating each the other's
gestures. For nearly half an hour, so far as I could
judge from what I learned later, these two men sat
opposite to one another, gesticulating wildly and aimlessly, using the most filthy language, and rocking

o

their bodies to and fro. They never took their eyes off one another for sufficient time for the strange influence to be broken, and, at length, utterly worn out and exhausted, first Sat, and then the Trĕnggânu man fell over, on the platform, in fits, foaming horribly at the mouth with thin white flakes of foam. Men came running to me for help, many having witnessed the end of this strange scene, and when I had doctored Sat and his companion back to consciousness, I tried to ascertain from them how they had come to fall victims to this seizure. They could tell me nothing, however, for they only remembered that before their trouble came upon them they had been chewing betel-nut. The matter was sifted out, none the less, and the small boy who had been the cause of the trouble again made the acquaintance of the piece of rattan, and to judge by his cries, found the interview an unusually painful one.

I have known so many cases of *látah*, during the years that I have spent wandering up and down the Peninsula, that I am tempted to multiply my instances indefinitely. The Malays have many tales of *látah* folk who have terrified a tiger into panic-stricken flight by imitating his every motion, and impressing him thereby with their complete absence of fear. I cannot say whether there is any sort of truth in these stories, but I can see no good reason for doubting them, since a sudden start, such as a tiger might well be expected to give to any one who came upon him unawares, would certainly induce a paroxysm of *látah* in a man suffering from the affliction, and a ludicrous caricature of the tiger's gait and movements would as certainly follow.

A tiger might well be supposed to be frightened out
of his life by such an unwonted spectacle. I have
myself seen a woman, stiff-jointed, and well stricken in
years, make violent and ungainly efforts to imitate the
motion of a bicycle, just as I once saw an old hag strip
off her last scanty garment because a chance passer-by,
who knew her infirmity, made a gesture as though he
was about to undress himself. But when one or two
examples have been given, the main features of this
affliction are made as clear to the reader as they would
be after a thousand instances had been examined, for
one *lâtah* person is very like another, the only difference
between them being one of degree.

I now come to the unscientific notions and theories
of which, as I warned my readers at the beginning of
this paper, I propose to unburden myself.

It has been remarked that people afflicted with
lâtah are as often found among the well fed and
gently nurtured, as among the poor and indigent.
Also that they are more frequently of the female
than of the male sex, and I may add that, so far
as my experience goes, they are invariably adults.
During the last fourteen years I have seen a great
deal of all classes of Malays, and I will go further
than all this, and say that to the best of my belief
every adult Malay of either sex is to some extent *lâtah*.
I do not mean to imply that they are all, or nearly all,
advanced instances of the affliction, such as those of
which I have been speaking, but I do most emphatically
state my belief that almost any Malay is capable of de-
veloping into a typical case of *lâtah*, if he be sufficiently
persecuted, teased, and harassed. To induce rudi-

mentary symptoms of *làtah* in a Malay it is only necessary to startle him violently.   Most human beings can be made to start or 'jump' involuntarily at a sudden noise, such as that caused by the loud slamming of a door, and Malays are peculiarly liable to these temporary nervous surrenders of self-control and of will-power, for in this light these involuntary movements must be regarded.   The man who is the victim of a sudden fright or nervous shock loses for a moment all control over his body, as completely as does the Malay on whom *làtah* has won its firmest grip.   The difference which exists between him and the *làtah* man is only one of degree, and that difference may often be more trifling than that which separates one *làtah* subject from another.   Imagine a start or 'jump' indefinitely prolonged, and you have the *làtah* state, about which so much has been said and written.

Any one who is inclined to doubt that incipient *làtah* lies hidden somewhere in most pure-blooded Malays, can experimentalise upon the vile bodies of any chance native who comes in their way.   For choice I would recommend a villager, one who has lived all his life among other Malays, and who has not had his sensations blunted by much intercourse with White Men.   Give him a sudden dig in the ribs when he knows not that any one is at hand, and though he is not *làtah* in the ordinary sense of the term, as Europeans understand its meaning, he will not only give a violent start, but will also shoot out some exceedingly coarse word, for which, in all probability, he will forthwith apologise.   When asked for an explanation, he will say simply that he was startled, and that a sudden shock always makes him *lâtah;* for the Malays see no reason for applying this word exclusively to those who suffer from the affliction in its more advanced and exaggerated forms. Unless you know the Malay upon whom you propose to experiment pretty intimately, I counsel you to be cautious how you try to extend your knowledge at his expense. His passionate love of science will not probably equal your own, and it is possible that then or later he may think it advisable to try what effect his knife will have on *your* ribs, which after all, from his point of view, is a sufficiently interesting experiment in its way.

As I have had occasion to say more than once in this paper, I have no pretensions to be regarded as a scientific man, and, therefore, in so far as the pathology of *lâtah* is concerned, I ask rather than offer an explanation ; but any one who desires to really account for this affliction must, I am convinced, begin by analysing and examining and explaining the pathology of the common start or 'jump,' to which we are all in a lesser or a greater degree subject. This must be the starting-point, and when this has been accounted for by some workable hypothesis,—supposing always that it admits of explanation at all in the present state of medical science,—then, and not till then, we may hope to arrive at some reason that must undoubtedly lie at the back of the fact that Malays, more than all other races of men, are so peculiarly liable to this species of seizure in its most exaggerated forms.

In the meantime, there are one or two suggestions that may be made, as tending to throw light upon the latter point. It is within the experience of every

European who has had occasion to sojourn long in the
Malay Peninsula, that his nerves have suffered somewhat from the 'climate.' He notices, no matter how
abstemious he may be in his habits, that he is apt to
grow what he calls 'jumpy.' He starts violently at
any sudden noise; finds it difficult to control the
trembling of his hands in moments of strong excitement; and is generally speaking less master of his
will, and over the movements of his body, than is his
wont. Now this may be the effect of any tropical
climate upon the system of a European; to some extent
this is no doubt the case, but I cannot but fancy that
this peculiar 'jumpiness' is more universal and more
severe in the Peninsula and in the Archipelago than in
other parts of the World. If this is so, we have at once
a tangible reason that may perhaps account for the
extraordinary sensitiveness of the Malays to sudden
sounds and shocks. If within a year or two Europeans
are able to note a marked change in their ability to
bear shocks and noises without 'jumping out of their
skins,' is it not easy to understand that a race, which
has inhabited these regions for many generations, is
very likely to have become morbidly susceptible to
these things? Once more, it is for the medical
authorities to say why the climate of the Malay Peninsula and Archipelago should have this strange effect
upon the nervous systems of the people who live in it.

There are two other matters to be considered
before I conclude these somewhat disconnected remarks
upon *látah*. The first of these is the question that
must naturally present itself, as to why adults alone are
subject to this affliction. The most natural explana-

tion would seem to be, that in the young the nervous system is not sufficiently developed to admit of this abnormal sensitiveness being experienced in its full force. It may be objected that little children start as readily at sudden noises as do adults, but I think that this ·cannot be regarded as in any way tending to weaken the probability of the suggestion that I have offered. The start or 'jumps,' as I have said, is to be looked upon as the germ from which *lâtah* springs ; and when we take into consideration the vast changes to the whole nervous organisation that occur at the age of puberty, it is easily conceivable that the seed of the affliction may have no chance of coming to maturity, so to speak, until the nerves of a boy or girl have passed their rudimentary stages. All this is the merest speculation, and I only put forward the hypothesis as a suggestion, on the validity of which some expert can finally pronounce.

The second point is, in some ways, more difficult to deal with. Every one who has spoken or written on the subject of *lâtah*, has drawn especial attention to the manner in which *lâtah* folk invariably try to imitate the actions, and often the very words, of those who happen to attract their attention while they are subject to one of their seizures. Why, it will be asked, if *lâtah* is really only a prolonged start or 'jump,' should this feature so constantly recur? To this I reply that the *lâtah* subject, having for the time being completely lost all controlling power over his will, is bereft of the faculty which is wont to regulate the motions of his body. The will is incapable of performing its proper functions ; and the helpless body,

abandoned to its own devices, looks about it for something to serve it as a guide. In this extremity, it
seizes upon the first moving object that catches its
sight, and follows slavishly every movement which it
makes. That there is no question of a weak will
surrendering itself to some stronger brain, is amply
proved by the fact that a *látah* person will mimic the
swaying motion of wind-shaken boughs just as readily
as the actions of a human being,—will follow their
movements in preference to those of a man, indeed, if
the former chance to attract his attention before the
latter. This shows that it is not a question of
surrender of will so much as a complete temporary
paralysis of the will-power,—similar, be it noted, to
that from which a man suffers when he performs some
wholly involuntary action because his will is, for a
moment, stunned by a sudden noise or shock. It is
not necessary to insist upon the fact that the actions of
a *látah* man, while he is in the grip of the affliction,
are in no sense voluntary. Sat did not thrust his hand
into the flame, or lay it upon the burning cooking-pot,
because he found it amusing ; and no woman of the
Malays,—the race beyond all others which is particular
to a fault about all matters of personal modesty,—
willingly dispenses with her last garment, in a public
place, at the casual invitation of a passing stranger.
Still less does a hag, who is racked with rheumatism,
try to prance along the high road in imitation of a
bicycle out of pure *gaieté de cœur*. The cause to
which I have attributed the alacrity of the *látah*
subject to imitate the actions of the moving things
about him may not be the correct one, but it is, at any

rate, I venture to think, a more likely and accountable one than any that I have hitherto seen advanced by writers on this subject.

I have spoken earlier in this paper of the possibility of the psychological condition of the *lâtah* man being, to some extent, accountable for his affliction. This, however, can only be guess-work, until such time as we know infinitely more about the real nature of the infirmity than we do at present. In the meanwhile, these notes may perhaps enable some more scientific observer than myself to direct his researches in the right course, with a view to discovering the true nature of what, rightly regarded, is a racial rather than an individual weakness.

Kneel down, fair Love, and fill thyself with tears,
Girdle thyself with sighing for a girth
Upon the sides of mirth,
Cover thy lips and eyelids, let thine ears
Be filled with rumour of people sorrowing;
Make thee soft raiment out of woven sighs
Upon the flesh to cleave,
Set pains therein and many a grievous thing,
And many sorrows after each his wise
For armlet and for gorget and for sleeve.

Swinburne.

ONE morning, some fifteen years ago, old Mat Drus, bare to the waist, sat cross-legged in the doorway of his house, in the little sleepy village of Kĕdòndong on the banks of the Pahang River. A single long blade of *lálang* grass was bound about his forehead, to save appearances,—for all men know that it is unmannerly to go with the head uncovered, and Mat Drus had mislaid his head-kerchief. His grizzled hair stood up stiffly above the bright green of the grassblade; his cheeks were furrowed with wrinkles; and his eyes were old, and dull, and patient,—the eyes of the driven peasant, the cattle of mankind. His lips, red with the stain of the areca-nut, bulged over a damp quid of coarse tobacco, shredded fine, and rolled into a ball the size of a marble. His jaws worked mechanically, chewing the betel-nut, and his hands were busy with a little brass tube, in which he was crushing up a fresh quid, for his teeth were old and ragged, and had long been powerless to masticate the nut without artificial aid. The fowls clucked and scratched about the litter of trash with which the space before the house was strewn ; and a monkey, of the species called *brok*, which the Malays train to pluck cocoa-nuts, sat on a box fixed to the top of an upright pole, searching diligently for fleas, with the restlessness of its kind, and occasionally emitting a plaintive, mournful cry. In the dim interior of the house, the voices of the women could be heard, amid the recurring clack of crockery ; and the fresh, pure, light-hearted laugh of a very young girl rippled out constantly, the soft and tender cadence of her tones contrasting pleasantly with the harsher notes of her older com-panion.

Presently a gaily dressed youngster entered the compound. He carried a *kris* at his belt, and in his hand was a short sword, with a sheath of polished wood.

' O Che' Mat Drus ! ' cried the new-comer, as soon as he caught sight of the old man in the doorway.

' What thing is it ? ' asked the latter, pausing in the preparation of his quid of betel-nut.

' The Chief sends greetings to thee, and bids thee come on the morrow's morn to the rice-field, thee and thine, to aid in plucking the weeds from amid the standing crop.'

'It is well,' said Che' Mat Drus, resuming his pounding stolidly.

'Also the Chief sends word that no one of thy household is to remain behind. The women-folk also are to come, even down to the girl Mînah, who has newly wedded thy son Dàman.'

'If there be no sickness, calamity, or impediment we will come,' said Mat Drus, with the caution of the Oriental.

But here a third voice took part in the conversation —a voice shrill, and harsh, and angry, which ran up the scale to a painful pitch, and broke queerly on the higher notes.

'Hast thou the heart, Kria, to bring this message to my man?' it cried. 'We both are of age, we both know and understand. The Chief shall die by a spear cast from afar, shall die vomiting blood, shall die a violent death, and thou also, thou who art but the hunting dog of the Chief.'

'Peace! Peace!' cried Mat Drus, in a voice betokening an extremity of fear. 'Hold thy peace, woman without shame. And Kria do thou tell the Chief that we will come even as he bids us, and heed not the words of this so childish woman of mine.'

'Indeed,' said Kria, 'I cannot trouble me to bandy words with a hag, but the Chief will be wroth if he learns of the things which thy woman hath spoken.'

'They matter not, the words of a woman who is childish,' said Mat Drus uneasily. 'Speak not of them to the Chief.'

'Then lend me thy spear with the silver hasp at the base of the blade!' said Kria, and when he had obtained possession of this weapon, which he had long coveted, he swaggered off to pass the word to other villagers that the Chief required their aid to weed his rice crop.

The sun stood high in the heavens, its rays beating down pitilessly upon the broad expanse of rice-field. The foot-high spears of *pâdi* received the heat and refracted it, while the heat-haze danced thin, and restless, and transparent over the flatness of the cultivated land. The weeders, with their *sârongs* wound turban-wise about their heads, for protection against the fierce sun, squatted at their work, men, women, and little children, the perpendicular rays dwarfing their shadows into malformed shapeless patches.

Near the centre of the field a hut had been erected, walled and thatched with palm-leaves, and the interior was gay with many-coloured hangings surrounding the mat and pillows of the Chief. Numerous brass trays containing food specially prepared for the occasion lay upon the flooring. In the interior of the Malay Peninsula, the luxury accessible to even the richest and most powerful natives is of a somewhat primitive order; but to the eyes of the simple villagers, the interior of this hut presented as high a degree of civilisation, as did the *chateau* of a French noble before '89 to the peasant who dwelt on his estate.

About noon the Chief emerged from the hut, and began a tour of inspection among the weeders, throwing a word to one or another, and staring boldly at the women, with the air of a farmer apprizing his stock.

Half a dozen fully-armed youths, dressed brilliantly in many-coloured silks, followed at the heels of their master.

Mat Drus and his son Dàman, with three or four women, sat weeding near the edge of the jungle, and Mînah, the girl who had recently married Dàman, edged her way towards her husband, as the Chief drew near.

'What is the news, Mat Drus?' asked the harsh, coarse voice of their Master.

'The news is good, O Chief,' replied Mat Drus, stopping his work, and turning submissively towards the speaker. All the rest of the little party acted in like manner, and the women-folk, squatting humbly with their men, bowed down their heads to avoid the hungry eyes of the Chief.

'Who is this child?' asked the great man, pointing to Mînah.

'She is the wife of thy servant's son,' replied Mat Drus.

'Whose daughter is she?'

'She is thy servant's daughter,' said an old and ill-favoured woman, who squatted at Mat Drus's elbow.

'Verily a *sâlak* fruit!' cried the Chief. 'An ugly tree, thorny and thin art thou, but thou hast borne a pretty luscious fruit.'

The weeders laughed obsequiously.

'How clever are the words of the Chief!' ejaculated Mat Drus, in a voice carefully calculated to reach the ears of the man he feared. The Chief did not even condescend to glance at him.

'Sweet Fruit,' he said addressing Mînah. 'Thou art thirsty with thy toil. Come to my hut, and I will give thee luscious sweetmeats to slake thy little parched throat.'

'Don't want to,' mumbled the girl.

'Nay come, I bid thee,' said the Chief.

'Go, girl,' said the mother.

'Don't want to,' repeated Mînah, nestling more closely to Dâman, as though seeking his protection.

'What meaneth this?' cried the Chief, whose eyes began to wax red. 'Come when I. bid thee, thou daughter of an evil mother!'

'She is afraid,' said Mat Drus pleadingly. 'Be not angry, O Chief, she is very young, and her fears are great.'

'May she die a violent death!' yelled the Chief. 'Come! Wait but a moment, and thou shalt be dragged thither!'

'Have patience, O Chief!' said Dâman sulkily. 'Let her be. She desires not to go.'

'Arrogant one!' screamed the Chief. 'Thou art indeed a brave man to dare to thwart me. Thou shalt aid to drag her to my hut.'

Dâman leaped to his feet. Like the rest of his kindred, he had squatted humbly in the dust during all the talk,—a serf in the presence of his lord,—but now he stood erect, an equal facing an equal, a man defending his women-folk from one who sought to put shame upon them.

'Peace, Dâman! Have patience!' cried Mat Drus nervously, but his son had no thought to spare for any save the Chief just then. His clear, young eyes looked boldly and angrily into the sodden, brutal, bloodshot orbs, set in the coarse self-indulgent face of his enemy, and the Chief faltered and quailed before his gaze.   Dàman's hand went to his dagger-hilt with a sounding slap, and the Chief reeled hastily backwards, nearly losing his footing, as he stepped blindly.   His youths surged up around him, and the coward felt his courage returning to him, when he realised that they were at hand.   No word was spoken for a little space, as the enemies eyed one another, and Mînah, crouching close to Dàman's mother, whimpered softly, though a thrill of love and admiration ran through her, as she marked the bearing of her husband.

Suddenly Kria, who stood somewhat to the right of the Chief, raised his arm in act to throw, and the bright sunlight glinted for a moment on the naked blade of a spear,—a spear with a silver hasp, which, until lately, had been the property of Dàman's father. Kria's eye sought that of the Chief, and the latter signalled to him to cast his weapon.   The long spear-handle, with its shining tip, flew forward with incredible velocity, like a snake in the act of striking, but Dàman leaped aside, and the weapon hissed harmlessly past him.

'Strike with the Paralyser !' cried the Chief, and at the word one of his youths ran forward, and stabbed swiftly and shrewdly at Dàman with a long uncanny-looking weapon.   It was a forked spear with two barbed blades of unequal length, and, after vain attempts to avoid the thrusts of his enemy, Dàman at length took the point in his chest.   He was now powerless, for the barbed tip could not be withdrawn, and the sharp point of the shorter blade prevented him from running up the spear, and killing his man, as has frequently been done in the Peninsula by one mortally stricken.

The women screamed shrilly, and Mînah sought to run to her man's aid, but those about her held her fast, while she shrieked in an agony of horror. The weeders clustered around, murmuring sullenly, but none dared interfere, and above all the tumult sounded the harsh, coarse laugh of the Chief.

'Verily a fish at the end of a fish-spear! Watch him writhe and wriggle!' he cried. 'Do not kill him until we have had our sport with him.'

But Dâman who had never uttered a sound, was not a man to die without a struggle. He soon found that it was impossible for him to wrench the barbed spear from his breast, and seeing this, he threw his *kris* violently in the face of the man who had stabbed him. The snaky blade flew straight as a dart, and the tip ripped open the cheek and eye-lid of Dâman's enemy. The latter dropped the end of the spear, which he had hitherto held firmly in both hands, and Dâman now strove manfully, in spite of the agony it occasioned him, to wrench the blade free. This was an unexpected turn for affairs to take, and the Chief's laughter stopped suddenly.

'Slay him! Slay him!' he yelled to his men, and, at the word, Kria, who had recovered his weapon, stabbed Dâman full in the throat, with the broad spear-blade. The murdered man sank to the ground with a thick, sick cough, and no sooner was he down, than the Chief's youths rushed in to wet their blades in his shuddering flesh.

Mînah, wild with fear, threw herself prostrate upon the ground, seeking to shut out the sight with her tightly clasped hands, and, as she lay on the warm earth, the wailing of the women, the rough voices of the men, and the soft *swish* of the steel piercing the now lifeless body of her husband, told her that all was over.

The day waned, darkness shut down over the land, and the moon rose above the broad, still river, pale and passionless, looking calmly down upon a world which, bathed in her rays, seemed unutterably peaceful and serene. But all through that night, and for many days and nights to come, the pitiful wailing of a girl broke the stillness of the silent hours, in the neighbour-hood of the Chief's compound. It was only Mînah mourning for her dead, and taking more time than her friends thought altogether necessary to become ac-customed to her new surroundings, as one of the household of the Chief.

Her new lord was not unnaturally annoyed by her senseless clamour ; and beating, he discovered, tended only to increase the nuisance. But crumpled rose-leaves are to be met with in every bed of flowers, and the Chief had, at any rate, the satisfaction of knowing that in future the season of weeding would be a merry time for him, and that all would be conducted seemly and orderly, without any risk of his peace or his pleasure being further disturbed by rude and vulgar brawls.

IN THE RUSH OF MANY WATERS

Our homes are whelmed 'neath a watery waste,
    Bestir ye, our Thousands, and flee !
Crawl, wriggle, and struggle, and haste, O haste !
    To the bough, and the branch, and the tree.
The purring flood is around and about,
    His waters are angry and red,
Quick ! Join in the tail of the labouring route,
    Ere half of our Thousands be dead !

The Song of the Ants.

THE broad Pêrak River was rolling down in flood.
For two days its waters had been rising steadily, and
my boat had sidled up stream, hugging the jungle-
covered bank, towards which the steersman kept her
head pointed, while three or four squealing Malays
propelled her by means of forked poles thrust firmly
against the yielding, swaying branches, and the leafy
shrubs. As the poles were withdrawn the boat would
move forward, reeling tipsily against the greenery of
the banks, so that protruding boughs forced their way
under the palm-leaf roof, scratching my face and hands
as I lay there, and littering my mat with heaps of
sodden trash. Ants and other creeping things had
come aboard in their thousands, running over me with

swarms of restless legs. Occasionally one or another of the boatmen would miss his aim as he prodded at the jungle on the bank, and a lurch which followed would send an even wave of water rippling over my mat. Therefore everything in the boat was wet through, and the physical discomfort of my surroundings was more than sufficient for my requirements.

We made little progress, of course, for the current was very strong, and the greenery on the banks gave but a poor hold to the punting-poles, and as I was in a hurry, I tied up my boat for the night in a pretty bad temper.

Three times before the dawn came we had to shift our moorings, for the waters were rising angrily, and when daylight broke, the river was a dozen feet above its banks. It was a lovely morning when the sun rose above the jungle, for the rain to which the flood was due had fallen in the mountains more than a hundred miles away, and here the sky was clear and bright. The river, red with earth stains, rolled along with here and there a swirling eddy on its surface, marking some submerged snag or rock. Its broad breast was flecked with drift,—a portion of a native shanty ; a giant tree, whirling helplessly round and round, while the water played in and out of its spreading branches to which the green leaves still clung, or rolled it over and over ; dry logs, long dead, which no flood had hitherto succeeded in dragging into the water, wallowed deeply as they sagged down stream ; and here and there some drowned buffalo, or dead beast of the forest. The river in its bed made a gentle purring sound as it rolled along, but on each bank the

water, tearing through the jungle, made a ceaseless
swishing noise, varied now and then by the dull splash
of a falling tree. And from above us the sun looked
down upon the dulled flood which glistened and shone,
but threw back no answering reflection from its ruddy
surface.

The boatmen sat philosophically chewing quids of
betel-nut, and gazing placidly at the world of water.
Progress in the face of such a flood was of course
impossible for my large boat, and a dug-out with a
couple of Malays in it, which whirled down to us
from the village below which we were moored, had
much ado to avoid being swept past us.

'If this be the likeness of the Male Flood, what
will that of the Female be?' ejaculated my Head
Boatman. In common with other Malays he held the
belief that floods, like other moving things, go in
couples. The first to come is the Male, and when he
has passed upon his way, the Female comes after him,
pursuing him hotly, according to the custom of the
sex, and she is the more to be feared, as she rushes
more furiously than does her fleeing mate.

It was important for me to reach Kuâla Kangsar,
—a township which lay some thirty miles up river,—
not later than the following evening ; and while the
morning meal was being cooked, I gazed sulkily at
the flood, and wondered how this was to be accomplished. Walking was out of the question, for the
river had broken bounds and the water stood ten feet
in the jungle on either bank. Then it occurred to
me that a dug-out might thread its way through the
submerged forest, where the current was broken by

the trees, and the obstructing underwood was well below the surface of the flood. Accordingly when our rice had been eaten, I embarked in the dug-out with Kûlop and Ngah, two of my men, and taking the steer-oar myself, set them to work the paddles.

We expected to spend the night in some native hut,—for the banks of the Pêrak River are set closely with little villages,—so we did not encumber the dug-out with food. A change of clothes for each of us, and a mosquito-net for me, was all the gear we considered necessary, except the tobacco and betel-nut which such of us as needed them carried about our own persons.

We fought our way through the racing water, which lined the jungle, and pushed through a tangle of boughs into the forest. Then we headed up stream, threading our way carefully between the close-set trees.

The forest, as I saw it that day, has left an impression upon me that I shall never forget. It resembled the depths of some enchanted wood such as an Evil Genius might have set about his castle in order to affright would-be intruders upon his solitude. The canopy of branches, interwoven and twined one about another, completely obscured the daylight, and cast an even and melancholy gloom about us. The sodden darkness which ever . clings about the forests of the Peninsula seemed to be intensified by the water in which the trees appeared to have taken root ; and an added stillness pervaded the silent woods. This, however, was an aspect of Nature by no means strange to me, but to-day the trees themselves were wholly un-

like any to which my eyes were accustomed. Some
were stained an angry red, others glistened with a
black sheen, while others again were of a dull and
lustreless colour, quite foreign to vegetable life. And
as I looked at them the bark of one and all seemed to
be endued with a strange power to move and crawl.
Then I saw the cause of the change that had come
over the forest. Every tree was covered with ants,
and insects of strange varieties, all seeking shelter from
the flood. One tree would be occupied by all the
inhabitants of a red ants' nest, the lanky, long-legged,
wasp - waisted creatures crawling restlessly over one
another, and occasionally missing their foothold, to fall,
struggling impotently, into the water beneath. On
many trees a fierce war was waging between ants from
rival nests, every inch of bark being covered by a
swarming, struggling mass of furious insects, fighting
cruelly, and with a viciousness which the complete
absence of all noise and outcry only seemed to emphasise. Here and there a great elephant ant, an inch
long, would be seen struggling bravely but helplessly
under a load of tiny assailants ; or a great flat wood-
louse floundered along with half a hundred insects
clinging to his scaly back. Clouds of cockroaches of
all shapes, sizes, and degrees of villainy, fluttered from
the branches against which we brushed, and ran over
our bodies with their loathsome legs.

But the semblance of an ˜enchanted wood was
chiefly given by the snakes. Over and over again as
we skirted a tree, or pushed past a low, hanging bough,
a cruel, lozenge-shaped head would dart out at us from
among the foliage, with wicked, glistening eyes, and

nimble, protruding tongue. We could see others coiled up in the branches overhead, and several fell into the boat, or splashed into the water around us during the course of the day. Now and then we would turn aside to avoid a water-snake wriggling along the surface of the flood, only to find another enemy coiled up in a branch into which we had backed.

Scorpions and centipedes, wasps and hornets, which nest in the earth, every kind of stinging and evil-smelling abomination crawled over or fluttered among the trees in which they had sought shelter. We killed two large, black, crab-like scorpions in the boat. I was myself stung by a centipede which fastened on to the back of my neck, and our skins were raw with the stinging and biting of ants and other lesser insects.

All that day we pushed on through the submerged forest, baling out water and wild beasts at intervals, and when the night began to shut down, we found ourselves far inland, with a very vague idea of our whereabouts, and no village in our neighbourhood. Broad patches of ground were here and there showing above the surface of the water, and on one of these we camped for the night. Supper there was none, and the mosquitoes came in clouds to feast upon us. The sounding slaps upon their bare skins, which the Malays made every second when the mosquitoes bit them keenly, disturbed my rest, and eventually we all three lay down side by side upon the bare earth under my curtain. My bedfellows were restless sleepers, and the ants were here as everywhere, so when the dawn came I was not only a very hungry, but also a very tired man.

Alas ! there was no morning meal to detain us while it was being cooked ; no fire even over which to linger warming ourselves after the cold dankness of our comfortless night ; so we made a very early start, stepping into our dug-out, and making our way once more through the insect- and reptile-covered trees. The jungle had been submerged for many hours now, and the fights between rival ants were mostly ended— even wounded friends had been cast ruthlessly into the water. Some depressed-looking monkeys sat cowering in the upper branches, and here and there the sharp face of a rat peered down at us with quick, curious glances. We were heading inland now, trying to find the edge of the flooded jungle, and about 11 A.M. we came to dry ground and went ashore.

The jungle was not thick in this place, and we pushed our way through it with little difficulty. This was just as well, for we had eaten no food for nearly thirty hours, and had passed a night which held. but little ease. We said hardly a word one to another, but we plied our wood-knives doggedly, and plodded patiently onwards. After an hour's tramp, Kûlop, who was leading, suddenly gave a grunt of dissatisfaction. In front of us the jungle was once more submerged, and looking through the trees, we could see no end to the stretch of water. I began to feel desperate. We had come too far inland to think of going back, for we were now walking against Hunger — that grimmest and most sure - footed of all competitors.

' Our fate is indeed accursed ! ' exclaimed Kûlop.

' What is now our stratagem ? ' I asked.

'Whatever the *Túan* pleases,' said my two companions.

I said a word or two to them, and then we all three fell to work, and in a few minutes had completed the construction of a tiny raft. Next we stripped to the skin, and, piling all our possessions upon the raft, waded into the stagnant water, pushing it carefully before us. We were soon out of our depths, but aiding one another we swam steadily onwards with the raft bobbing and rolling in front of us. Ngah was faint for want of food, and we had to make many halts, clinging to the trunks of the trees, or the overhanging branches for support, before that weary swim was finished. The swamp proved to be about half a mile across, and we were all more or less exhausted before we gained the far side.

At last, dragging the raft after us, we floundered out of the shallows, three naked men, with here and there a black and shiny band six inches long clinging to our water-puckered skins. These were horse-leeches, breakfasting happily, and when we had wrenched them from their holds, the blood ran in widening scarlet streaks and patches down our wet bodies.

Shivering and chattering with cold, stained with the foul water, raw with the bites and stings of insects, and bleeding in many places, we began to tumble into our clothes. We were very sorry for ourselves. It was now that I discovered that my shoes had disappeared. When they fell off the raft we could not say, but they were gone past all hope of recovery. I cut my trousers off at the knee with my wood-knife, for the flapping bottoms would afford too good cover for the jungle leeches, and I think I cursed a little to myself as I started forward once more. I had been in charge of a District the year before where the swamp water was so poisonous that it made one's feet swell hideously. Therefore during some months I had been driven to do my jungle travelling without the aid of the boots into which my feet declined to fit, so I now found little difficulty in picking my way barefoot through the forest.

Twice again we had to cross swamps, but neither of them was so broad as that which we had already encountered. Standing on the grassy bank of the last one, while we plucked a fresh batch of horse-leeches from our bleeding limbs, I saw the mountains which divide the Pêrak Valley from Larut showing above the jungle. Directly in front of us was Gunong Arang Para—the Mountain of Soot—and a little behind it rose the summit of Gunong Bubu—the Fish-Trap—with its angular peak flanked by the long, flat ridge. I could see each round tree-top on the mountain sides, and the bungalow among the coffee shrubs on the upper slopes of Arang Para. This showed me that we were already some five miles inland, and I knew that if we pressed forward towards the hills, we should, sooner or later, strike a charcoal-burners' path leading along the foot of the mountains to the high-road. This thoroughfare joins Kuâla Kangsar to Taiping, and I calculated that we should strike it some five miles from the former place. This gave me hope, and we all three plunged into the jungle, heading for the mountains with renewed energy.

The Malays lagged somewhat, and I pressed on alone. There had once been a path leading inland from this point, but it was now much overgrown, and my wood - knife was constantly needed to help me force my way through the thick brushwood. Here and there a monster tree, which in its fall had dragged others to the ground, obstructed the path, and over it I had to climb laboriously. In places the faint trail disappeared utterly, and I had to make numerous casts on one side and on the other, before I could find a means of again moving forward. It was weary work, and I was faint with hunger, but I pushed on doggedly, and after some hours, which seemed like weeks, I came out upon a charcoal-burners' path. It had only been cleared sufficiently to enable the slow buffaloes to drag their clumsy sledges along it, and the passage of many hoofs had stamped the yielding earth into a quagmire. It was heavy walking for a weary, famished man, and the two miles which separated me from the high-road were almost too much for me.

At last the welcome streak of yellow—the dusty, metalled road winding through the green walls of jungle on either hand—showed me that civilisation was drawing near; and my bare feet trod its flint-set surface with a boundless satisfaction. A Chinaman's booth stood by the roadside, a few hundred yards away, and from rattan lines stretched across the window depended little clusters of yellow bananas. The Chinaman could speak no known language, so I could not explain my position to him, but when I sat down and devoured the whole of his fruit with such eager delight he smiled at me compassionately, and doubtless told himself that the

'Red-Headed Foreign Devil' was mad. I am afraid that I confirmed him in this opinion by the lavish manner in which I paid for my meal; but indeed I was grateful to him, and would readily have parted with my birthright that day in exchange for the least savoury mess of pottage.

Then I got some Malays together, and sent them back, with such food as they could collect, to seek for Kûlop and Ngah. I afterwards learned that they found them lying down, quite exhausted, about half a mile from the charcoal-burners' track.

When the search party had started, I set off to walk into Kuâla Kangsar, and in three hours' time I once more saw the waters of the Pêrak River. The angry stream rolled down swollen and ruddy, measuring nearly half a mile across. The whole of the low-lying township was flooded, and even in the shops on the higher roads the people were camping on the roofs. On the hills around the town the Malays were living under all manner of crazy shelters, and the smell of the evening meal, which all were engaged in cooking, fell gratefully upon my nostrils as I threaded my way among the huts.

Many of my friends were homeless and outcast that day, and a draggled and woebegone crowd they were to look upon, but my own figure was, perhaps, the most ruffianly of all. My broad felt hat was a limp and shapeless mass; my flannel shirt was torn down the back, and hung in sodden tatters about me; my trousers were sawn off raggedly at the knee; my legs and feet were bare. Here and there a patch of red showed where the blood from a leech bite had stained my clothes. The dirt of the jungles clung about me from head to foot, and the white dust of the road was caked over all. Never was respectable man reduced to an aspect more disreputable !

Pĕrak is a peaceful land, from which the knife and the spear have for ever departed ; but so long as Nature plays her pranks with us, a man may accumulate unpleasant experiences even in places where Pax Britannica is an idol unbroken.

The Dream came to me as I lay
   Beneath the waving palm,
It led me forth upon my way,
   It broke upon my calm,
It whispered to me as I went
   Beneath the forest green,
The Message that my God had sent
   To break my sleep serene.

Ah me! I travailed brave and strong,
   To set the wry World right,
To succour those who suffered wrong,
   To fight the Holy Fight ;
And if the Wicked win the day
   'Tis Allah's will, I wean,
Glad to His peace I'll pass away,
   Who have His Vision seen !
                  The Song of the Dreamer of Dreams.

In the East men not infrequently suffer sadly because they are so unfortunate as to possess ideas. In the West, on the other hand, a man may hold all manner of extravagant theories without necessarily being brought by them to an evil end. The reason of this is very plain. The less excitable European does not always think it incumbent upon him to put all his theories into practice, whereas the ideas which come to an

Oriental have a habit of running away with their owner, leaving him no peace, until they have succeeded in landing him in some very unsavoury place, such as the Andaman Islands, or the Central Gaol.

The White Man, looking calmly at the age into which he has been born, and at all the circumstances of his surroundings, may tell himself that the times are not yet ripe for the adoption of his more advanced theories.   This is a comforting view to take, for the man who looks upon life and its difficulties in this common-sense light runs no risks, while he has further the consolation of thinking that he is blessed with an intellect more far-seeing than those of his fellows.   If he has ideas very badly indeed, he may sit down and write about them ; and we all know that the profuse ink-flux is an exceedingly efficient safety-valve.   By its means large quantities of bile and other disagreeable fluids may be carried off, which, without some such relief, might conceivably hurry their victim into impossible action, dangerous to society, and still more hazardous to himself.   The inability of the Celt to appreciate the fact that half a hundred excellent reasons may exist for not putting a beautiful theory into practice without more ado, is one of the qualities that make the most Westerly people of Europe so incongruously like the nations of the East.   The Russians, being to all intents and purposes an Oriental race, share this inability with other Asiatic peoples.

But the majority of Brown Men go further than this, for they can see no steps between the inception of an idea and its realisation.   Their natures are so constructed that they cannot easily be made to under-

stand that all really sound theories are sure to be tried
upon their merits, if you only wait long enough, but
that for this to happen, the theory itself must have
some intrinsic value of its own. Even could they
appreciate this fact, it would not help them, for they
are impatient of delay. They want to see their
theories put into practice now, at once, during their
own lifetime. They are unable to look forward calmly
to the days when their children's grandchildren will
enjoy many good things to which they must ever
remain strangers. 'Why should we do so much for
Posterity? What has Posterity done for us?' was
the impassioned exclamation of the excellent Sir Boyle
Roach, and the feeling expressed in this remarkable
phrase finds an echo in many an Oriental heart.

Moreover the Man with an Idea, if he belong to an
Asiatic race, never stays to ask himself whether his
theory is really for the good of the greatest number.
An intense belief in its merits comes to him with the
idea itself, and his utter faith in it is thus, from the
very first, both firm and unquestioning.

Now in Europe and Asia alike, the first object or
the political theorist is to break down the Present; but
while the White Man peers eagerly into the Future,
and his hands itch to fashion it according to his heart's
desire, the Brown Man's eyes are fixed dreamily upon
the Past. The White Man seeks to build up What
Ought To Be; the Brown Man longs to reconstruct
What Has Been; and since the unlettered Oriental
has none of the safety-valves which may bring relief
to the European, the Idea is wont to hurry him into
ill-considered and ill-advised action. Then, if the

Q

Present chances to be presided over by the British Government, that unwieldy monster lifts up its foot, and stamps upon the Man with an Idea ; and he and those who have followed him thereafter suffer many and heavy things because of the faith that is in them.

In the Malay State of Pahang there was once a Man with an Idea. He had begun life as dog-boy to a Prince ; and the latter, after many wars, wrested the throne from its rightful owners, and became a King. As the new Monarch was a keen sportsman, and appreciated the skill of the dog-boy, it followed that the latter presently found himself the possessor of a high-sounding title, a long and straggling river, and a steady income, derived from 'squeezing' the couple of thousand peasants who had their homes in the valley through which this river ran.   In an independent Malay State, jobs on this magnificent scale excite no adverse comment ; and the simple villagers bowed down before the ex-dog-boy, and feared him exceedingly, as one who held unlimited power in his hands.

I knew him well in those days, and he certainly was a remarkable man. His knowledge of wood-craft was unsurpassed, even among the aboriginal tribes of jungle-dwellers, with whom, at certain seasons, he was wont to herd, garbed, like them, in a scanty loin-cloth, fashioned from the bark of the *trap* tree. He was gifted with great physical strength, invincible courage, much cunning, and a really marvellous imagination. This latter possession is of no small value to a Malay of the Peninsula, for in no land, and among no other people, may a man more easily induce others to take him at his own valuation. A huge granite boulder, weighing some five tons, is still pointed out, lying high up on the bank of the river, over which the ex-dog-boy ruled, and the traveller, who passes it, is told how the Chief plucked it with one hand from the river bed, and cast it aside where it now lies, because it chanced to obstruct the passage of his dug-out. The Chief himself was responsible for this remarkable statement, and no man dreamed of doubting his word. Like the man who was the bravest Knight in France, 'he said so, and *he* ought to know.'

Thus the ex-dog-boy's reputation waxed very great in the land, and he flourished exceedingly ; and the good old times ran gaily through the hour-glass in the bad old way, until Pahang became a Protected State, and the servants of the British Government began the ungrateful and laborious task of teaching an un-regenerate people the elementary differences between right and wrong, and between *meum* and *tuum*.

The bulk of the people were well pleased, for peace and plenty—strangers in their villages—began to draw near, and to smile upon them. But the Chiefs could not, of course, regard matters in quite the same light. When a large district lies before him, from which he may pick and choose all that his heart may desire, without asking absurd questions as to ownership ; when his income is what he may elect to exact in fine and cess from the cowed villagers, who dare not resist him ; when he is not cursed with a conscience ; and when he has no bowels of compassion in his anatomy,—

even though he be married half a dozen deep, a man may succeed in living very much at his ease. But when all these things, upon which he has learned to rely, sink away suddenly from under him, as the Earth drops downwards as you gaze at it from the car of a rising balloon; when power, and wealth, and cherished manorial rights,—such as were wont to make life so sweet to him, so exceeding bitter to his neighbours, —are all reft from him in a moment; when he is called upon to live up to a standard of morality with which he has no sympathy; and when his only compensation is a monthly stipend,—the very regularity of which robs life of half its excitement,—a man is apt to become morose and taciturn, and to spend much time in dreaming of the good old days.

Such was the experience of the ex-dog-boy; and upon a certain day, as he lay tossing upon his mat, and pondering moodily upon the Past, the Idea came to him. Then, in that hour, several hundreds of souls —men, and tender women, children at their mothers' skirts, and little babies at the breast—were doomed to terrible suffering, and, in too many instances, to a lingering and untimely death.

The Idea was, of course, that the ex-dog-boy and his people should rise up against the representatives of the British Government, and should drive them screaming from the land. The ex-dog-boy had nothing to scale things by, and he knew that the White Men and their followers were few. The matter seemed easy, and he counted on the other Chiefs, who shared his grievances, and his love of the good old times, to join him, and share also in his risks. The peasants, he knew, would follow the Chiefs in a war directed against their best interests, from sheer force of habit, and because the feudal feeling was still strong within them ; and in so judging the event proved him to be right. But the other Chiefs lacked his courage, so the rising never became general, though aid was lent to the ex-dog-boy by every secret means that could suggest themselves to his numerous well-born sympathisers.

And here it is that the Muhammadan has the advantage of the Christian. If the latter wars with the Powers that Be, he may be an Anarchist, or a Socialist, or a Nihilist, but he is by no means necessarily regarded as a Christian Hero. Some Christians may be found to sympathise with him, but their sympathy is in no sense connected with their religious beliefs. But with the Muhammadan it is different. If those against whom he rebels chance to belong to any other Faith, no matter what the cause of quarrel, no matter how lax the rebel's own practice may be, his revolt against authority is at once raised to the dignity of a *Sabil Allah*, or Holy War against the Infidel. It becomes a reproach to any Muhammadan to side against him ; all who aid him thereby serve God and His Prophet ; and in this lies the real strength of a Muhammadan population.

Wonderful it is how powerful are those words ' *Sabil Allah*,' among even the least fanatical of Muhammadans. Men who never pray, not even on Friday ; men who break the Fast of Ramathân for thirty days each year ; men to whom the Faith is nothing but a name, and whose knowledge of its tenets would disgrace an ignorant European, can still be fired to enthusiasm, when the sorriest and most selfish rebel among them dignifies his storm in a tea-cup by calling it a Holy War.

This merely affords one more instance of the marvellous cohesion of the Muhammadans. Their Faith, which is hedged about by pride and hate, causes them to regard the professors of all other religions with a passion of disdain, such as no modern Christian can easily realise ; and it has, withal, the power to bind men one to another, as nothing else can do. The old, simple, unquestioning Faith of the Middle Ages, when the two thousand odd Christian Sects were as yet uninvented, and when, speaking broadly, all men held the same teaching upon all points of theology, may have had some very similar effect upon its professors ; but the warlike Creed of Muhammad has for its very marrow a desire to ex-terminate all other Faiths—putting infidel men to the sword, and leading their women-folk captive,—a spirit which is certainly not to be found in the Gospels of Christ.

This is the rough outer edge which Muham-madanism presents to those who are not of the Faith ; but among themselves, those who believe in Allah and the Prophet, exercise to one another a large and generous charity, that may well put to shame the Christians, to whom that virtue, in its highest practice, should surely belong.

The ex-dog-boy opened the game by firing upon a party of Europeans from the heavy jungles which fringed the banks of the narrow river over which he had once ruled supreme. He killed a few people, and wounded some others. Then he chanced to catch Sikh, who had lost his way in the jungle, and him he strangled with a rattan, after making him, while still living, the victim of nameless mutilations. Thus the first blood was to him ; and his people followed him like sheep, with their old fear of him, and their belief in his prowess waxing strong within them.

But his next move in the game was a mistake. Malays chiefly conduct their warfare from behind stockades, the attacking party constructing their rude works at a safe and convenient distance from those of the enemy. Much breath is expended in shouts and vaunting challenges, and large quantities of gunpowder are burned, but after war has raged for many months a mere handful of casualties have to be counted, for no attempt is made to rush a stockade so long as any watch is kept within it. The ex-dog-boy believed that White Men fought upon a like principle ; so when he took the field, he built numerous forts, all of which were promptly destroyed.

I shall not follow him through the various stages of the campaign which ensued, but eventually he became convinced that he and his people must make their way out of Pahang if they would win to safety. He dared not travel by any known route, but his skill in wood-craft has been spoken of. He took to the jungle, with some six hundred men, women, and children, and during the space of five months he wormed his way through untraversed forests, guiding himself wholly by the knowledge which he possessed

of the river-systems of the country, until after many
adventures, and almost unparalleled hardships, the
strange journey was accomplished, and the miserable
remnant, that had survived the march, won clear of
the country.

If you know the East Coast of the Malay Peninsula
well, you can make your way up and down it, and
across and across, and through and through, by following the net-work of narrow footpaths which thread
the jungles here, there, and everywhere. Travelling
in this fashion is not easy, for the trails are almost
blind in places, and every now and then a wood-knife
must make a way through the forest before a man
may pass. But the fugitives dared not follow well-
known paths, or any paths at all, save in the wildest
and least frequented parts of the forest, and even then
they were constantly harassed by their enemies. For
the rest, they cleared their own way through the
depths of a Malayan jungle, which is more like one
enormous thick-set hedge, bound fast by ropes in-
numerable, stayed at every point by giant trees, than
anything else which the untravelled Englishman can
easily imagine. Half a mile a day was a good journey
in such country; and when the food failed, a few
yards was almost more than the stricken wretches could
accomplish. Their line of march was marked by
bâyas and *îbul*, and other wild palms, which had been
felled, that men might fill their empty stomachs with
the edible shoots. At every point the earth had been
grubbed up, as by a thousand moles. This marked
the places where jungle roots and yams had been dug
for. At spots where the *kěpâyang* fruit grew plenti-

fully the refugees had camped for over a week, and many new graves marked their resting-place, for the *këpâyang* bears an ill name.

> Këpâyang fruits so green and fair,
> How like my Love are they!
> To eat thereof I do not dare,
> Yet cannot throw away!

says the Malay rhyme; but those who run from the grip of the Law are foredoomed to the suffering of many things, and by a starving stomach no food, no matter how unhealthy, may be lightly rejected.

For the first three months or so the rebels kept more or less together, for deserters were dealt with severely by the Chief, and at night-time, round the fires of the camp, he told blood-curdling tales of the vengeance of the White Men, filling his simple followers with a fear that made them prefer a lingering death in the forests to even a chance of capture. But when the cruel grip of hunger began to wring their empty stomachs, those among the rebels who still had the strength to do so, pushed on, devouring the jungle foods as they went, while the weak and feeble lagged hopelessly behind in a land where there was no gleaning.

The forests were dotted with little knots of stragglers, and we gathered them in, filled them with good food, and sent them home to their villages, with peace upon their faces, and in their eyes glad wonder at the treatment meted out to them. We followed up the main body of the rebels, and fought them again and again in the blind jungles, where nought could be seen save trees and dripping greenery, with the thick, white smoke-clouds bellying through between trunks and leaves, or hanging low in the still air. Here men were struck dead not seeing the hand that smote them, while the rifles sang out sharply, and clearly, and fiercely, breaking through the forest in a thousand echoes, amid the discordant war-yells of the enemy, and the answering roar of our own people.

Towards the end of the fifth month the chase grew hotter, and the little bands of survivors dwindled daily in number. We followed them up relentlessly, for Pahang stood at gaze, irresolute concerning the action which it would be wise for it to take while the success or failure of the Government hung uncertainly in the balance. Sometimes we lost all trace of the fugitives for weeks together ; sometimes, for a day or two, we were hot upon their trail, and we had a stirring little brush with them in those dreary forests every other hour. The stragglers became more and more numerous, while the Chief and his fighting-men pressed forward with increased eagerness as they neared the Kělantan boundary. The distress of the fugitives became daily more acute, and never shall I forget the horror of those days, and the heartrending scenes of which I was a witness.

Sometimes it would be a small knot of stragglers, mostly women and ghastly little children—children whose care-worn faces seemed to bear the weight of a hundred years of pain and sorrow. We would find them sitting huddled together, in utter, dull despair, looking at us almost calmly from out the awful hollows of their deep-set eyes. How well I know that miserable, squalid group, and the sick passion of pity which

the sight of it awakens ! They never doubt but that
death awaits them, but even that seems to them to be
preferable to any prolongation of the keen yet lingering
agony from which they are suffering. They are in
the last stages of famine. Their skulls show sharp and
angular, with knobs of protruding temple, and prominent cheek-bones visible beneath the taut, dry skin.
Their knees, their elbows, every joint in their shrunken
bodies, are bosses of bone, huge, and round, and ugly,
from which depend brittle, stick-like limbs, hanging
feeble and inert. Their feet and hands resemble the
talons of some unclean night-fowl, and their ribs rise
clear, each one of them as separate and as distinctly
marked as the bold, black stripes upon a tiger's hide.
Their stomachs alone are swollen and inflated, dread-
fully out of all proportion to their wasted frames, but
the roundness is that of disease, not the curves of health.
Their eyes are the eyes of wild beasts when food is set
before them, and like animals they throw themselves
upon it, seizing and tearing it in the fury of their
hunger. But when the first few mouthfuls have been
devoured, their strange, feeble listlessness returns, and
the slow, painful languor of their movements makes
them resemble more and more closely a weird band of
spectres in some ugly Dance of Death

Sometimes we would find a man, sitting with his
head fallen forward between his knees, with his back
against a tree, with his arms pendent and nerveless,
and his legs drawn convulsively up against his empty
stomach. His body would be a mere bag of bones,—
slender, frail bones, in a wofully tight casing of yellow,
fever-parched skin. Such an one would too often be

beyond all human aid, his shrunken gullet refusing to swallow the brandy which we forced through his set teeth. His mouth would be half full of some horrible trash, with which he had tried to stay the pangs of his hunger, stuff which he had lacked the power even to eject. His glassy eyes would stare horribly into our pitying faces, and without a word he would pass away while we stood around him.

Wonderful devotion was shown to one another by some of these poor folk in their common necessity. Once we found a man sitting gaunt and grim, by the side of one whom he had loved. He was too weak to be able to bury his dead, but he would not leave the useless skin and bone, which hunger had transformed into a mummy, for the beasts of the forest to devour. He would neither eat nor move until the body had been washed and buried, according to the rites of the Muhammadans ; and those who did these last offices told me that the dead man's mouth was full of rice which he had been unable to swallow,—the last hoarded handful that the starving father had forced upon his dying son !

On another occasion we found a little party of three, a man and his wife, with their baby at her breast. All were in sore straits for lack of food, and the woman had quite lost the use of her legs. The man carried her upon his bowed back, bound to him by an old *sàrong* or native waist-cloth. In his hands were two bundles, containing all that remained to them of the wreck of their household goods. The woman nursed the fretful baby in the hollow of her left arm, and with her disengaged hand she sought to clear the way for her man, hacking feebly at the lower branches of the trees, and at the thick underwood with a clumsy wood-knife. She was quite a young girl, while the man was middle-aged, and neither of them were at all good to look upon, but when they gazed at one another I saw the love-light well up in their eyes. Just before we chanced upon them this poor family had struggled, in the manner which I have described, over the summit of a hill nearly a thousand feet in height, whence they had again descended into the plain. I know not how long this part of their journey had taken them, nor what measure of toil, and pain, and heart-breaking effort had been the man's ere half his self-imposed task had been accomplished ; but whatever he may have suffered, and however great the strain that he had put upon his endurance, I know that his first care was for the woman, when we set food before them. I re-member, too, that he insisted upon helping to carry the litter upon which we laid her, though he could hardly stagger along unaided when the strain to which he had nerved himself had been removed. When we got the girl to one of the field hospitals he watched beside her, tending her with a constant care and gentleness very pitiful to see ; and even in her last agony her eyes followed him lovingly. But though he failed to stay the life that ebbed so fast away from her, I cannot think that his love, and his labour, and his suffering, and his pain, were utterly wasted.

But, perhaps, the saddest incident of all was that which befell at the very end of the Disturbances, when we were hunting the vanguard of the rebels through the forests that cluster around the borders of Kĕlantan.

They had still a few of their women and children with them, but the men were nearing safety and plenty, so those who sank by the way, too utterly worn out to make a further effort, were now often deserted even by their own kinsfolk.

We were close upon the track of the rebels, whose footsteps we had been following all day, and we were expecting every moment to come up with them. The afternoon was far advanced, and we hoped to find them in camp. Some of the tracks were so fresh that water was still oozing into the depressed toe-prints, and the Dyak trackers in front were beginning to bristle with excitement, like hounds on a hot scent. The evening hymn, which all the jungle creatures join in singing as the sun sinks, was ringing through the forest, the parrots calling shrilly one to another as they swooped upon the clouds of flying insects, the birds thrilling and quavering upon almost every tree, while the *cicada* raised their strident tocsin to tell that the day was dead.

Suddenly, through all the tumult of the animal and insect world, there broke upon our ears a cry that made our heart-beats quicken. It was the whine of a little child; but to us it meant that a camp which we hoped held the advance party of the rebels—the men whom we had so long pursued, yet had never once taken unawares—was close at hand. We crept forward as noiselessly as we were able, turning into the bed of a stream and wading down the shallows. Presently the Dyak trackers, who were leading, stiffened like pointers, and the next moment four of them fired a volley. Their orders had been to hold their fire until they received the word, but Dyaks are ill to hold when the chance of killing presents itself. I rushed forward, and came up with the Dyaks in time to see that they had fired into a small camp on the river bank, and pushing past them I ran into the little cluster of temporary sheds. One man lay dead with a bullet through his stomach ; another, huddled up under a torn and shabby velvet coverlet, was squirming with fear, and crying to us to slay him speedily, if indeed we desired to take his life.

In the centre of the camp sat a woman with a little child, a girl of perhaps five years of age, clinging convulsively to her. Both mother and child were screaming in a manner most pitiful to hear. I turned the man with the coverlet over with my foot, and bade him hold his peace, as no man had any intention of harming him. He was in the last stages of dropsy, brought on by the hardships which he had endured in the damp, comfortless jungles, and he sat there, a horrible sight, calling upon his bloated carcase to burst if he were in thought or deed inimical to the British Government.

Disregarding him, I pushed on to where the woman sat, and strove to reassure her.

'Peace, Sister !' I said. 'There is no one here who desireth to hurt thee.'

'Not hurt me ?' she cried, with a fresh outburst of screams. 'Not hurt me? Behold !'

She had been sitting cross-legged on the ground, but as she spoke, she kicked her left leg forward, and it opened in the middle of her shin, until the heel snapped limply against the inside of her knee. A red

chasm opened like the mouth of a shark, wide, and
gaping, and horrible to see, and a spurt of warm blood
spattered me from head to foot. She rolled over on
her back in a dead faint. The bones of her leg were
both sundered by the cruel Snider bullet, which to all
intents and purposes is an expanding missile, and the
severed arteries pumped the blood out in little eddying
jets. The ground on which she lay speedily became
covered with a broad patch of scarlet, clotting in
cracking blebs and blisters, upon which a thousand
flies settled and feasted horribly, and while we strove
vainly to staunch the flow of blood, the little girl sat
placidly at her mother's side, munching a captain's
biscuit, which we had given to her, clasping it greedily
between her tiny hands. The utter insensibility of
the child to her mother's sufferings, and the case with
which · food distracted her attention from all other
things, was not the least ghastly feature of that painful
scene.

Presently the wounded woman began slowly to
recover consciousness. Her head rolled restlessly from
side to side, a low groan escaped her, and her eyes
opened and fixed themselves upon me as I knelt by her
side leaning over her. The look they wore—the look
of some tender, hunted animal gazing despairingly at
her captor—made the lump rise queerly in my throat.
Her lips were painfully forming words, and I bent low
to catch them. They came faint, and halting, and
broken with suffering, but even in that moment of
agony the mother's heart was with her child.

'Wilt . . . thou . . . slay . . . my . . . child . . . in
like manner?'

'O Sister!' I cried, in the familiar vernacular phrase which makes all folks akin. 'O Sister, thou knowest that we had no desire to harm thee. It was a bullet that had gone astraying, a bullet that had lost its way which did thee this hurt. Have no fear for thy child.'

'If thou slayest her not,' came the painful whisper, 'she is still as one already dead, living as she will do, having neither father nor mother, nor any relative to tend or love her.'

'Peace, Sister!' I said. 'I myself will tend and love her. Have no fear for her.'

The woman looked up at me wonderingly, stupidly, until the meaning of my words at last forced itself upon her tortured brain. Then, with a supreme effort, she raised herself into a half-sitting posture.

'Say that again!' she screamed, and I repeated the words of my promise.

'Swear that thou wilt tend her!' she cried next, and I swore solemnly in the name of God. Then she sank back exhausted, but with peace upon her face.

'It is well,' she murmured, 'and now leave me with my child for a little space before I die.'

I left her, and as I turned away I saw her draw the emaciated little creature to her heart, while her face spoke of love unfathomable, and her lips moved painfully, as they formed the words of the baby language —that tenderest of all tongues—which only mothers and little children, the purest of our kind, know and understand.

We camped on the opposite side of the stream, and

R

the night fell dark and impenetrable. At about eight o'clock a pure baby's voice broke the stillness.

'Come and fetch me,' it cried. 'Come and fetch me, for my mother is dead!'

And presently the poor little starving girl, whose sad experience had taught her so early.to recognise death, was carried across the stream in the arms of one of my Malays, and was laid to sleep beside me upon my mat. Next day she was put into a knapsack, fashioned of rattan, and sent to the rear; and, as I write these lines five years later, the sound of a merry laugh is borne in to me from the place where the children of my native followers are playing together in my compound. The laugh rings out in the shrill pure treble of happy childhood, and when I hear it I pause in my work, and wonder whether the child's mother looks down upon her little one, and is satisfied that after all her life has not been quite a loveless one.

THE STRANGE ELOPEMENT OF CHÂLING THE DYAK

The Woods are old, and vast, and wide,
These Forest Lands, through which we stride;
We've known them long, we've known them well,
Their every secret folks may tell.
And yet, and yet, these Woods are strange,
These Forest Lands, through which we range,
For though we know them through and through,
They still hold marvels wondrous new.
The Song of the Old Hunters.

THIS story was told to me by the Pĕnghûlu of the Dyaks, as he sat cooling his feet in the running waters of a little stream in the interior of Trĕnggânu, and tenderly arranged the broken peacock feathers of his head-dress, like a draggled bird pluming itself. He wore a Government *khaki* uniform, stained green, and black, and yellow, by much hard wear in damp jungles, and a mangy tiger's skin, with a hole cut in its centre, through which his head was thrust, hung down his back and chest, like the chasuble of a Catholic priest. He was tattooed with faint lines in pale indigo, and the lobes of his ears consisted mainly of two vast holes, so that the lower rims of flesh depended limply, almost to his shoulders. His voice was harsh and grating, and his words came with the curious jerky intonation of the Dyak people; and, since he had little skill in story-telling, and as his Malay was crude, I shall take the words out of his mouth, and shall relate the strange things, to which he bore testimony, in a manner of my own choosing.

In what follows, I believe that I have not omitted anything material, and that I have myself inserted nothing at all; though the tale, as I write it, is more connected, and more exact in detail, than was the tale as I heard it told at any one time. Natives of the lower class lack the power to narrate any story in such a manner that the facts follow one another, in the order in which they actually occurred. Also, they tell their tales with a baldness that will not bear reproduction. If a man would fill in the rude outlines, thus supplied to him in the beginning, he must listen to constant repetitions, must ask countless questions, and must trust to picking up a stray fact or detail here and there, until, at last, he can piece the thing together into a more or less connected whole.

The following story is a specimen of this kind of verbal patch-work.

The interior of the Dyak hut was plunged in obscurity, dimly relieved by the dull, red glow of the smouldering embers, and by the flecks of light cast by the pale moonbeams struggling through the interstices of the high-pitched, thatched roof, and the wattled walls. The married couples within the single long room, of which the hut consisted, were three in number :—the father and mother, owners of the house, and their two married sons with their wives—each couple lying packed away under dingy mosquito curtains, only giving evidences of their presence, now and again, by a restless movement, a many-jointed, hard-fought snore, or by the sleepy, fretful cry of an infant at the breast, quickly soothed into silence again by the gentle words of comfort whispered by its tired, patient mother. But, though the night was very far advanced, though the cool dawn-wind was whispering through the fruit trees of the compound, and even making a little stir among the bed-curtains of the sleepers, two figures sat facing one another in the obscurity, still wide awake, and happy, as only lovers can be, who find each moment ugly that is not spent in one another's company.

If you study the manners and customs of the various races of the Earth with a little care, you will find the ways of humanity strangely similar, though the men you watch be clad in loin-cloths or in dress-coats, though the scene be a French *salon* or a Malay hut. The continental system of arranging marriages between young folk, who have barely seen one another, finds its counterpart in many savage lands. But the Dyak custom of allowing unmarried girls to receive their own guests, and to practically manage all the preliminaries to their own marriages with the youth of their choice, without reference to, or interference from, their elders, more nearly approximates to the American system, and would seem to show that even the emancipated girls of that energetic race have not got so very far ahead of primitive people and their

beginnings, as one might at first be inclined to
suppose.

Châling the Dyak had come to this particular hut
to *ngayap*, or court, Mînang, and, though he had been
refused admittance on the first one or two occasions,
he had, later, been allowed to pay his nocturnal calls
with great regularity. Before she had become convinced of his earnestness, Mînang had treated Châling
with the scant courtesy that a Dyak maiden finds
necessary, if she is to preserve her self-respect. Once
or twice she had suddenly affected to be wearied by
his presence, and had abruptly bidden him depart, and
when, declining to believe that she really desired
him to be gone, he had stubbornly kept his seat,
she had stepped quickly to the fireplace, and, with
a few deft strokes of the bellows, had set flames
leaping, which cast a lurid light throughout the
hut. Then Châling had fled precipitately, for all
men know what is implied when a damsel throws
unnecessary light upon the situation, and Châling had
no desire that any one should look upon his face, and
recognise that he was the youth who had bored a girl
to desperation. Later, when she had begun to love
him, and when there no longer remained any doubt in
her mind as to Châling's passionate devotion to herself,
she had invited him to stretch himself to rest upon the
mat beside her, and Châling had lain there, listening
to her even breathing, longing for the time when she
would be his wife, but fearing to touch even the edge
of her garment, lest the cry which rouses a maiden's
men-folk should be uttered, and he should be cast out
of the hut, with the door barred against him, his body

covered with wounds and bruises, and his head broken
in many places ; for such is the custom of the Dyak
people ; and severe is the probation which a lover
must undergo before he is deemed to have proved himself worthy of her he desires to have to wife.

But, lately, things had taken a turn for the better.
Mînang had been kinder and gentler, at each successive
meeting, and, this evening, when Châling had played
his best and sweetest upon the little Jew's harp, and
had begun the fragmentary conversation that is permitted before the girl takes her turn with the music-
maker, the consent to allow Châling to make a formal
proposal to her people, which Mînang in her coyness
had long withheld, had at length been given. Then
Châling had clasped her about the waist for a moment,
and the twain now sat whispering together 'In that
New World which is the Old.'

Next day, Châling had an interview with the parents
of his lady-love—that *mauvais quart d'heure* which
helps to knock the romance out of so many lovers' day-
dreams—but he was a mighty hunter, and his hut was
well stored with gear of his own earning, so the questions asked by Mînang's father, and the rather mercenary
demands which he made as the price of his consent,
were answered and complied with satisfactorily enough.
The date was fixed, upon which all the house should
be invited to partake of the *pûding sîrih*, and Châling,
with his heart uplifted, as it had never been before,
betook himself to the jungle to seek for wild swine.

He was a dapper little fellow, with well-formed
sturdy limbs, the face of a London street-arab, and

only one eye.   A thorn had pierced the pupil of its
fellow long ago, when Châling was a little naked
baby roaming about, with other tiny brown puff-balls,
bathing in the streams, and playing catch-as-catch-can
in the brakes of jungle near the villages.   None the
less, his sight was nearly as keen as that of other
Dyaks, which means an acuteness of vision that we
civilised men, whose organs have been blunted by
long disuse, regard as little short of miraculous.

He wore about his waist a twisted loin-cloth of
scarlet cotton with a gold thread running through the
fabric, and, by his side, hung a curved, wooden sheath,
brave with beads and red horsehair, in which reposed
the long, keen-edged Dyak knife, without which he
never went forestwards.   He went all alone, like
Young Lochinvar, for the pork he sought was destined
to be a present to his future mother-in-law ; and he
was not willing that any one but himself should have
a hand in the killing.   He passed quickly through
the forest, placing one foot exactly in front of the
other at each step, as is the manner of all jungle
creatures, and soon the scant traces of human habitation
were left far behind him, and Châling found himself
in the deep, dead jungle, with only the babble of a
brook, and the gentle distant murmur of the forest
flies and insects, to disturb the utter stillness.

There was an unusual stir in the house of Mînang's
people when, after two days—ample time for a man to
slay more wild swine than the village-folk could eat
in a month—Châling still failed to return, and the
hour appointed for the eating of the *puding sirih* drew

near. The friends and relations of the bride had been invited in their scores, and Mînang's father and mother waxed very wrathful, indeed, when they thought of the shame that must fall upon them if Châling was too late to keep his appointment. Mînang's brothers girded their loins anew, and, with their swords at their sides, set off upon Châling's track, in a state of anger which boded ill for the treatment that their prospective brother-in-law might expect, if he chanced to fall into their hands. Little Mînang sat within her father's hut weeping furtively, a shamed maiden, and her mother shook her head sadly, for all Dyak women know that suicide is the only proper medicine for a girl who has been the subject of a public slight, such as this. Her brothers returned bringing with them Châling's sword, which they had found in the jungle, and they told strange stories of broken boughs overhead, and of a sudden cessation of Châling's foot-prints, as though he had suddenly soared upwards through the branches. They said that he had been caught up to the sky by the hand of the Jungle Fiend, for one and all swore that no wild beast had seized him, since no tracks were to be found. Needless to say, no man placed credit in their words, for they had good reason to wish that their sister's shame might be hidden. And Mînang, weeping very bitterly, in the still, sad night, knew that her brothers' talk was foolish-ness; writhed in body and spirit when she thought of the shame that had been put upon her; and shuddered at the open door of self-inflicted death, through which she knew that she ought now to pass, because, even without Châling, and with a fame that was besmirched, life was still sweet while the young blood pulsed so warmly through her veins.

As for the shameless Châling, he had eloped with a lady, or, to be more accurate, a lady had run away with him ; and he now sat bruised, and sore, and naked, high up amid the tree-tops, eyeing his new-found mistress with extreme disfavour. He kept continually asking himself whether he was really awake, hoping against hope that this vile thing, which had happened to him, was an evil dream such as the bad spirits send to a man when he lies stretched to sleep upon 'hard ground,' where the devils love to dwell. But his sores, and cuts, and scratches, and bruises, and the aching pains in every bone, told him unmistakably that he was wide awake, and that this unspeakable thing was true. He rehearsed in his mind, again and again, the order in which the events had occurred, and he almost went mad with impotent fury when he thought of the horror of the situation in which he now found himself, and of his utter powerlessness to escape from it. The morning when, amid the peaceful birds' chorus, he had left the Dyak village, and had passed into the forest, that glistened with undried dew, when his soul had been at rest, and his heart uplifted with joy in his love for Mînang, seemed incredibly far away ; and he himself had aged, he felt, and was now transformed into a being strangely different from the light-hearted, cheery creature whom he had known as Châling so few hours ago.

He had sat down to rest at the foot of a large tree, in a spot where the jungle was, if anything, more thick and entangled than elsewhere, for the day was hot, and he found the shade grateful. He had pulled out his knife, and, with it, had peeled the rind from a length of sugar-cane, which he had brought with him, and, when he done with it, he had laid it aside, without putting it back into its sheath. Then he had fallen to thinking of Mînang, of the soft, sweet words she had whispered to him in the dim firelight, of the look her face had worn when he told her of his love, and asked her to be his wife. The better to see her dear features on the retina of his mind, he had closed his eyes, and the craving for sleep, that the long watching during the previous night had brought to him, aiding the soft, warm midday air, in the fragrant forest, had lulled him to slumber before he even knew that he was drowsy.

He was rudely awakened—startled into a wide-eyed alertness without any previous gradation from sound sleep to intense clearness of perception—by his right arm, and the back of his neck being violently seized from behind. He could see nothing, for the vice-like grip on his neck kept his head immovable, but he felt that his assailant was not a wild animal, but a human being, for he could count the fingers that pressed into his flesh. The things which grasped him were *hands*, hard, bony, long-nailed *hands*, with palms rough as the hide of a skate, and with muscles of enormous power, but, none the less, the hands of a human being. Châling smelt a keen, pungent odour, like that of ill-kept swine, and, during that terrible moment—it seemed to him an age—while he could see nothing but had power to feel, with a keenness of fear, that he

had never before experienced, every tale of the Spectre-
Huntsman, of the Forest-Demons, of Giants and Ogres
and Devils and Spirits, that Châling had ever heard told
by the elders of his village, ran riot through his
frightened brain. Vainly he tried to screw his head
round one half inch, so that he might see the creature
behind him ; vainly he struggled to release his right
arm from the grip of the unseen hand that held it
drawn painfully back ; vainly he sought with his left
hand to reach the knife, whose blade shone amid the
carpet of brown dead leaves, with which the earth of
the forest is always strewn to a depth of many inches.
He could do nothing. The knife looked very near,
yet it was as hopelessly out of reach as it would have
been had the metal that formed its blade still lain
untouched in the bowels of the earth. Châling
stretched out a prehensile foot to grasp the knife,
for, like most Dyaks, he could on occasion pick a
sixpence off the ground with his toes, but he missed
it by a fraction, and the semblance to a bad dream
seemed now to be complete. All these actions, and
the hurrying thoughts that prompted them, occupied
fewer seconds than it is easy to conceive, for the mind
works with extraordinary rapidity when the stimulus
of deadly fear comes to aid it, and, at such times, the
limbs follow the dictates of the brain, even before the
soul of the man is well aware that a plan of any kind
has been formed in the mind.

A moment later, Châling felt himself lifted clear
from off his feet, hard held by neck and arm, in the
grip of hands that were still invisible to him. His
head was slightly depressed, and, in a flash, he saw the

sodden jungle leaf-carpet drop from under him, saw his feet dangling limply, saw the blade of his knife glisten where it lay, and heard his neck crack again, as the strain of supporting most of the weight of his body was put upon it. He was swung lightly upwards into the lower branches of a tree, resisting and struggling fiercely, but with as much effect as the efforts of a bird might have had to free itself from the grip of a hand that held it firmly. A pause followed, during which Châling's eyes started prominently from his head, and his breath came in hard, sobbing gasps. Then, once more he was swung upwards, and again upwards, until he found himself upon a huge bough, some fifty feet above the ground. He was not giddy, and he balanced himself instinctively upon the limb of the tree, on which he was now seated, for the Dyaks have never quite deserted the arboreal habits of the human race, and they are still as much at home among the branches and tree-tops, as is possible for a people who have learned to build huts upon the ground.

Then, suddenly, the grip upon his arm and neck relaxed, and, a moment later, two vast hairy arms were wound about his body, and a long, leathery face, like a human countenance covered with a taut mask fashioned from goldbeater's skin, was thrust forward over Châling's shoulder. The hair on the iron arms was red and shaggy; the hair on the head was a straggling mass of ruddy wires; the nails were horny tips to fingers that seemed made of steel; the thumbs were disproportionately small compared to the size of the rest of the hand; and the palms were rough and hard where they touched Châling, so that they rasped his flesh painfully. But it was the monster's face, which was thrust round to look at him, that filled Châling with a fear and a loathing that made him sick. It was the colour of bad parchment, with brutal creases and wrinkles, that seemed to mark every evil passion known to man. It measured nearly nine inches across, and the eyes set in it, under lowering brows and a low, narrow, animal forehead, were red and angry, and filled with a horrible eagerness. The small flat nose, with its two gaping nostrils, seemed to point upwards, and Châling found himself wondering whether the rain water fell into it, and thence into the interior of the beast's head, when the weather chanced to be wet. At a moment of the greatest mental tension, it is always the most trivial and incongruous thoughts that hurry through the mind. But it was the prominent, bestial mouth, the heavy brutal jaw, the long yellow fangs, and the dwarfing effect that the protruding muzzle had upon the rest of the face, that made Châling tremble with fear as the monster thrust its head forward against his cheek, and licked him with its rough hot tongue.

After this for a space, Châling remembered little. Later on, he had a confused recollection of climbing from tree to tree, and of making his way along a maze of branches, with the creature forcing him onwards, swinging him now upwards, now downwards, now back, now forward, and occasionally halting to crush him to its hairy breast in a horrible embrace that filled Châling with loathing, and drove the breath from his body, while his ribs cracked and groaned under the pressure. How far they travelled on this strange journey, Châling never knew, but, when the sun was beginning to sink, the captive found himself squatting disconsolately upon a bough, high up among the tree-tops, mechanically watching his keeper building a rude nest with a skill that seemed more than half human.

The tree, in which they were perched, was a giant of the forest, a good hundred feet of gray-white trunk separating its lower branches from the ground, which was densely covered with thick underwood. The brute had chosen the very highest point available, and it now sat breaking off large branches, with a sharp turn of its mighty wrist, and laying them across and across one another, until a rude platform, screened by the leaves, which still grew upon the severed boughs, had been constructed.

While the beast was working quickly and deftly at the construction of this nest, Châling had time to observe it more closely. It, or rather she, was a full-grown female Mais—an *òrang-útan*, to use the ludicrously misapplied Malay phrase, which has been embodied into European languages without reference to its proper meaning of 'jungle dweller,' and is usually given more vowels and consonants than it can possibly know what to do with. She measured nearly four feet in height, and the spread of her arms, from finger tip to finger tip, could not have been less than six feet. Her legs were disproportionately short, and this caused her to assume a semi-erect attitude as she moved about among the branches, now and again walking on all-fours with the knuckles and back of her hands, not the palms, serving as the soles of her front feet. Every now and then she paused in her work to cock an evil, cunning, brutal eye at Châling, and, though he longed for escape, as he had never before longed for anything, he knew that any attempt at flight would be useless while that ugly glance was upon him. She was very quiet even in her movements and never once did she articulate a sound; and this complete silence, in a creature so strangely, hideously human, filled Châling with an added dread, for which he found it difficult to account.

When her work was completed, the Mais put out a leisurely arm, and, seizing Châling in an iron grip, swung him into the nest without visible effort. Then she threw herself down by his side, and pressed him fiercely against her great hairy body. Her limbs wound about him, crushing him with a strength of which their owner was quite unconscious. The rough, shaggy masses of hair forced their way into Châling's mouth and throat, choking him, and causing him to cough painfully. The reek of the beast filled his nostrils with a horrible odour, and the black jungle ticks, with which she was covered, began to swarm over the thin-skinned body of the man. Châling felt no hunger, for fear takes all longing from a man's stomach, but his throat was parched with thirst, and, since he dared not attempt to creep away to the brook, which he heard babbling through the forest beneath him, he was fain to lick the dew from the leaves around the nest. The Mais was an uneasy bedfellow, for she constantly woke up, or changed her grip upon her victim, and now and again she tore at her hairy hide with an energy that set the tree-top rocking. At such times Châling would be nearly thrown out of the nest, and, long before morning, he was black and blue with the bruises received from the beast's jerking elbows. While she was awake, her attentions to the man were unremitting, and Châling was driven to a state bordering upon frenzy, by her horrible blandishments, and by the acute physical pain which her clutching grip caused him. None the less, exhausted nature would have its way, and Châling slept fitfully upon his rough couch, and, for a space, till the inevitable nightmare seized him, he was able to forget the miseries of his horrible slavery.

The dawn-wind, faintly breathing over the forest, was gently swaying the tree-tops when Châling finally awoke, and the first thing that he saw was the hideous head of the Mais pillowed upon his shoulder, blinking sleepy, bleary eyes at him, through a tangle of sparse red hair. To Châling the beast represented all the Fates and Furies rolled into one, and, when the full horror of his helplessness broke freshly upon him, he burst into a passion of weeping. The Mais snuggled up against him, blowing hot, fetid breaths over his face, and licking his cheeks, till they were sore, with her rough, feverish tongue. Then she began picking the ticks off him, causing him intense pain, for these crab-shaped insects drive their prongs into nerve centres, and any attempt to remove them by force is an agony. Soon sharp despairing cries mingled with Châling's sobs and tears, and, at length, in a fit of utter recklessness, he struck the Mais full in the face. As his hand clapped upon her leathery countenance, Châling felt more keenly than ever how completely impotent his little strength was against this hairy giantess. The Mais snarled, and showed her teeth.

S

Then she apparently came to the conclusion that this was a game, and presently the flat of her iron hand told loudly on the man's tender face. It was a stunning blow, though she only struck half-handedly, without any attempt at real violence, and Châling's one eye was almost closed by it, and then came large purple bruises, swelling rapidly, so that his face was soon a shapeless, discoloured mass.

Then Châling cowered down upon the rude platform, and moaned aloud, and the Mais pawed him mercilessly, with rasping hands, much as a child treats a favourite and long-suffering kitten.

Later, when the sun began to rise, the Mais set off on her daily roaming through the forest. She moved along at a leisurely pace, swinging from tree to tree, walking along branches, but always keeping at some distance from the ground, and she took Châling with her wherever she went. The pinch of hunger was gripping him now, and his mind dwelt most insistently on the fat rice, and roots, the rich pork, and the fish, and the condiments, which he knew were that day cooking, in the house of Mînang's parents. His heart, no doubt, was very much in Mînang's keeping, but his stomach was a free agent, and it stimulated his imagination into constantly conjuring up alluring visions of the sweet human viands for which his whole being now craved unceasingly. The Mais seemed to feed upon almost every fruit that grew, but she appeared to be specially addicted to those which were most sour, acrid, and astringent. Hunger drove Châling to partake of such food as the Mais permitted him to approach, and it must be confessed that he made the acquaintance of

more unpleasant tastes, during the time that he was
with her, than he had hitherto known to exist in all
the world. But Châling's sufferings did not end here.
The Mais never bathed in the streams which, every
now and again, Châling could see glistening below
them, as he looked downwards through the tree-tops,
and often, for days together, she never drank at all.
The unfortunate Châling was forced to do what the
Mais regarded as right and proper, wherefore he had
to slake his thirst as best he could, by lapping up the
water he occasionally found lying in the hollows of
trees, and in other similar uncleanly places. For the
rest, he sucked the dew-drenched leaves that, at night-
time, formed his bed-curtains, and prayed fervently, to
every Demon in the Dyak Mythology, for deliverance
from his terrible slavery.

Châling never knew clearly how long his captivity
lasted. It seemed to him that the whole of his life
had been spent in wandering through the forest, with
his horrible companion. Ever since he could remember anything at all, so he sometimes thought, his
bones had been racked with aches, his skin had been
covered with abrasions, his stomach had been consumed
with importunate longings for food, and his heart filled
with a wild desire for escape. It would not have been
so difficult to bear, if only the Mais had not been
so horribly, so clumsily attentive to him. Doubtless,
with the kindest of intentions, she insisted upon
forcing the most repulsive objects down the man's
unwilling throat, nearly strangling him the while with
the brawny grip she fixed upon his neck. When she
waxed playful, and she was often a most hilarious

creature, she was really the worst of company, for she had no notion of her own strength, and she bruised and tore the man's soft body, with a cruel indifference to the sufferings which she occasioned. She travelled through the jungle in a very leisurely fashion, sometimes spending an hour or more upon one tree, before quitting it for the next, and thus Chǎling, as he sat huddled up on a bough, like a sick bird, had many hours at his disposal during which to mourn over the hardness of his lot, and to plan wholly impracticable schemes of revenge, and of escape.

One day, the Mais dragged Chǎling down to the ground, at a spot where there was a large brake of bamboos, and began tearing up the great round stems, in order to get at the edible shoots. Her giant hands rent the shrieking bamboos, with as much ease as a child might rend long grass, and Chǎling, watching her sullenly, saw herein the chance for which he was always looking. He had long ago abandoned as hopeless all idea of saving himself by flight, for the Mais, he knew, had the legs of him in the jungle, and, since he had no weapon, he could do nothing to render her unable to pursue him. But, in the shivered bamboos, Chǎling thought that he saw, at last, a means of supplying himself with a fairly good substitute for a knife. He knew that the edge of a newly split bamboo is as keen as tempered steel, and, in the wreckage around him, he had a wide choice of weapons. He selected two long splinters, which particularly commended themselves to him on account of their superior strength and sharpness, and, when, late in the afternoon, the Mais quitted the bamboo-brake, and again ascended into the trees, Châling carried the two fragments of wood, held cross-wise in his mouth, as he climbed.

The Mais made the hut-like nest, as usual, and, as the night drew on, she composed herself to sleep, under the covering of *pandanus* leaves with which she sometimes provided herself, for the purpose. Châling lay very still, feigning sleep, until the heavy breathing of the unclean monster, at his side, showed him that the Mais was slumbering profoundly. Then, moving with extreme caution, he sat up, and very gently raised the *pandanus* leaf from the beast's face. The moon was near the full, and the pale rays, struggling through the canopy of foliage overhead, showed Châling the face of the sleeping brute, as clearly as if it had been day. The Mais lay upon her back, with arms and legs extended widely, and her hideous, leathery face looked strangely and most repulsively human. Her mouth was wide open, and her evil-smelling breath came in heavy snoring grunts, like that of a drunken man. Châling looked at her very carefully, for he knew that everything depended upon no mistake being made, at this critical moment. Like all jungle-dwellers, the Dyak had a fair working knowledge of anatomy, and he was anxious to make the incision he contemplated in the exactly correct spot. For perhaps five minutes, Châling sat thus gazing at the upturned face of the Mais, and gently running his light fingers along the surface of the creature's extended throat. Then, suddenly, putting out all his force, he drew the keen edge of the bamboo swiftly and firmly across the beast's neck, severing the jugular artery. The bamboo knife was so sharp that, as is the case when a cut is a very clean one, the Mais, for the moment, did not feel a pang; and Châling had time to drop over the edge of the nest-platform, before the creature was fairly awake. Then the Mais leaped up, and started in pursuit. A warm jet of blood burst downwards as the animal looked over the edge of the nest at the descending man, and the pungent, reeking stream struck Châling full in the face, temporarily blinding him. He could hear the Mais crashing through the branches above him, and giving vent to sick, thick coughs. He could hear all the noises of the jungle night plainly and distinctly, but for a moment he could see nothing. He was now in an agony of fear, and terror lent speed to his descent. Hardly knowing how he did it, he half climbed, half fell through the branches, and never paused until he felt the solid earth once more beneath his feet. He halted then, for an instant, but the sounds overhead, that told him that the Mais was in pursuit, soon drove him again into headlong panic-stricken flight.

All that night, and all the next day, Châling made his way through the forest, until, in the fulness of time, he came out upon a track, which he recognised as one that led to a village with which he was acquainted. He spent the night in this place, and, after eating as he had never eaten before, and obtaining the loan of some old clothes, he next day pushed forward to his own village.

On his arrival here, he at once sought the Headman, and reported to him the extraordinary misfortune of which he had been the victim. He came in time to save Mînang from the suicide which, as befitted a well-educated Dyak girl, she had been by way of contemplating, ever since her lover failed to put in an appearance at the marriage feast, but his future parents-in-law were not to be so easily satisfied. The immutable Dyak customs provide punishment by fine for recalcitrant *fiancés*, and no excuse can be accepted in extenuation or mitigation of the offence. Thus it came about that the luckless Châling found his sojourn with the Mais almost as expensive as it had been unpleasant. It was in vain that he pleaded that he had been the victim of circumstances over which he had had no control; for, as the Headman shrewdly remarked, all the young men in the Dyak country would be running away with the beasts of the forest, if thereby they might avoid paying the price of their infidelities. The girls of the village did their best to shame Mînang out of marrying Châling, but in this attempt they failed. What did it matter to her, she said, that Châling should have been forced to mate with a Mais, whom he assured her that he had never loved? Was it not yet one more proof of his beauty and attractiveness that even the animals in the jungle fell in love with him at first sight? And would not these other girls, who jeered at her, willingly forsake their own miserable men-folk, if thereby they might win Châling for themselves? So Mînang and Châling were married, with great state, in accordance with the ancient Dyak custom and ritual, and their after years were probably of little interest to any one except themselves. The *Pênghûlu* of the Dyaks, when he told me the story, said that he could remember Châling, who was then a very old man, being pointed out to him, in the far off days, when the *Pěnghûlu* himself was a child, and, so far as he could recollect, there was nothing remarkable in his appearance. That is the worst of your hero of romance ;—he is usually so very commonplace to look at.

THE END

Printed by R. & R. CLARK, LIMITED, *Edinburgh.*

BY THE SAME AUTHOR.

IN COURT AND KAMPONG:

Being Tales and Sketches of Native Life in the
Malay Peninsula.

By HUGH CLIFFORD

British Resident at Pahang.

Large Crown 8vo.   Cloth.   7s. 6d.

The Athenæum.—"The chief aim is to portray character, to reveal to the European thoughts, passions, and aspirations which unfold themselves but slowly even to him who for long years has lived the life of his Asiatic associates in places remote from the sound of Western civilisation. . . . In this effort Mr. Clifford has achieved a considerable success; and as he writes also in a bright style, which has a distinctly literary flavour, his work is not less welcome for the information which it gives than interesting as a story-book."

The Speaker.—"Mr. Clifford undoubtedly possesses the gift of graphic description in a high degree, and each one of these stories grips the reader's attention most insistently.   The whole book is alive with drama and passion; but, as we have said, its greatest charm lies in the fact that it paints in strikingly minute detail a state of things which, whether for good or ill, is rapidly vanishing from the face of the earth."

The Saturday Review.—"The chapters dealing with 'The East Coast' and 'Among Fisher Folk' have rarely, if ever, been surpassed as word-pictures."

The Pall Mall Gazette.—"These tales Mr. Clifford tells with a force and life-likeness such as is only to be equalled in the stories of Rudyard Kipling.   Take, for instance, the gruesome story of the were-tiger, man by day and man-eater by night. . . . Every one of these tales leaves its impression, dramatic yet lifelike.   Moreover, they are valuable as giving a picture of strange, distorted civilisation which, under the influence of British residents and officials, will soon pass away or hide itself jealously from the gaze of Western eyes."

The Glasgow Herald.—"Mr. Clifford's book is very welcome, and we cordially recommend it for glimpses of strange ways of life and thought in a far-off corner of the world."

Mr. T. P. O'Connor in *The Weekly Sun.*—"Mr. Clifford's book is the key to a great, new, and intensely interesting kingdom of human beings and human emotions."

The Birmingham Daily Gazette.—"Has not only the charms of excellent style, and quiet humour, but also the rarer attractions of complete novelty."

St. James's Budget.—"This book has an indescribable fascination that holds the reader enchanted . . . and many people will turn again and again to these pages that are instinct with life and actuality."

GRANT RICHARDS, 9 HENRIETTA STREET,
COVENT GARDEN, W.C.

I

2

"OLD MAN'S" MARRIAGE.

By G. B. BURGIN.

Crown 8vo.　Cloth.　6s.

The Times.—"There is none to vie with Miss Wilks. It is a strong thing to say that this female is the most interesting specimen of her class that has ever been portrayed in fiction, but it is literally true."

The Speaker.—"Temperaments and incidents are deftly interwoven, and Mr. Burgin may be congratulated upon having produced one of those books which are not only entertaining in themselves, but which leave a good taste in the mouths of their readers."

The Standard.—"Mr. Burgin's best qualities come to the front in ' "Old Man's" Marriage.' . . . Miss Wilkes has nearly as much individuality as any one in the story, which is saying a good deal, for reality seems to gather round all the characters in spite of the romance that belongs to them as well . . . the story is fresh and full of charm."

The Daily Telegraph.—"Mr. Burgin's humour is both shrewd and kindly, and his book should prove as welcome as a breath of fresh air to the weary readers of realistic fiction."

Mr. COULSON KERNAHAN, in the *Star.*—" ' "Old Man's" Marriage' is told with such humour, high-spirit, simplicity, and straightforwardness that the reader is amused and entertained from the first page to the last. Once I had begun it I had to go on to the end ; when I put it down it was with a sigh to part with such excellent company. . . . As thoroughly enjoyable and racily written a story as has been published for a long time."

Manchester Guardian.—" It would be difficult to speak too highly of the delicate pathos and humour of this beautiful sketch of a choice friendship in humble life. . . . A study at once simple and subtle and full of the dignity and sincerity of natural man."

Birmingham Gazette.—"We pant for more books like ' "Old Man's" Marriage,' and we hope our thirst may soon be assuaged."

Daily Mail.—"The gem of the book is the mule. Never since the days of Rosinante was any animal so tenderly dealt with in fiction. Even Stevenson's Modestine did not get her whim studied and her temperament psychologically analysed as does this wonderful Miss Wilkes."

The Spectator.—"'Old Man' is a particularly admirable person, and 'Miss Wilkes,' his mule, is a worthy companion. We know no more entertaining animal in all the *fauna* of fiction. Mr. Burgin has a very pretty gift of humour."

By the same Author—THE CATTLE-MAN.　6s.

GRANT RICHARDS, 9 HENRIETTA STREET,
COVENT GARDEN, W.C.

Mr. GRANT RICHARDS'S PUBLICATIONS.

GRANT ALLEN.

AN AFRICAN MILLIONAIRE: Episodes in the Life of the Illustrious Colonel Clay. With over 60 Illustrations, by GORDON BROWNE. Crown 8vo. Cloth. 6s. *[Eighth Thousand.*

THE EVOLUTION OF THE IDEA OF GOD: An Inquiry into the Origins of Religions. Demy 8vo. Cloth. 20s. net.

LAURENCE ALMA TADEMA.

REALMS OF UNKNOWN KINGS: Poems. Fcap. 8vo. Paper Covers. 2s. net. Buckram. 3s. net.

A. G. B. ATKINSON, M.A.

ST. BOTOLPH, ALDGATE: The Story of a City Parish. Compiled from the Record Books and other ancient documents, with a Supplementary Chapter by the Vicar. Crown 8vo. Cloth. 5s. net.

EDWARD CLODD.

PIONEERS OF EVOLUTION FROM THALES TO HUXLEY, with an Intermediate Chapter on the Causes of Arrest of the Movement. With Portraits in photogravure of Charles Darwin, Professor Huxley, Mr. A. R. Wallace, and Mr. Herbert Spencer. Crown 8vo. Linen. 5s. net. *[Second Edition.*

GEORGE FLEMING.

LITTLE STORIES ABOUT WOMEN. Crown 8vo. Cloth. 3s. 6d.

R. MURRAY GILCHRIST.

A PEAKLAND FAGGOT: Tales told of Milton Folk. Fcap. 8vo. Cloth. 2s. 6d.

LAURENCE HOUSMAN.

SPIKENARD: A Book of Devotional Love-Poems. With Cover designed by the Author. Small 4to. Gilt. Paper Boards. 3s. 6d. net.

VICTOR HUGO.

HERNANI: A Drama translated into English, with an Introduction by R. FARQUHARSON SHARP. Small 4to. Paper Boards. 3s. 6d. net.

EDWARD VERRALL LUCAS.

A BOOK OF VERSES FOR CHILDREN: An Anthology. With Cover, Title-page, and end-papers designed in colours by F. D. BEDFORD. Crown 8vo. Cloth. 6s. *[Third Edition.*

GRANT RICHARDS, 9 HENRIETTA STREET, COVENT GARDEN, W.C.

DUMPY BOOKS FOR CHILDREN.

1. THE FLAMP, THE AMELIORATOR, and THE SCHOOLBOY'S APPRENTICE: Three Stories. By EDWARD VERRALL LUCAS.

2. MRS. TURNER'S CAUTIONARY STORIES. Edited by EDWARD VERRALL LUCAS. With end-papers designed by Mrs. FARMILOE. 18mo. Cloth. 1s. 6d. each.

VERNON LEE.

LIMBO AND OTHER ESSAYS: with Frontispiece. Fcap. 8vo. Buckram. 5s. net.

MRS. PERCY LEAKE.

THE ETHICS OF BROWNING'S POEMS. With Introduction by the BISHOP OF WINCHESTER. Fcap. 8vo. Cloth. 2s. 6d.

EUGENE LEE-HAMILTON.

THE INFERNO OF DANTE TRANSLATED INTO ENGLISH VERSE. Fcap. 8vo. Cloth. 5s. net.

RICHARD LE GALLIENNE.

RUBAIYAT OF OMAR KHAYYAM: A Paraphrase from several Literal Translations. From the press of Messrs. T. and A. Constable of Edinburgh. Long Fcap. 8vo. Parchment Cover. 5s.

A LIFE OF THE PRINCE.

H.R.H. THE PRINCE OF WALES: An Account of his Career, including his Birth, Education, Travels, Marriage and Home Life; and Philanthropic, Social, and Political Work. Royal 8vo. Cloth. 10s. 6d. With 100 Portraits and other Illustrations.

MAURICE MAETERLINCK.

AGLAVAINE AND SELYSETTE: A Drama in Five Acts. Translated by ALFRED SUTRO. With Introduction by J. W. MACKAIL, and Title-page designed by W. H. MARGETSON. Globe 8vo. Half-buckram. 2s. 6d. net.

LEONARD MERRICK.

ONE MAN'S VIEW: A Novel. Crown 8vo. Cloth. 3s. 6d.

THE ACTOR-MANAGER: A Novel. Crown 8vo. Cloth. 6s.

ALICE MEYNELL.

THE FLOWER OF THE MIND: A Choice among the best Poems. With Cover designed by LAURENCE HOUSMAN. Crown 8vo. Buckram. 6s.

GRANT RICHARDS, 9 HENRIETTA STREET,
COVENT GARDEN, W.C.

W. T. STEAD.

REAL GHOST STORIES. Crown 8vo. Cloth. 5s.

W. J. STILLMAN.

THE OLD ROME AND THE NEW, AND OTHER STUDIES.
Crown 8vo. Cloth. 5s.

WILL ROTHENSTEIN.

ENGLISH PORTRAITS: A Series of Lithographed Drawings.
With short Texts by Various Hands. In twelve parts, each in
a wrapper designed by the Artist. 2s. 6d. each net.

MARIE AND ROBERT LEIGHTON.

CONVICT 99: A Novel. With eight full-page Illustrations by
STANLEY L. WOOD. Crown 8vo. Cloth. 3s. 6d.

HELMUTH SCHWARTZE.

THE LAUGHTER OF JOVE: A Novel. With Cover designed by
W. H. HORTON. Crown 8vo. Cloth. 6s.

EDWARD SPENCER ("Nathaniel Gubbins").

CAKES AND ALE: A Memory of Many Meals; the whole interspersed with various recipes, more or less original, and anecdotes,
mainly veracious. With Cover designed by PHIL MAY. Small
4to. Cloth. 5s. [*Third Edition.*

LOUISA SHORE.

HANNIBAL: A Drama. Crown 8vo. Cloth. 5s. net.

LAURENCE BINYON.

PORPHYRION, AND OTHER POEMS. Crown 8vo. Buckram.
5s. net.

FREDERIC BRETON.

TRUE HEART: A Novel. Crown 8vo. Cloth. 6s.

GRANT RICHARDS, 9 HENRIETTA STREET,
COVENT GARDEN, W.C.

GEORGE EGERTON.

THE WHEEL OF GOD: A Novel. Crown 8vo. Cloth. 6s.

HALDANE MACFALL.

THE BLACK VAGABOND: A Novel. Crown 8vo. Cloth. 6s.

MARTIN LEACH WARBOROUGH.

TOM, UNLIMITED: A Story for Children. With Fifty Illustrations by GERTRUDE BRADLEY. Globe 8vo. Cloth. 5s.

GEORGE BERNARD SHAW.

PLAYS PLEASANT AND UNPLEASANT. With Portrait of the Author. Two vols. 5s. each.

BECKLES WILLSON.

THE TENTH ISLAND: Being some Account of Newfoundland, its People, its Politics, and its Peculiarities. With an Introduction by Sir WILLIAM WHITEWAY, K.C.M.G., Premier of the Colony, and an Appendix by Lord CHARLES BERESFORD. With Map. Globe 8vo. Buckram. 3s. 6d.

R. S. WARREN BELL.

THE CUB IN LOVE: In Twelve Twinges. With six additional Stories. With Cover designed by MAURICE GREIFFENHAGEN. Tauchnitz Size. Paper Cover. 1s. 6d. Copies also obtainable in cloth. 2s.

THE ETHICS OF THE SURFACE SERIES.

By GORDON SEYMOUR. 16 mo. Buckram. 2s. each.

1. THE RUDENESS OF THE HONOURABLE MR. LEATHERHEAD.
2. A HOMBURG STORY.
3. CUI BONO?

GRANT RICHARDS, 9 HENRIETTA STREET, COVENT GARDEN, W.C.

CATALOGUE OF BOOKS PUBLISHED by Mr. GRANT RICHARDS AT 9 HENRI-ETTA STREET, COVENT GARDEN, LONDON.

This List includes Books by Grant Allen, Miss Alma Tadema, G. B. Burgin, Edward Clodd, George Egerton, George Fleming, R. Murray Gilchrist, Vernon Lee, Eugene Lee-Hamilton, Richard le Gallienne, Maurice Maeterlinck, Leonard Merrick, Mrs. Meynell, Will Rothenstein, G. Bernard Shaw, W. T. Stead, W. J. Stillman, and Sidney Webb.

For the convenience of Booksellers a List of these Books classified according to price appears at the end of the Catalogue.

ALLEN, GRANT.

The Evolution of the Idea of God : an Inquiry into the Origins of Religions. Demy 8vo. Cloth. 20s. net.

Grant Allen's Historical Guides :

Paris.   [*Ready.*

Florence.   ,,

The Cities of Belgium.   ,,

Venice.   [*In preparation.*

Rome.   ,,

Fcap. 8vo.   Cloth.   3s. 6d. each, net.

" Good work in the way of showing students the right manner of approaching the history of a great city. . . . These useful little volumes."—*Times.*

" Those who travel for the sake of culture will be well catered for in Mr. Grant Allen's new series of historical guides. . . . There are few more satisfactory books for a student who wishes to dig out the Paris of the past from the immense super-incumbent mass of coffee-houses, kiosks, fashionable hotels, and other temples of civilisation, beneath which it is now submerged. Florence is more easily dug up, as you have only to go into the picture galleries, or into the churches or museums, whither Mr. Allen's guide accordingly conducts you, and tells you what to look at if you want to understand the art treasures of the city. The books, in a word, explain rather than describe. Such books are wanted nowadays. . . . The more sober-minded among tourists will be grateful to him for the skill with which the new series promises to minister to their needs."—*Scotsman.*

" Mr. Grant Allen, as a traveller of thirty-five years experience in foreign lands, is well qualified to command success in the task he has set himself, and nothing in the two volumes under notice is more striking than the strong sense conveyed of his powers of observation and the facility with which he describes the objects of art and the architectural glories which he has met and lingered over. . . . It would be a pity indeed were his assiduous researches and the fruits of his immense experience, now so happily exemplified, to pass unnoticed either by 'globe trotters' or by students of art and history who have perforce to stay at home."—*Daily Telegraph.*

" No traveller going to Florence with any idea of understanding its art treasures, can afford to dispense with Mr. Grant Allen's guide. He is so saturated with information gained by close observation and close study. He is so candid, so sincere, so fearless, so interesting, and his little book is so portable and so pretty."—*Queen.*

" That much abused class of people, the tourists, have often been taunted with their ignorance and want of culture, and the perfunctory manner in which they hurry through, and 'do' the Art Galleries of Europe. There is a large amount of truth, no doubt, but they might very well retort on their critics that no one had come forward to meet their wants, or assist in dispelling their ignorance. No doubt there are guide-books, very excellent ones in their way, but on all matters of art very little better than mere indices ; something fuller was required to enable the average man intelligently to appreciate the treasures submitted to his view. Mr. Grant Allen has offered to meet their wants, and offers these handbooks to the public at a price that ought to be with-in the reach of every one who can afford to travel at all. The idea is a good one, and should insure the success which Mr. Allen deserves."—*Morning Post.*

" Not only admirable, but also, to the intelligent tourist, indispensable. . . . Mr. Allen has the artistic temperament. . . . With his origins, his traditions, his art criticisms, he goes to the heart of the matter, is outspoken concerning those things he despises, and earnest when describing those in which his soul delights. . . . *The books are genuinely interesting to the ordinary reader, whether he have travelled or not, and unlike the ordinary guide-book may be read with advantage both before and after the immediate occasion of their use.*"—*Birmingham Gazette.*

An African Millionaire : Episodes in the Life of the Illustrious Colonel Clay. With over Sixty Illustrations by Gordon Browne. Crown 8vo. Cloth. 6s. [*Fifth Edition.*

"It is not often that the short story of this class can be made as attractive and as exciting as are many of the Colonel's episodes. Let us be thankful for these, and hasten to commend 'An African Millionaire' to the notice of all travellers. We can imagine no book of the season more suitable for an afternoon in a hammock or a lazy day in the woods. And the capital illustrations help an excellent dozen of stories on their way."—*Daily Chronicle.*

"For resourcefulness, for sardonic humour, for a sense of the comedy of the situation, and for pluck to carry it through, it would be difficult to find a more entertaining scoundrel than Colonel Clay."—*Daily News.*

"A volume which, excepting to those devoid of humour, will have afforded some wholly genuine amusement."—*Morning Post.*

"The interest of the book never flags, and it is perfectly clean and wholesome, no book of detective stories could be more suited for drawing-room reading."—*Queen.*

"When Mr. Grant Allen is not elevating the human mind, but only instructing or amusing it, one knows few pleasanter writers. He is equally at home with the scientific essay, or the short story, and by no means holds a back seat as a novelist. This book is a good example of his talents. It is only a collection of tales describing how a very rich man is again and again victimised by the same adventurer, but it has not only plenty of dramatic incident, but of shrewd and wise reflection, such as is seldom found in the modern novel."—Mr. JAMES PAYN, in the *Illustrated London News.*

ALMA TADEMA, LAURENCE.

Realms of Unknown Kings : Poems. Fcap. 8vo. Paper Covers. 2s. net. Buckram. 3s. net.

BELL, R. S. WARREN.

(*See* Henrietta Volumes.)

BURGIN, G. B.

"Old Man's" Marriage : A Novel. (A Sequel to "The Judge of the Four Corners.") Crown 8vo. Cloth. 6s.

"Mr. Burgin's best qualities come to the front in '"Old Man's" Marriage.' . . . Miss Wilkes has nearly as much individuality as any one in the story, which is saying a good deal, for reality seems to gather round all the characters in spite of the romance that belongs to them as well . . . the story is fresh and full of charm."—*Standard.*

"Mr. Burgin's humour is both shrewd and kindly, and his book should prove as welcome as a breath of fresh air to the weary readers of realistic fiction."—*Daily Telegraph.*

"'Old Man's' Marriage is told with such humour, high-spirit, simplicity, and straightforwardness that the reader is amused and entertained from the first page to the last. Once I had begun it I had to go on to the end; when I put it down it was with a sigh to part with such excellent company. . . . As thoroughly enjoyable and racily written a story as has been published for a long time."—Mr. COULSON KERNAHAN in the *Star.*

"It would be difficult to speak too highly of the delicate pathos and humour of this beautiful sketch of a choice friendship in humble life. . . . A study at once simple and subtle and full of the dignity and sincerity of natural man."—*Manchester Guardian.*

CLIFFORD, HUGH (British Resident at Pahang).

In Court and Kampong: being Tales and Sketches of Native Life in the Malay Peninsula. Large Crown 8vo. Cloth. 7s. 6d.

"The chief aim is to portray character, to reveal to the European thoughts, passions, and aspirations which unfold themselves but slowly even to him who for long years has lived the life of his Asiatic associates in places remote from the sound of western civilisation. . . . In this effort Mr. Clifford has achieved a considerable success; and as he writes also in a bright style, which has a distinctly literary flavour, his work is not less welcome for the information which it gives than interesting as a story-book."—*Athenæum*.

"Mr. Clifford undoubtedly possesses the gift of graphic description in a high degree, and each one of these stories grips the reader's attention most insistently. The whole book is alive with drama and passion; but, as we have said, its greatest charm lies in the fact that it paints in strikingly minute detail a state of things which, whether for good or ill, is rapidly vanishing from the face of the earth."—*Speaker*.

"These tales Mr. Clifford tells with a force and life-likeness such as is only to be equalled in the stories of Rudyard Kipling. Take, for instance, the gruesome story of the were-tiger, man by day and man-eater by night. . . . Every one of these tales leaves its impression, dramatic yet lifelike. Moreover, they are valuable as giving a picture of strange, distorted civilisation which, under the influence of British residents and officials, will soon pass away or hide itself jealously from the gaze of Western eyes."—*Pall Mall Gazette*.

CLODD, EDWARD.

Pioneers of Evolution from Thales to Huxley, with an intermediate chapter on the Causes of Arrest of the Movement. With portraits in photogravure of Charles Darwin, Professor Huxley, Mr. A. R. Wallace, and Mr. Herbert Spencer. Crown 8vo. Linen. 5s. net. [*Second Edition.*

"We are always glad to meet Mr. Edward Clodd. He is never dull; he is always well informed, and he says what he has to say with clearness and incision. . . . The interest intensifies as Mr. Clodd attempts to show the part really played in the growth of the doctrine of evolution by men like Wallace, Darwin, Huxley, and Spencer. Mr. Clodd clears away prevalent misconceptions as to the work of these modern pioneers. Especially does he give to Mr. Spencer the credit which is his due, but which is often mistakenly awarded to Darwin. Mr. Clodd does not seek in the least to lower Darwin from the lofty pedestal which he rightly occupies; he only seeks to show precisely why he deserves to occupy such a position. We commend the book to those who want to know what evolution really means; but they should be warned beforehand that they have to tackle strong meat."—*Times*.

"The goal to which Mr. Clodd leads us in so masterly a fashion in the present volume is but the starting-point of fresh achievements, and, in due course, fresh theories. His book furnishes an important contribution to a liberal education."—*Daily Chronicle*.

"There is no better book on the subject for a general reader, and while its matter is largely familiar to professed students of science, and indeed to most men who are well read, no one could go through the book without being both refreshed and newly instructed by its masterly survey of the growth of the most powerful idea of modern times."—*Scotsman*.

DUMPY BOOKS FOR CHILDREN.

1. **The Flamp, the Ameliorator, and the Schoolboy's Apprentice: Three Stories.** By Edward Verrall Lucas.

2. **Mrs. Turner's Cautionary Stories.** Edited, with a Chapter on Bad and Good Children, by Edward Verrall Lucas.
With end-papers designed by Mrs. Farmiloe. 18mo. Cloth. 1s. 6d. each.

EGERTON, GEORGE.

Detached: a Novel. Crown 8vo. Cloth. 6s.
[*In preparation.*

ETHICS OF THE SURFACE SERIES.

1. **The Rudeness of the Honourable Mr. Leatherhead.**
2. **A Homburg Story.**
3. **Cui Bono.**

By Gordon Seymour. 16mo. Buckram. 2s. each.

"The stories are remarkable for their originality, their careful characterisation, their genuine thoughtfulness, and the sincerity of their purpose. They certainly open up a fresh field of thought on the problems set by the philosopher of the superficial, problems which, though they seem to lie on the surface, strike their roots deep down into human life; and they make us think for ourselves (though perhaps somewhat gropingly), which is more than can be said for the general run of modern novels."—*Pall Mall Gazette.*

"An able and well written little bit of fiction. . . . Amongst the short descriptive portions of the book there are some excellent examples of graceful prose, and if the dialogues occasionally resolve themselves into disquisitions on life and society too elaborate for the reader who is chiefly concerned to get the story, they will repay the reader who can appreciate the analysis of delicate shades of thought and feeling.' —*Aberdeen Free Press.*

"The book is altogether an ingenious one, and is also interesting as being a kind of modern revival of the old-time 'moral tales' and other old-fashioned ways of combining instruction with entertainment."—*Perthshire Advertiser.*

FLEMING, GEORGE.

Little Stories about Women. Crown 8vo. Cloth. 3s. 6d.

"All novel readers must welcome the decision which has caused these stories, many of which are gems, to appear in volume form. . . . Story is hardly the name to employ in the case of these impressionist pictures. They have the suggestive merit of the school and none of its vagueness."—*Morning Post.*

"It is impossible to read 'Little Stories about Women' without a feeling of blank astonishment that their author should be so very little more than a name to the reading public. . . . It is difficult to imagine anything better in its way—and its way is thoroughly modern and up to date—than the first of the collection, 'By Accident.' It is very short, very terse, but the whole story is suggested with admirable art. There is nothing unfinished about it, and the grip with which the carriage accident which opens it is presented never relaxes."—*World.*

GILCHRIST, R. MURRAY.

(*See* Sylvan Series.)

6

HENRIETTA VOLUMES, THE

The Cub in Love: in Twelve Twinges; with Six additional Stories. By R. S. Warren Bell. With Cover by Maurice Greiffenhagen. Tauchnitz size. 1s. 6d. (*Copies also obtainable in Cloth.* 2s.)

"Light and amusing withal is Mr. Warren Bell's sketch of a very young man suffering from the bitter-sweet of an unrequited affection. . . . The Cub seems to be a near relation of Dolly (of the 'Dolly Dialogues'), and the sprightliness of his dialogue makes him worthy of the kinship."—*Pall Mall Gazette.*

"Under the title 'The Cub in Love' Mr. Grant Richards sends out the first of a series of light stories to be styled 'The Henrietta Volumes.' The writer is Mr. R. S. Warren Bell, and his bright colloquial style, lightened by flashes of wit and abundant humour, makes this story of the love-sickness of a healthy well-to-do young Englishman infinitely entertaining. . . . The book makes excellent reading for travelling or a holiday, or, indeed, for any occasion on which amusement is the thing desired. If the subsequent volumes of the Henrietta series are up to this standard, there need be no question of their success."—*Scotsman.*

"This is one of the most brightly written books we have read for some time. . . . We cannot conceive a more enjoyable book for a couple of hours' reading at the seaside."—*Belfast Evening Telegraph.*

H.R.H. the Prince of Wales: an Account of His Career, including his Birth, Education, Travels, Marriage and Home Life, and Philanthropic, Social, and Political Work. Royal 8vo. Cloth. 7s. 6d. With over Sixty Portraits and other Illustrations.

LEAKE, MRS. PERCY.

The Ethics of Browning's Poems. With Introduction by the Bishop of Winchester. Fcap. 8vo. Cloth. 2s. 6d.

LEE, VERNON.

Limbo and other Essays: with Frontispiece. Fcap. 8vo. Buckram. 5s. net.

"The brilliant and versatile writer who adopts the pseudonym of Vernon Lee affords a dainty feast to her readers in this charming little volume."—*Times.*

"For charm, that 'delicate and capricious foster-child of leisure,' Vernon Lee's latest work, small as it is, is the equal of anything that she has yet produced."—*Morning Post.*

"This little volume might be called a manual of the cultivated soul adventuring among masterpieces of art and natural beauties. It brings to the enjoyment of these a power of association which traverses seas and years, and refreshes the mind with images summoned from the recesses of memory. They are pitched in a pleasant conversational way, frankly, even daringly, personal, and are strewn with vivid descriptions of Italian scenes and places. . . . A quiet strain of genuine feeling and genuine discernment runs through these essays, and it would be thankless to deny their charm as companions for a summer afternoon."—*Manchester Guardian.*

"'Limbo and other Essays' is amongst the most welcome of recent books. . . . Few essayists see so many beautiful things as Vernon Lee, and fewer still, having seen them, say so many beautiful things about them."—Mr. RICHARD LE GALLIENNE in the *Star.*

7

LEE-HAMILTON, EUGENE.

The Inferno of Dante translated into English Verse. Fcap. 8vo. Cloth. 5s.

LE GALLIENNE, RICHARD.

Rubaiyat of Omar Khayyam: a Paraphrase from several Literal Translations. From the press of Messrs. T. and A. Constable of Edinburgh. Long Fcap. 8vo. Parchment. 5s. Also a very limited Edition on Japanese vellum, numbered and signed by the author. 15s. net.

LEIGHTON, MARIE CONNOR, and ROBERT LEIGHTON.

Convict 99: a Novel. With Eight full-page Illustrations by Stanley L. Wood. Crown 8vo. Cloth. 3s. 6d.

LOWNDES, FREDERIC SAWREY.

Bishops of the Day: a Biographical Dictionary of the Archbishops and Bishops of the Church of England, and of All Churches in Communion therewith throughout the World. Fcap. 8vo. Cloth. 5s.

"While the assembly of nearly 200 Bishops of the Anglican Communion at the Lambeth Conference makes the publication of the volume at the present time especially opportune, Mr. Lowndes's work is likely to command a more permanent interest. It gives a full and lucid sketch of the career of each Bishop, without any suggestion of partisan bias on the part of the author."—*Times*.

"Few works of reference could be more acceptable to Churchmen of the present time. . . . Plenty of dates of the right sort, as well as matters of more human interest."—*Guardian*.

"The work is thoroughly up to date, as one may see from the Episcopal events of 1896 and 1897 here recorded. It abounds in personal incidents and anecdotes not to be found elsewhere, and evidently derived from original and accredited sources. . . . Much valuable information on Church matters generally incidental to Episcopal administration."—*Morning Post*.

"Mr. Lowndes has spared no pains to make his compendium as perfect as possible. . . . This book is, as far as we can know, the first of the kind that has been published, and supplies, in good time, a want that would have soon become urgent."—*Standard*.

"Valuable for reference on account of much of the information contained in the neatly got-up volume being supplied by the prelates themselves."—*World*.

"The book should be bought and read at once. There is no Churchman whom it will not interest, and it contains a sufficiency of blank spaces to admit of MS. additions, which may record the inevitable changes brought about by death or by translation. Mr. Lowndes deserves our very cordial thanks for a piece of work which few would have undertaken, and none could have achieved more perfectly."—*Sheffield Daily Telegraph*.

LUCAS, EDWARD VERRALL.

A Book of Verses for Children: an Anthology. With Cover, title-page, and end-papers designed in colours by F. D. Bedford. Crown 8vo. Cloth. 6s.

"The principle of this Anthology, Mr. Lucas explained at length in the *Fortnightly Review* for September 1896, in an article entitled 'Some Notes on Poetry for Children.' The *Daily Chronicle*, commenting in a leading article on this, says, 'Very wise, as well as very witty notes they are. . . . If the new 'Child's Anthology' is going to be of this sample, we should like to subscribe to a copy in advance. . . . Why should not Mr. Lucas compile it himself? No one, clearly, is better fitted for the task."

(*See also* Dumpy Books for Children.)

MAETERLINCK, MAURICE.

Aglavaine and Selysette: a Drama in Five Acts. Translated by Alfred Sutro. With Introduction by J. W. Mackail, and Title-page designed by W. H. Margetson. Globe 8vo. Half-buckram. 2s. 6d. net.

"To read the play is to have one's sense of beauty quickened and enlarged, to be touched by the inward and spiritual grace of things. . . . Mr. Sutro is the most conscientious, and at the same time the most ambitious, of translators; not content with reproducing the author's thought, he strives after the same effect of language—the plaintive note, the dying cadence, the Maeterlincked sweetness long drawn out. And more often than not he succeeds,—which is saying a good deal when one considers the enormous difficulties of the task."—Mr. A. B. WALKLEY, in the *Speaker*.

"The book is a treasury of beautiful things. No one now writing loves beauty as M. Maeterlinck does. Sheer, essential beauty has no such lover. He will have nothing else."—*Academy*

"Mr. Alfred Sutro's careful and delicate translation of Mr. Maurice Maeterlinck's new play gives readers of English every opportunity of appreciating a work which, so to speak, is at the tip of the century. . . . The book, as a whole, is perhaps the best yet published by which an English-speaking stranger to M. Maeterlinck could make his acquaintance."—*Scotsman*.

MERRICK, LEONARD.

One Man's View: a Novel. Crown 8vo. Cloth. 3s. 6d.

"A novel over which we could at a pinch fancy ourselves sitting up till the small hours. . . . The characters are realised, the emotion is felt and communicated."—*Daily Chronicle*.

"An uncommonly well written story. . . . The men in the book are excellent, and the hero . . . is an admirable portrait."—*Standard*.

"Mr. Leonard Merrick's work is exceptionally good: his style is literary, he has insight into character, and he can touch on delicate matters without being coarse or unpleasantly suggestive. 'One Man's View' is keenly interesting. . . . 'One Man's View' is one of those rare books in which, without a superfluous touch, each character stands out clear and individually. It holds the reader's attention from first to last."—*Guardian*.

"Mr. Merrick's fascinating story—a story written in a vivacious style, containing many humorous and pathetic passages, and pervaded throughout by a high and pure tone. . . . There is not a dull passage in the story, and the character of the brave, unselfish, magnanimous barrister is admirably drawn."—*Aberdeen Free Press*.

MEYNELL, ALICE.

The Flower of the Mind: a Choice among the best Poems. With Cover designed by Lawrence Housman. Crown 8vo. Buckram. 6s.

" Partial collections of English poems, decided by a common subject or bounded by the dates and periods of literary history, are made more than once in every year, and the makers are safe from the reproach of proposing their own personal taste as a guide for the reading of others. But a general Anthology gathered from the whole of English literature—the whole from Chaucer to Wordsworth—by a gatherer intent upon nothing except the quality of poetry, is a more rare attempt."—*Extract from Introduction.*

ROTHENSTEIN, WILL.

English Portraits: a Series of Lithographed Drawings. With short texts by various hands.

Part I.—Sir Frederick Pollock; Mr. Thomas Hardy.

Part II.—Sir F. Seymour Haden; Mr. William Archer.

Part III.—Rt. Rev. Dr. Creighton, Bishop of London; Marchioness of Granby.

Part IV.—Mr. W. E. H. Lecky, P.C., M.P.; Mr. John Sargent, R.A.

Part V.—Mr. W. E. Henley; Mr. A. W. Pinero.

Part VI.—Miss Ellen Terry; Mr. Sidney Colvin.

[*These parts are now ready.*

In Twelve Parts, each in a Wrapper arranged by the Artist. 2s. 6d. each, net; or, the subscription to the Series of Twelve, post free with a Case for binding, designed by the Artist, 30s. net.

"Admirably life-like, . . . and the style of publication makes it very attractive."
—*Speaker.*

"The drawings are lithographs, rough sketches rather than elaborate drawings, but they show that Mr. Rothenstein has thoroughly mastered his method and knows how to use it with most commendable self-restraint. They are admirable examples of the style of drawing which he has made his own, and which has much to recommend it. The drawings are accompanied by the briefest personal paragraphs."—*Scotsman.*

"The portraits, which are of a large portfolio size, are vivid likenesses, and their appearance is a gratifying indication of the revival of lithography in fine art."—*Aberdeen Free Press.*

"The introductory examples fulfil to the full the promises made in the publisher's announcements, and it is certain that the series will be keenly appreciated by art lovers."—*Dundee Advertiser.*

SCHWARTZE, HELMUTH.

The Laughter of Jove: a Novel. Crown 8vo. Cloth. 6s.

SEYMOUR, GORDON.

(*See* Ethics of the Surface Series.)

SHAW, GEORGE BERNARD.

Plays, Pleasant and Unpleasant.

I. Unpleasant.

II. Pleasant.

These Volumes will contain all Mr. Shaw's Dramatic work, acted and unacted, with special Introductions, and Prefaces to Each Play. Fcap. 8vo. Cloth. 5s. each.

(*See also* Politics in 1896.)

SHORE, ARABELLA and LOUISA.

Poems by A. and L. Crown 8vo. Cloth. 5s. net.

SPENCER, EDWARD ("Nathaniel Gubbins.")

Cakes and Ale: a Memory of Many Meals; the whole interspersed with various recipes, more or less original, and anecdotes, many veracious. With cover designed by Phil May. Small 4to. Cloth. 5s.
[*Third Edition.*

" A book from which every restaurant-keeper can, if he will, get ideas enough to make a fortune. Sportsmen, stock-brokers and others with large appetites, robust yet sensitive palates, and ample means, will find it invaluable when they are ordering the next little dinner for a select party of male friends."—*Saturday Review.*

" Exceedingly readable, clever, and, moreover, highly informative. . . . From racy chapter to racy chapter the reader is irresistibly carried on. . . . The mistress of the house will read it carefully for the sake of the valuable recipes and hints, and mine host will esteem it for the smart style in which it is written, and for the plenitude of humour displayed in anecdote, story, and reminiscence."—*Dundee Advertiser.*

" Allow me to say that it is a little book on a great subject that deserves to occupy an honourable place in every library, on the same shelf as Kettner's ' Book of the Table,' Sala's ' A Thorough Good Cook,' and perhaps that over-praised but undoubtedly entertaining classic, ' Gastronomy as a Fine Art,' by Brillat-Savarin."—*Sporting Life.*

" This little volume should have its place among the wedding presents of every bride."—*Lady's Pictorial.*

" There are many useful hints on table matters, and the recipes are all eminently practical. No country house should be without it."—*Guardian.*

STEAD, W. T.

Real Ghost Stories: A Revised Reprint of the Christmas and New Year Numbers of the "Review of Reviews," 1891-92. With new Introduction. Crown 8vo. Cloth. 5s.

STILLMAN, W. J.

The Old Rome and the New, and Other Studies. Crown 8vo. Cloth. 5s.

SYLVAN SERIES, THE

A Peakland Faggot: Tales told of Milton Folk. By R. Murray Gilchrist. Fcap. 8vo. Cloth. 2s. 6d.

"Not only are the sketches themselves full of charm and real literary value, but the little volume is as pleasant to the eye and to the touch as its contents are stimulating to the imagination. . . . We do not envy the person who could lay down the book without feeling refreshed in spirit by its perusal. . . . We cannot give our readers better counsel than in advising them to procure without delay this charming and cheery volume."—*Speaker.*

"We have no hesitation in saying that this is the very best work which Mr. Gilchrist has given us. As studies of Black Country character it is superb. In fact he is a master of our feelings and emotions in this daintily produced little volume, and 'A Peakland Faggot' will solidify that reputation which he has been steadily building up of late years. The style is thoroughly poetic. . . . Our hearty congratulations to Mr. Murray Gilchrist upon this performance—the magic he has used is the magic of true genius."—*Birmingham Gazette.*

"The writer who gives us glimpses into the psychology of the poor and illiterate ought always to be welcome. . . . Mr. Murray Gilchrist has introduced us to a new world of profound human interest."—Mr. T. P. O'Connor, in the *Graphic.*

"I have read no book outside Mr. Hardy's so learned in such minutiæ of country 'wit' and sentiment."—Mr. Richard le Gallienne, in the *Star.*

TROUBRIDGE, LADY.

Paul's Stepmother, and One Other Story. With Frontispiece by Mrs. Annie Hope. Crown 8vo. Cloth. 3s. 6d.

"There is a fine natural interest in both these stories, and Lady Troubridge recounts them so well and gracefully that to the critical reader this interest is greatly enhanced."—*Dundee Advertiser.*

"It is with a genuine feeling of pleasure that the reader will linger over 'Paul's Stepmother,' a story that one is inclined to wish were longer. . . . The pathos of the situation is treated with real feeling, and there is not a discordant note throughout the story. . . . Both stories are marked as the work of a fine and cultured writer.' —*Weekly Sun.*

TURNER, ELIZABETH.

(*See* Dumpy Books for Children.)

WALDSTEIN, LOUIS, M.D.

The Subconscious Self and its Relation to Education and Health. Fcap. 8vo. Cloth. 3s. 6d.

WARBOROUGH, MARTIN LEACH.

Tom, Unlimited: A Story for Children. With Fifty Illustrations by Gertrude Bradley. Globe 8vo. Cloth. 5s.

WEBB, SIDNEY.

Labour in the Longest Reign (1837-1897). Issued under the Auspices of the Fabian Society. Fcap. 8vo. Cloth. 1s.

" It is, considering the source from which it comes, a singularly temperate and just review of the changes in the lot of the labourer which the reign has brought."— *Scotsman.*

" Mr. Sidney Webb has set forth some expert and telling comparisons between the condition of the working-classes in 1837 and 1897. His remarks on wages, on the irregularity of employment, on hours of labour, and on the housing of the poor, are worthy of earnest consideration."—*Daily Mail.*

WHELEN, FREDERICK (Editor).

Politics in 1896. With Contributions by H. D. Traill, D.C.L. ; H. W. Massingham ; G. Bernard Shaw ; G. W. Steevens ; H. W. Wilson ; Captain F. N. Maude ; Albert Shaw and Robert Donald. Globe 8vo. Cloth. 3s. net.

" For more reasons than one Mr. Whelen's Political Annual, of which the present is the first issue, deserves a welcome. Not only does it constitute a handy work of reference, that besides merely enumerating the political wants of the past year shows also the light in which they are regarded by various shades of public opinion, but it calls for recognition as a record of the development of political thought, that, if regularly issued, will be of value to the future historian. . . . The book has attractions for those who wish to understand the various ideas actuating contending parties, and such readers will certainly find entertaining matter in the several contributions." —*Morning Post*

" Mr. Whelen has undertaken a difficult task, but the volume which he has just issued is a very interesting and useful retrospect, and all who are interested in contemporary affairs will be glad to know that it is intended to be an annual. The plan is simple and comprehensive. . . . Mr. Whelen has done a useful work in starting this adventure, and we wish him all success."—*Daily Chronicle.*

" Those who can afford it, which includes at least every Labour Club, ought to possess a copy for their library."—Mr. KEIR HARDIE, in the *Labour Leader.*

WHITTEN, WILFRED.

The London - Lover's Enchiridion: An Anthology of Prose and Poetry inspired by London. With an Introduction. Crown 8vo. Buckram. 6s. *[In Preparation.*

WILLSON, BECKLES.

The Tenth Island; Being some Account of Newfoundland; its People, its Politics, and its Peculiarities. With an Introduction by Sir William Whiteway, K.C.M.G., Premier of the Colony, and an Appendix by Lord Charles Beresford. Globe 8vo. Buckram. 3s. 6d. With Map.

1s.
Labour in the Longest Reign (1837-1897).

1s. 6d.
The Cub in Love.   (Paper.)

Dumpy Books for Children.

    I. The Flamp, and other Stories.
    II. Mrs. Turner's Cautionary Stories.

2s.
The Ethics of the Surface Series.

    I. The Rudeness of the Honourable Mr. Leather-
      head.
    II. A Homburg Story.
    III. Cui Bono.

The Cub in Love.   (Cloth.)

2s. net.
Realms of Unknown Kings.

2s. 6d.
A Peakland Faggot.
The Ethics of Robert Browning's Poetry.

2s. 6d. net.
English Portraits.   (Twelve Parts.)
Aglavaine and Selysette.

3s. net.
Realms of Unknown Kings.   (Buckram.)
Politics in 1896.

3s. 6d.
The Tenth Island: An Account of New-
    foundland.
Convict 99.
The Subconscious Self.
Little Stories about Women.
One Man's View.
Paul's Stepmother.

3s. 6d. net.

Grant Allen's Historical Guides.

I. Paris.
II. Florence.
III. Cities of Belgium.
IV. Venice.   *[In Preparation.*
V. Rome.   *[In Preparation.*

5s.

Real Ghost Stories.
Rubaiyat of Omar Khayyam.
The Old Rome and the New.
Tom, Unlimited.
The Inferno of Dante translated into English Verse.
Cakes and Ale.
Bishops of the Day.
Plays, Pleasant and Unpleasant.

I. Pleasant.
II. Unpleasant.

5s. net.

Poems by A. and L.
Pioneers of Evolution.
Limbo, and other Essays.

6s.

The Flower of the Mind.
A Book of Verses for Children.
The Laughter of Jove.
" Old Man's " Marriage.
An African Millionaire.

7s. 6d.

H.R.H. the Prince of Wales.
In Court and Kampong.

20s. net.

The Evolution of the Idea of God.

16

www.ingramcontent.com/pod-product-compliance
Lightning Source LLC
Chambersburg PA
CBHW020845020726
47497CB00005B/1267